A SHORT HISTORY

OF

ENGLISH LITERATURE

IN THE

NINETEENTH CENTURY

BY

WILLIAM HENRY HUDSON

STAFF LECTURER IN LITERATURE TO THE
EXTENSION BOARD, UNIVERSITY OF LONDON

LONDON

G. BELL AND SONS LTD.

1919

First Published, 1918
Reprinted, 1919

Wordsworth & the Lyric
Keats & the Narrative Poem

713. H. McD. Innes
15th Nov. '20.

ENGLISH LITERATURE
IN THE NINETEENTH CENTURY

PREFACE

I HAVE tried to make this little volume, so far as the limits imposed upon me would permit, a fairly comprehensive sketch of English literature during the nineteenth century. To this end I have included a good many minor authors who are little read to-day except by special students of the period, and are commonly ignored in books of this kind, but who none the less, on account either of the intrinsic merit of their production or of its historical interest, seem to me important enough to warrant consideration. On the other hand, I have economised space by the exclusion of writers whose work does not, as a whole or in part, properly fall under the head of General Literature. Hence, scientists, philosophers, theologians, and for the most part even historians, find no place in my survey. The exceptions which I have occasionally admitted to this rule will, I think, justify themselves.

It is perhaps unfortunate that no history of literature can well be written without some valuation of the writers dealt with, and the consequent intrusion of the personal factor. But wherever critical estimates are perforce introduced it is evident that they should at least be the honest expression of the historian's independent opinions. I am aware that the views recorded in this book will be found to differ, in certain cases rather widely, from those generally current, but as they are my own views I am bound to let them stand. I should wish, however, to apologise if a dogmatic tone is anywhere suggested in my criticism. One cannot be continually loading one's pages with qualifying phrases —" I think," " It seems to me," " In my opinion," and the like ; but I will ask the reader to remember that whenever in this book judgment is registered, some such qualification is to be understood.

WILLIAM HENRY HUDSON.

CONTENTS

PART I

THE AGE OF THE REVOLUTION

1798–1830

PART II

THE VICTORIAN AGE

THE EARLIER PERIOD

1830–1872

vii

CONTENTS

PART III
THE VICTORIAN AGE
THE LATER PERIOD
1872–1900

PART I

THE AGE OF THE REVOLUTION

1798–1830

CHAPTER I

INTRODUCTORY

WHEN the English literature of the nineteenth century is considered in its totality and the changes which came over it in successive generations are taken into account, it is seen that its history falls very naturally into three periods, which may be described respectively as the Age of the Revolution, the Earlier Victorian Age, and the Later Victorian Age. To delimit these periods by actual dates is of course impossible, but we shall not go far wrong if we choose the years 1830 and 1872 as the landmarks of our study.

It will, however, be understood that this division refers only to successive generations and the large movements of literature, and must as a matter of practical convenience be disregarded in the treatment of individual writers, each of whom will be dealt with in the period to which his main activity belongs. The necessity for this procedure is obvious, as otherwise the work of many authors would have to be broken up into parts. Save in a few exceptional cases (as, *e.g.*, that of Carlyle), in which there is good reason for departing from it, our rule will be to include all writers born before 1800 in the first period, those born between 1800 and 1850 in the second, and those born after 1850 in the third.

Our point of departure is the publication by Wordsworth and Coleridge of the *Lyrical Ballads* in 1798, which

historians are at one in treating as the real beginning
of our nineteenth-century literature.   It is true, indeed,
that even here some qualification is required, for the
Ballads were received with contempt or neglect by
critics and readers alike, and as a result some years
elapsed before their influence made itself felt.   None
the less they heralded, if they did not at once ensure,
that great change of taste which we have in mind when
we speak of the fundamental difference between the
literature of the Age of the Revolution and that of the
preceding century.   For this reason there is no ground
for protesting against the long-accepted view of their
epoch-making importance.

At the same time we must safeguard ourselves against
the possibility of misapprehension in yet another way.
The change of taste in question, though we are in the
habit of associating it directly with the *Ballads*, was
after all not initiated, far less created by them.   In
current phraseology the Age of the Revolution is defined
as that of the triumph of romanticism.   But this triumph
had been long prepared.   The reaction against all the
dominant ideals of the so-called Augustan school, and
with this the romantic revival, had begun well back in
the eighteenth century, and had grown steadily in
strength and volume in the thirty years before the
Ballads appeared.   Aggressively original as they seemed
to their first readers, neither in matter nor in manner,
neither in spirit nor in style, was there anything absolutely new in their contents.   They merely represent
the culmination of tendencies already prevalent.   Such
writers as Gray and Collins, Macpherson and Chatterton,
Percy with his *Reliques of Ancient English Poetry*, and
even more notably, Blake, Crabbe, and pre-eminently
Burns and Cowper, were all in various ways and along

many different lines the forerunners of Wordsworth and Coleridge, and though it does not fall within our province to enter upon the discussion of origins, it is still necessary to insist in passing upon the vital connection between the older generation and the new. The later eighteenth century was indeed the seed-time of the early nineteenth-century harvest, and we must remember this, though it is the harvest alone that has to be dealt with here.

Thus much it has seemed well to premise in the interests of historical perspective. To attempt any preliminary epitome of the general characteristics of the age of triumphant romanticism is unnecessary, since these will become clear as we proceed with our detailed study. A few words must, however, be said about the social forces at work in it.

The fact that the period between 1798 and 1830 is known as the Age of the Revolution will serve to suggest the immense importance of such social forces. Broadly viewed, the great French upheaval itself was only the chief expression in the field of politics of a vast general movement in every department of life and thought— a movement the keynote of which was emancipation, or the assertion of individuality against the restraints by which it had long been repressed. This was the keynote also of the contemporary literature of England no less than of that of the Continent. Romanticism was fed by many influences and assumed many forms, and we need not now try to reduce its various characteristics—its intense subjectivity and emotionalism, its love of nature and the picturesque, its mediaeval leanings, and so on—to any single formula. But at bottom it was, as Victor Hugo put it, " liberalism in literature." Its impatient rejection of prescribed rules and conventions — its repudiation of the trim correctness of the classic school—its quest for fresh subjects and fresh modes of treatment—its belief in " nature," genius, and inspiration as opposed to conscious art—its insistence upon spontaneity and the central principle that every man has a right to utter his own thoughts in his own language and in whatever way he may deem best : all these conspicuous features of it are but aspects of the extreme individualism which marked the revolutionary spirit at large. The very variety which bewilders us in our literature of the romantic period, and which makes it difficult for us at times to see its different parts in their relations to one another and to the whole, was itself an inevitable result of this individualism.

We have, however, to go further than this, and to recognise not only the general connection between politics and literature during the revolutionary age but also the direct influence of the former upon the latter. Stage by stage that influence is very clear, particularly in the changing spirit of our poetry. Twelve years before the nineteenth century opened, the fall of the Bastille, hailed by Fox as "the greatest event which ever happened in the world," and the excitement which ensued, had stirred the nations of Europe with a mighty new hope. That hope was shared by many in England, to whom, as to their Continental contemporaries, it seemed as if the hour of deliverance and regeneration, long foretold by prophets and dreamers, was now actually at hand, and humanity, freed from the shackles of the past, was about to advance at once into an era of realised democratic ideals—of liberty, brotherhood, and the rights of man. Conservative opinion, voiced especially in the passionate eloquence of Burke, had indeed from the first run strongly against the popular cause. But young, ardent, generous natures, impatient of all the evils which were being done under the sun, easily caught fire. While to hostile critics the Revolution figured only as a wanton attack upon law, order, and the fabric of society, they saw in it, in Mr. Frederic Harrison's phrase, a movement of the race towards a completer humanity. For them, therefore, the moment was one of boundless promise. As Southey long afterwards told a friend, it was impossible for one who had not himself lived through the experience to understand the feelings of those who in the years of opening manhood were inspired to enthusiasm by the idea that all old things were passing away and that everything would soon be made new. As Wordsworth wrote, looking back into his own youth :

> "But Europe at that time was thrilled with joy,
> France standing at the top of golden hours,
> And human nature seeming born again";

and once more :

> "Bliss was it in that dawn to be alive,
> But to be young was very heaven."

But before the century closed, popular sympathy with the Revolution had already waned, and the early years of the new era were marked by the spread of that spirit of depression which, in nations as in individuals, often follows intense excitement. The madness and crimes of the Reign of Terror—the military aggressions of the Republic—the rise of Napoleon—the long struggle with France—the restoration of the Bourbons—the determined attempt of the crowned heads of Europe to undo the work of the Revolution and set back the hands on the clock : all these things in their combination were naturally productive of vast disturbances in thought and feeling. In a large sense, indeed, no Congress of Vienna or Holy Alliance could really undo the work of the Revolution, for the humanitarianism which it had kindled and the democratic ideals which it had proclaimed were alike indestructible. But for the moment the minds of men everywhere were most impressed by the failure of France to make good the splendid promises of '89. While risings in Spain, Portugal, Italy, Greece, like rumblings of distant thunder, showed that the great storm had by no means rolled away, all over Europe progressive movements suffered a temporary check, and in England, till the years immediately preceding the passing of the Reform Bill, such check was almost complete. This strong conservative counter-revolution profoundly affected the temper of English society. As I have elsewhere written : " Many of the older generation abandoned their early faith, and for a time the principles of progress and popular government suffered eclipse. The complacency of toryism, however, was impossible to many of the more fiery spirits among the younger men. Growing into manhood just in time to realise the full meaning of what seemed to be the failure of the democratic cause, they found themselves in a world which had emerged from the long strain of revolutionary excitement, exhausted but not satisfied. The old enthusiasms and hope had gone, and their collapse was followed here by apathy and indifference, there by the cynicism which often results from exploded idealism, and there again by the mood of disappointment and aimless unrest. Such were the conditions which naturally weighed heavily upon the English poets who were born into the later revolutionary age." [1]

[1] *Outline History of English Literature*, pp. 235, 236.

Summarised in broadest outline, this was the course of political events during the period with which we are first to be concerned, and to understand the poetry of that period in its historical relationships and bearings we must always bear them in mind. Their influence will become apparent as we turn to the poets whose activity lies in the main between 1798 and 1830.

CHAPTER II

THE OLDER POETS

In dealing with the poetry of the Age of the Revolution we will arrange the writers to be considered, according to date of birth, in two groups, taking the year 1780 as the line of demarcation. Though this division is adopted mainly as a matter of convenience, it has a real basis in fact, since for reasons already suggested it is a division between two literary generations.

William Wordsworth was born at Cockermouth, Cumberland, on 7th April 1770, and was educated at the **Words-** Hawkshead Grammar School and at Cambridge. **worth.** While still an undergraduate his mind was so deeply stirred by a walking tour in France and Switzerland which he made with a friend during his third summer vacation (1790), that on leaving the University he again crossed to France where, chiefly at Orléans and Blois, he spent more than a year (November 1791– December 1792). He now became an ardent supporter of the popular cause, which he espoused the more readily, as he explains, because his early life among the simple dalesmen and shepherds of Cumberland and his sojourn in the scholarly republic of Cambridge had already built the revolutionary principles of equality and the inborn nobility of all men into the fabric of his thought (*Prelude*, ix. 125 ff.), and prepared him to accept, as a thing of course, " the government of equal rights and individual worth." He was in Paris a month after the September massacres, and there became intimate with the leaders of the Girondist party ; and their fate at the hands of the Jacobins a little later would doubtless have been his had not a timely summons from anxious friends at home compelled him to return to England.

The rapid course of political events soon precipitated a crisis in his thought. Pitt's declaration of war against France involved him in a terrible struggle of conflicting emotions, for his sympathies were on one side and his patriotism on the other. But the Reign of Terror shook his faith in the revolutionary movement, and the policy of military aggression, on which the Republic now entered, and presently the rise of Napoleon, completed his alienation from it. This total collapse of his early ideals reduced him almost to despair. It was largely through the influence of his beloved sister Dorothy, whose name is indissolubly linked with his own, and through the soothing power of nature, which she helped him once more to feel, that his faith and hope were gradually restored. But though he regained perfect trust in the providential order he never went back to his revolutionary creed. The current of his thought had taken a different turn, and he became, and remained to the end, a strong conservative.

Meanwhile he had opened his career as a poet with the publication in 1793 of two poems entitled *An Evening Walk* and *Descriptive Sketches*, dealing, the one with the familiar landscape round Hawkshead and Ambleside, the other with scenes and memories from his pedestrian tour on the Continent three years before. Both these poems are in the orthodox classic couplet and contain much to remind us of the eighteenth-century manner and style, but they are at the same time prophetic by reason of their descriptions of nature and especially their wealth of specific detail.

Relieved of immediate financial anxiety by a legacy left him by a friend, Wordsworth now settled with his sister, first at Racedown in Dorsetshire, and then at Alfoxden among the Quantock Hills. His friendship with Coleridge, which dates from this time, introduced a new influence into his life—an influence, according to his own statement, second only to Dorothy's. The first-fruits of this friendship was the small volume of verse entitled *Lyrical Ballads* (1798). Out of their endless talk about the aims and powers of poetry the thought (Coleridge tells us) had emerged that "a series of poems" might be composed of two kinds: "in the one, the incidents and agents were to be, in part at least, supernatural," while "for the second class, subjects were to be chosen from ordinary life." The *Lyrical Ballads* were designed to illustrate both these kinds. Coleridge took the supernatural part of the joint enterprise, his chief contribution to it being *The Ancient Mariner*. Wordsworth exemplified the poetry of common things by *Simon Lee, We are Seven, The Thorn, The Idiot Boy*, and other pieces of the same general character, though the poem with which the collection closed, the superb *Lines composed a Few Miles above Tintern Abbey*, was entirely independent of the theoretical scheme. Wordsworth's work, therefore, represents the movement towards naturalism which had been a marked feature of later eighteenth-century poetry, as that of Coleridge represents the parallel movement towards romance. But it is important to appreciate the difference between Wordsworth's handling of themes taken from common life and that of a pure realist like Crabbe. Crabbe's method (in *The Village*,

1783, *The Newspaper*, 1785) had been that of hard, uncompromising literalism. Wordsworth's aim, on the other hand, was to transfigure his material "by the modifying colours of the imagination," and thus to touch even the commonplace, which seems commonplace only because it is familiar, with the charm of the unfamiliar and the ideal. There was thus a closer connection between the two sides of the *Lyrical Ballads* —the romantic and the naturalistic—than might at first sight be supposed. Both Coleridge and Wordsworth sought the interest of wonder, freshness, mystery. But Coleridge found it in the remote and strange, Wordsworth in the sphere of everyday life.

A visit to Germany (September 1798–April 1799) followed the publication of *Lyrical Ballads*, after which Wordsworth settled for good in his native Lake Country : fiist at Dove Cottage, Grasmere (1799–1806), and finally, after several migrations, at Rydal Mount (1813), his home for the rest of his long life. In 1802 he had married his cousin, Mary Hutchinson, and when presently the needs of a growing family began to tax his slender resources, he was fortunate in obtaining an appointment as distributor of stamps for his district, the salary of which sufficed for his modest wants.

With his establishment among the Lakes Wordsworth entered definitely upon the practice of the art which was henceforth to be his chief occupation. In 1800 he brought out an enlarged edition of *Lyrical Ballads* containing an important Preface, to which further reference will be made directly. A little later he completed (1805), though it was not published till after his death, a long autobiographical poem, *The Prelude, or Growth of a Poet's Mind*, the purpose of which was "to record in verse the origin and progress of his own powers," and which thus provides a valuable introduction to the body of his work. Another long poem, *The Excursion*, setting forth his philosophy of life in nine books of blank verse, appeared in 1814, and in 1815 a romantic narrative poem, *The White Doe of Rylstone*, which for once brings him into comparison with Scott. His deep interest in political affairs (marked by his prose pamphlet on the Convention of Cintra) prompted many fine occasional sonnets, while the great *Ode on Intimations of Immortality* (1807) is the crowning example of the poetry in which he continued to express his thoughts on the ultimate problems of life. The re-reading of Vergil with his son presently brought a new influence—that of classic story—into his work, and to this we are indebted for three noteworthy poems—*Laodamia* (1814), *Dion* (1814), and the *Ode to Lycoris* (1817). But by the time of the last-named Wordsworth's inspiration was on the wane. For more than thirty years he went on writing with all his characteristic devotion and industry, but though he much increased the bulk he added little to the value of his output. Occasionally the old spirit came upon him, as in the verses *Composed upon an Evening of Extraordinary Splendour and Beauty* (1818), and here and there in the *Sonnets on the River Duddon* (1820). But speaking generally, his really great work was now done. Among his later productions mention may be made of the series of *Ecclesiastical Sonnets* (1822), in which he traces the history of the Church in England from the introduction of Christianity down to his own day.

The chief external events of his placid life were the visits which he paid from time to time to Scotland and the Continent, and which furnished much material for verse (e.g., *Memorials of a Tour in Scotland*, 1814 ; *Memorials of a Tour on the Continent*, 1820 ; *Memorials of a Tour in Italy*, 1837). Advancing age brought with it compensations in the shape of growing recognition on the part alike of the critics and of the public. For many years he had been treated with neglect or outspoken contempt. But at last the current began to turn in his favour. Honorary degrees from Durham and Oxford—the placing of his name on the Civil Pension List—his appointment in 1843 to the laureateship made vacant by the death of Southey : these were but outward signs that he was gradually coming into his own. His robust health continued almost to the end. He died, after only a few days' illness, on 23rd April 1850.

In his Preface to the second edition of *Lyrical Ballads* Wordsworth defined " good poetry " as " the spontaneous overflow of powerful feeling." This definition was itself a protest against that mechanical conception of poetry as a thing made according to " rules," which, though already challenged, maintained its place in the orthodox critical creed. In the same essay he explained his own aims in writing in words which, while they were meant to refer immediately to the *Ballads*, have also an interest in connection with all his work. " The principal object, then, proposed in these Poems," he declares, " was to choose incidents and situations from common life, and to relate or describe them throughout, as far as possible, in a selection of language really used by men, and, at the same time, to throw over them a certain colouring of imagination, whereby ordinary things should be presented to the mind in an unusual aspect " ; and he goes on to say that " humble and rustic life was generally chosen because," for reasons which he details, "in that condition the essential passions of the heart find a better soil in which they can attain their maturity, are less under restraint, and speak a plainer and more emphatic language" than elsewhere. In this statement there are three propositions which demand attention. In the first place, Wordsworth deliberately seeks his themes among the elemental, universal, and permanent interests of human life. Whether he was right or wrong in supposing that such interests are to be found mainly among the rural peasantry and that they are destroyed or at least obscured by the culture and refinements of civilisation, is a question which we need not now discuss. The point to emphasise is the poet's determination to penetrate through what is merely artificial and factitious to "the very heart of man" and to find inspiration, not in human nature as it has been fashioned by the conventions of society, but in "men as they are men within themselves" (*Prelude*, xiii. 231 ff.). In the second place, this return to nature and reality is further illustrated by his contention that the proper language for such poetry as he designed to write is, with certain modifications, the language of actual life. Under this head he delivers a spirited attack upon the pompous and rhetorical diction—the "gaudiness and inane phraseology"—by which our poetry had long been vitiated. His polemical purpose prompted him, indeed, to push his theory of poetic style much too far, and it was fortunate therefore that, save in a few early and disastrous experiments, it had little direct influence upon his own manner of writing. But historically it is important because it challenged the eighteenth-century tradition of artifice and convention and threw the stress upon the primary virtues of naturalness and simplicity. Thirdly, it will be observed,

Wordsworth expressly guards himself against the possible assumption that his return to naturalness and simplicity involved bald and prosaic literalism. This is a vital point, but as it has already been referred to, it need not detain us here.

The foregoing considerations provide a key to the greater part of Wordsworth's narrative and descriptive poetry. But he was not merely a narrative and descriptive poet. In his own view he was essentially a philosophical poet: "Every great poet is a teacher," he wrote to his friend Beaumont; "I wish either to be considered as a teacher or as nothing." The larger part of his work was, therefore, inspired by a directly didactic aim, and even his narrative poems generally carry a moral. In analysing his philosophy of life we may conveniently regard him, first as a poet of nature, and then as a poet of man.

Though Wordsworth has been justly described as "the keenest-eyed of all modern poets for what is deep and essential in nature," the distinctive quality of his nature-poetry is not love of natural beauty nor specific accuracy of description, but rather the mystical and religious element by which it is pervaded. Nature for him was the embodiment of the Universal Spirit, the presence of which he felt in the living world about him and at the same time (for the human soul is at one with the soul of nature) "in the mind of man" (*Tintern Abbey*). This sense of the spirituality of nature and of the kinship of nature and man lay at the basis of his thought, and from it arose his conception of communion with nature as the great means of attaining that knowledge of transcendental truth which is for ever beyond the reach of science and the "meddling intellect." His early simple and half-sensuous love of nature had thus been heightened and transfigured into mystical rapture and religious passion ; nature for him had become "the anchor" of his "purest thoughts," "the nurse, the guide, the guardian" of his heart, the "soul" of all his "moral being." Here we reach the most essential part of Wordsworth's message to the world. He taught men, "barricadoed evermore within the walls of cities," that they might find in nature not only beauty, not only infinite sources of joy and consolation, but also spiritual certainties and moral power. Nature he proclaimed as the greatest of all teachers.

The transition is easy from Wordsworth the poet of nature to Wordsworth the poet of man. Though he early repudiated his revolutionary creed, one great revolutionary idea remained at the core of his teaching —that of the innate and essential dignity of man. It was doubtless instinctive sympathy that led him to choose his types of manhood—his Leech-gatherer, his Michael, his Pedlar in *The Excursion* — from the peasantry of his native district ; yet moral purpose too had much to do with such selection, for in these humble and obscure characters he saw examples of strong elemental manhood, bred by nature and unspoilt by the sophisticating influences of an artificial society. His stress is thus thrown upon individual worth, irrespective of all the factitious differences of fashion and the world ; he teaches equality, not indeed in the political, but in the higher spiritual sense. Part of his avowed mission was to breathe "grandeur upon the very humblest face of human life "—to consecrate the commonplace, to reveal the value and beauty of the primary affections, to persuade his readers that the simplest things are after all the most divine. This is the ethical side of his romanticism. As a moralist, he endeavours to turn our minds away from "sanguine schemes" and "ambitious projects" to seek "for present good in life's familiar face." He insists upon the power which each man has within himself to lift himself by fortitude and conscious effort above the depressing influence of mere circumstance (e.g., *Resolution and Independence*). He dwells upon the thought that obedience to the moral law, while it must necessarily involve struggle, has its ultimate reward in a peace of soul which the world can neither give nor take away. Austere in temper as his poetry habitually is, it is at bottom a poetry of happiness —not of the transient and superficial satisfaction which may be found in exceptional conditions, but "of joy in widest commonalty spread."

As a poet of man and ethical teacher, Wordsworth thus everywhere reveals his vital connection with some of the underlying principles of the Revolution. In practical politics he had become a reactionary. But his work from first to last, with its emphasis upon the simplification of life and the essential worth of human nature, must still be regarded as part and parcel of the general democratic movement of his time.

His limitations are very marked. His outlook upon life was narrow; his interests were extremely circumscribed; he had little narrative or dramatic power; while too much engrossed by the moral truths he was solicitous to enforce, he frequently, especially in his later years, allowed his poetry to degenerate into the most prosaic didacticism. But within his restricted sphere he holds his place secure. He is great because he makes us feel the tranquillising beauty of nature and the sanctity of common life; because he touches what he handles with a peculiar and winning charm; and because in his really supreme moments the simple nobility of his thought is wedded to a simple nobility of style.

Wordsworth's brother poet, Samuel Taylor Coleridge, was born in the vicarage of Ottery St. Mary, on 21st October 1772, and after ten years at Christ's **Coleridge.** Hospital went up to Cambridge, which he left in April 1794 without a degree. By this time he had been completely carried away by enthusiasm for the Revolution, the outbreak of which he had already welcomed in some crude verses on the *Destruction of the Bastille*, while still at school. There was little real human feeling behind this enthusiasm, for Coleridge, who once significantly confessed to a friend that, though he read everything, he did " not like history," was always more at home with the speculations of metaphysics than with the concrete facts of life. His interest in the popular cause was indeed inspired far less by sympathy with an oppressed people than by certain abstract principles, like that of freedom, which the revolutionary movement involved. But though bred rather in the head than in the heart, his ardour knew no bounds, and always fertile in projects, he now conceived a visionary scheme of an ideal commonwealth to be founded by a company of congenial spirits on the banks of the Susquehanna River under the high-sounding title of Pantisocracy. Visiting Oxford in June 1794, he sought out Robert Southey, of whom he had heard, and made him the confidant of his plans ; and there, and a little later at Bristol, the two young dreamers discussed the undertaking in all its details. But practical difficulties soon became manifest, and Pantisocracy took its place among the world's unrealised utopias. In the meantime Coleridge and Southey had married two sisters, of the Fricker family of Bristol (1795), and had collaborated in a three-act play, *The Fall of Robes pierre*. Early in the year following his marriage Coleridge also published a small volume of *Poems on Various Subjects*, which included a *Monody on Chatterton* and a " desultory poem " entitled *Religious Musings*, a bombastic production in which the Revolution is justified as a triumph of " infinite love."

Sanguine as he was in the intervals between his recurrent fits of depression, even Coleridge could hardly expect to support a family by poetry, and he accordingly tried various ways of making a living—among others, journalism, lecturing, and preaching in Unitarian pulpits. Happily for him, however, friends came to his rescue ; one providing him with a cottage and garden at Nether Stowey and money enough to enable him to tide over his immediate troubles ; two others granting him an annuity of £150 on the simple condition that he should devote himself entirely to poetry and philosophy. It is proof of the essential weakness of Coleridge's character that even as a young man he should have been willing to live mainly on charity. All through life this ineffective dreamer was largely dependent upon the kindness of more practical people.

The eighteen months at Nether Stowey (1797–98) were the great flowering time of Coleridge's poetic genius : nearly all that is best in his verse dates from this brief period of inspiration and fertility. On the eve of his settlement at Stowey he had already indicated the change which was rapidly coming over his feelings in regard to the Revolution in an *Ode on the Departing Year* (1796). This change was now fully declared in the splendid *France : an Ode* (1798), first published in *The Morning Post* under the significant title of *The Recantation*. The poem called *Fears in*

Solitude (1798), written " during the alarm of an invasion," is also interesting on the political side, but is even more noteworthy because, like *This Lime-Tree Bower my Prison* (1797), *Frost at Midnight* (1798), and *The Nightingale* (1798), it is full of tender domestic sentiment and of the beauty of the Quantock landscape which forms the idyllic background of the poet's meditations.   The marvellous dream-fragment, *Kubla Khan*, *The Ancient Mariner*, and the first part of *Christabel* also belong to these halcyon days.   A more ambitious work, the tragedy *Osorio*, from which he had a faint hope of gaining some substantial reward, also engaged his attention.   It was, however, rejected at the time by Sheridan, to whom it was offered, though in 1813, in a revised form and under a new title—*Remorse*—it ran for twenty nights at Drury Lane.

We have already spoken of Coleridge's collaboration with Wordsworth in the *Lyrical Ballads*.   The significance of his principal contribution to this joint-work, *The Ancient Mariner*, must now be considered.   Wordsworth, as we have seen, had taken his subjects from real life, but had sought to give " the interest of novelty " to them " by the modifying colours of imagination." Coleridge's effort, on the other hand, was directed to " persons and characters supernatural or at least romantic " ; but in dealing with these he endeavoured " to transfer from our inward nature a human interest and a semblance of truth " to his " shadowy creations and the strange scenes through which they move."   Thus in *The Ancient Mariner*, while the incidents as such are in the last degree weird and wonderful, the attention is really centred upon the spiritual experiences of the mariner himself, and a story which would otherwise have been a tissue of extravagances is humanised by the prevailing presence of psychological truth. Once more, therefore, we can see that Coleridge's work, while apparently the antithesis, was really the complement of that of his friend and collaborator. Wordsworth's aim was to touch fact with imagination, and so save naturalism in poetry from degenerating into hard literalism ; Coleridge's was to unite imagination with human interest and so save romanticism from becoming, as indeed it had already become in the hands of " Monk " Lewis and Anne Radcliffe, a mere orgy of crude sensationalism.

Coleridge accompanied Wordsworth and his sister to Germany in September 1798, but parted from them at Hamburg, and went on by himself to Ratzeburg and Göttingen, where he steeped himself in German metaphysics. Returning to England in July 1799, he busied himself for a time with political articles for *The Morning Post* and with a translation of Schiller's *Wallenstein*. In 1800 he settled at Greta Hall, Keswick, in order to be near the Wordsworths, who were now living at Grasmere ; and there he wrote the second part of *Christabel*. The damp climate of the Lake region, however, affected his constitution, already undermined by serious illnesses ; he suffered much from rheumatic gout and other ailments ; and matters were made worse by the practice of opium-taking, to which he had previously had recourse and which now became habitual. As a result he lost his powers of work and fell into deep melancholy, while chronic misunderstandings with his wife filled the cup of his sorrows to the brim. The beautiful and pathetic *Dejection* is a record of his feelings during this miserable time. With funds provided by Wordsworth and Sir George Beaumont he went south in quest of health, but his sojourn in Malta (April 1804–1806) was

of little benefit to him.   For the next ten years he led a
wandering life, neglecting his wife and children and still
largely depending for means upon his friends, and
especially upon his brother-in-law, Southey, whose
forbearance and generosity are beyond praise.   He
once more experimented in journalism (his periodical,
The Friend, ran to twenty-seven numbers between June
1807 and March 1810), and also gave several courses of
lectures on Shakespeare and the drama.   By this time,
as he confessed in a letter (1814), his nerves were
shattered and his life endangered by " the one crime of
opium."   Happily, in 1816 he placed himself in the
hands of a Dr. Gillman of Highgate, in whose house,
nominally as patient, really as guest, he spent the remainder of his life.   Under Gillman's influence he conquered the opium habit and gained back a measure of
health and peace of mind, though he was still haunted
at times by the bitter thought of wasted energies and a
futile career (see *Youth and Age*, 1823 ; *Work without
Hope*, 1827).   His reputation during his last years was
very great.   His occasional prose writings (e.g., *Aids to
Reflection*, 1825) made him widely known as an interpreter of German idealism and a force in breaking down
the dry rationalism which had long dominated English
thought.   But his power was exerted rather through
the spoken than through the written word.   The house
on Highgate Hill became a Mecca, and many ardent
disciples of the younger generation repaired thither to
sit at the prophet's feet and listen to his marvellous and
inspiring if nebulous talk (see Carlyle's *John Sterling*,
Part I.).   He died on 25th July 1834.

While we are here chiefly concerned with Coleridge
as a poet, the importance of his work in criticism must
still be recognised.   Unsystematic, capricious, and in-

conclusive, that criticism is none the less remarkable for its frequent flashes of penetrative insight and for its suggestiveness. His *Biographia Literaria* (1817), though rambling, chaotic, and in places choked with pedantry, is one of the most stimulating books of the kind in the language, and historically it is valuable as the most philosophical interpretation of the principles underlying the romantic movement. In his discursive *Lectures on Shakespeare* he inaugurated a new era in the English criticism of our greatest dramatist. Following the lead of the German writers Lessing and Schlegel, he repudiated the eighteenth-century conception of Shakespeare as a rude and untutored genius, and set out to show that even his so-called " irregularities " were the results of " consummate judgment " and the finest constructive art. He was not, however, satisfied with straightening the crooked tree ; he bent it violently in the contrary direction. In his protest against the narrow pseudo-classic view of Shakespeare he, like other romanticists, went to the opposite extreme, asserting the universal pre-eminence of Shakespeare quite as uncritically as the pseudo-classicists themselves had asserted that of the Greek and Latin masters. For this reason, and also because of his habit of dealing with his text according to his own " inner lights," his influence on later Shakespeare criticism was on the whole unfortunate.

As a poet Coleridge was essentially romantic, and nowhere in our literature does the spirit of romance find purer expression than in some of his verse. His treatment of the supernatural is indeed unique in its combination of elusiveness and actuality ; the world conjured up by his imagination is as unsubstantial as the world of our dreams, yet as often happens with the world of our dreams, it has a curious reality and consistency of its own.   Another feature of his poetry—the pervading presence of psychological truth in it—though already mentioned, must still be re-emphasised.   We have seen how such psychological truth is of the very essence of *The Ancient Mariner*.   It is of the very essence no less of *Christabel*.   Full as this is of the subtle suggestions of mystery and terror, yet here again, as Dowden has said, the supernatural and the human elements interpenetrate each other.

But though Coleridge's most distinctive work is to be found in his romantic poetry he was not merely a "footless bird of paradise."   He often descended to the common earth.   The tender charm of the purely personal poems written at Stowey and the poignant pathos of those in which, later, he dwelt upon the tragedy of his life, must never be forgotten in any general estimate of him ; nor must we overlook the greatness of some of his verse (like the *Ode to France*) inspired by public events.   Yet while the domestic note in his poetry is at times clear and strong, his love of man in the wider sense of the term had little in it of Wordsworth's intimate sympathy with human life. His poetry of nature is rich in sensuous beauty, touched here and there with mystical radiance, and it has often (as in the Stowey poems) a fidelity of detail which reminds us of Wordsworth.   But it is noteworthy that he was quite as much at home in the scenery of *The Ancient Mariner* as in that of his "green and silent spot" among the Quantock Hills, for he saw pictures with his eyes shut (*A Day Dream*) and trusted to his imagination more than to his memory (*Table Talk*). It must be added that one salient feature of his poetry is the peculiar beauty of the versification, which is full of music and verbal magic.

Though the third and youngest of the so-called Lake Poets, Robert Southey, does not rank among the greater poets of his time, his close personal connection with Wordsworth and Coleridge makes it convenient for us to group him with them here. Born in Bristol on 12th August 1774, he entered Westminster School in 1788, but having been expelled in 1792 for publishing an article against flogging, went up to Oxford with his head full of Rousseau, *The Sorrows of Werther*, and the scepticism which he had imbibed from Gibbon. Of his relations with Coleridge in the scheme of Pantisocracy we have already spoken. Meanwhile he had found a poetic channel for his radicalism in an epic, *Joan of Arc*, inspired by his sympathy with the Republic then at war with England, and in the crude drama *Wat Tyler*. After this, two visits to Portugal turned his mind from utopian dreams to the romance of the past, and opened up for him a field in which later much of his work was to be done—that of the history and literature of the Peninsula. Then he settled at Greta Hall, Keswick, to a life of steady industry in book-making, translating and reviewing, by the proceeds of which, supplemented presently by a Government pension, he supported not only his own family but also the wife and children of the vagrant and irresponsible Coleridge. *Thalaba the Destroyer*, an Arabian tale of a son's efforts to avenge his father, appeared in 1801 ; *Madoc*, dealing with the adventures of a mythical Welsh prince among " barbarous powers," in 1805 ; *The Curse of Kehama*, a Hindoo story full of fantastic marvels, in 1810 ; *Roderick the Last of the Goths*, the scene of which is laid in Spain at the time of the Arabian invasion early in the eighth century, in 1814. Long before this, Southey had turned

Southey.

Tory, and had thus no compunction about accepting the laureateship in 1813. His *Vision of Judgment*, a fulsome eulogy of George III., is now remembered only as the occasion of Byron's brilliant reply.

Southey's work in verse, though great in bulk, represents, however, only a small part of his incessant activity. His prose writings, always noteworthy for their pure and pleasant style, are too numerous to be catalogued here ; but mention may be made of the admirable lives of Nelson (1813) and Wesley (1820), and of that curious medley of narrative, out-of-the-way learning, gossip, whimsical humour, and reflection, *The Doctor* (1834–38).

His last years were clouded with sorrow. He lost his wife in 1837, and though in 1839 he married Caroline Bowles, herself a writer of verse, he never recovered from the blow. Then brain disease set in ; his mind gradually gave way ; and death came as a happy release on 21st March 1843.

As a poet, Southey lives chiefly by virtue of a few short poems, such as *The Holly Tree, The Battle of Blenheim*, and *The Scholar*. Some of his ballads (e.g., *Rudiger, Lord William, The Inchcape Rock*) are also meritorious, and are further interesting because they were in part inspired (like Scott's early work) by German romanticism. His huge narrative poems, which he himself regarded as the sure foundations of a lasting fame, and which were much praised at the time by men like Scott, Landor, and Shelley, are to-day little more than names. Interesting as stories and full of passages of picturesque description, they yet testify on the whole to the writer's laborious patience and extraordinary erudition rather than to real poetic power. Historically, however, they have some importance. They are portions of Southey's ambitious design,

conceived when a schoolboy from a reading of Picard's
Religious Ceremonies, of turning " all the more prominent
and poetical forms of mythology " into verse " by
making each the groundwork of an heroic poem." They
thus illustrate the tendency of the romantic movement
to abandon classic mythology, long worn threadbare
by continual use, and to seek fresh subjects in unfamiliar
fields. In two of them, moreover, we mark an extreme
reaction against the regularity of eighteenth-century
versification. *Thalaba* is in unrimed verse, the lines
of which vary in length and metrical cadence,[1] and
though in *Kehama* rime is added, the structural irregu-
larity is retained. A further point in connection
with these " romantic epics " is that they show that
Southey depended for his inspiration almost entirely
upon books. This is true even in regard to his treatment of nature. When he took his daily walk for
exercise it was always book in hand. Thus the real
landscape of the Lake district is hardly suggested in
his poetry. The scenes which give local character to
his narratives are for the most part built up out of
materials furnished by his richly-stored library.

While for the reasons explained we have associated
Southey with Wordsworth and Coleridge, in order of actual
importance as well as of date " the Wizard of the North "
comes next on our list.

Born in Edinburgh on 15th August 1771, Walter
Scott, though his father was an attorney and his mother
the daughter of a University professor, was
Scott. remotely connected on both sides with ancient
and " gentle " families which had long figured in the

---

[1] This irregular blank verse was adopted by Southey from a certain
Dr. Sayers of Norwich, and was in turn imitated by Shelley in *Queen
Mab*.

annals of the Border : a fact which he always recalled with satisfaction, for in him pride of blood was rooted deep in that strong imaginative feeling for the past which was the inspiration of so much of his work. A good deal of his childhood was spent at his grandfather's farm at Sandy-Knowe, where he learned to love the wild Border country, with all its associations and traditions, and where his fancy was fired by the tales told to him during the long winter evenings of feuds and superstitions, and the great Jacobite risings of 1715 and 1745 (see *Marmion : Introduction to Canto III.*). His regular education at the Edinburgh High School and University counted little in his making as poet and novelist ; but meanwhile he learned to read French, Italian, and Spanish, and eagerly devoured all the romantic literature in these languages on which he could lay his hand. He himself regarded his first acquaintance at the age of thirteen with Percy's *Reliques of Ancient English Poetry* as marking an epoch in his life. The *Reliques* stirred his interest in popular poetry, and he soon began to collect ballads on his own account.

In 1786 he entered on the study of law, and in 1792 he was called to the Bar. During the interval the French Revolution had shaken Europe from end to end, and had, as we have seen, made a deep impression on Wordsworth, Coleridge, and Southey. On Scott its influence was very slight and purely negative. It aroused him to no humanitarian enthusiasm or prophetic visions of a regenerated society. It only deepened his constitutional hatred of democracy, and threw him back with fresh ardour upon the romantic past. Scott was a born Tory, and all his sympathies were with the old order which the Revolution threatened at its very foundations.

In 1797 Scott married Charlotte Margaret Charpentier, the daughter of a French royalist refugee ; in 1799 he was appointed Sheriff-Depute of Selkirkshire ; in 1806 he received in reversion the Clerkship of the Court of Session, though he did not begin to enjoy the emoluments of this office till the retirement of the actual incumbent in 1812.   Wealth as well as fame soon came to him from his writings ; yet for many years he continued to discharge his official duties with regularity and thoroughness.   The wonderful rapidity of his production becomes more wonderful when we remember that authorship was not the main business of his life. It was part of his practical creed that literature should be " a staff and not a crutch."

We must now turn back to the beginnings of his career as a poet.   In 1788 a paper on the German drama, read by Henry Mackenzie, " the Man of Feeling," before the Royal Society of Edinburgh, aroused his interest in German literature.   He at once devoted himself to the study of the German language, and was soon deep in its romance and poetry.   This led a few years later (1794) to what he himself called his real introduction to the " feverish trade of poetry "—the translation of Bürger's famous ballad *Lenore*.   Other translations followed, including one of Goethe's drama *Goetz von Berlichingen* (1796), and some original ballads (*Cadyow Castle, Glenfinlas, The Eve of St. John, The Gray Brother*), which, though not altogether free from eighteenth-century mannerisms, have much of the strength and simplicity of the genuine old ballad type.   Then shortly after the appearance of *Goetz*, Scott arranged with an old schoolfellow, James Ballantyne, now a printer at Kelso, for the publication of a small book of selections from the mass of old ballads and popular poems which year by year had been growing on his hands. But the undertaking rapidly expanded beyond the limits of the original design, and at length developed into the three large volumes of *The Minstrelsy of the Scottish Border* (1802–1803)—a work which evidently owed its existence to the inspiration received from Percy's *Reliques* long before. Out of this in turn sprang the first of Scott's romances in verse. While he was busy with the third volume of the *Minstrelsy*, the Countess of Dalkeith brought to his notice the old Border legend of Gilbert Horner, the goblin page, and asked him to put it into a ballad for her. He willingly complied ; but as soon as he began to work, his imagination took fire ; the goblin's pranks sank into a subordinate place in his mind ; he awoke to the poetic possibilities of the immense body of illustrative material which he had collected for the *Minstrelsy* ; and in the end the proposed ballad became a long narrative poem of fighting and love which, though sadly wanting in continuity as a story, was full of vivid descriptions of Border life and manners in feudal times. Such was the origin of *The Lay of the Last Minstrel* (1805), which may thus be regarded as the poetic outcome and efflorescence of the loving labours which for many years he had given to the study of Border antiquities.

Notwithstanding the immense success of this poem, three years elapsed before Scott followed it up with other work of the same kind. Then came *Marmion : a Tale of Flodden Field* (1808) and *The Lady of the Lake* (1810). Both these poems more than sustained his popularity, and while the critics were on the whole agreed that they showed an immense advance upon the *Lay* in construction, narrative interest, and power of characterisation, the general reading public was specially delighted by the melodramatic plot of the one and the sentimental love-story which runs through the other. But Scott was never again to repeat these triumphs in verse. *Rokeby* (1813), the scene of which was laid in Yorkshire at the period of the Civil War, is in comparison laboured and tame ; *The Bridal of Triermain* (1813), though a pretty story, is of slight importance ; *The Lord of the Isles* (1815), a tale of the Bruce, was written, as he afterwards confessed, unwillingly and in haste ; while the last of the series, *Harold the Dauntless* (1817), was rightly regarded as a failure. It was a happy thing for Scott, therefore, that before this he had found a fresh field for his genius in prose fiction, the financial rewards of which were even greater than those which he had gained from verse. For some years success continued to attend all his efforts, and in 1819 his worldly fortunes were crowned by a baronetcy. But in the winter of 1825–26 the entire collapse of two firms in which he was deeply interested as a sleeping partner—the printing house of Ballantyne and Constable's publishing business—entailed his own ruin. Faced by an indebtedness of £117,000, he refused to shield himself behind the Bankruptcy Act, and, determined that not one of his creditors should be a penny the worse through fault of his, sat down to wipe off his liabilities with his " own right hand." For six years he kept up the heroic struggle. But his strength finally gave way under the terrific strain. In the winter of 1831 he went to Italy in search of health ; but home-sickness fell upon him ; he was brought back to his beautiful home, Abbotsford, in the following summer ; and there, with the " gentle ripple " of his beloved Tweed in his ears, he died on 21st September 1832.

In the *Introduction* to the third canto of *Marmion*

3

Scott has himself described the influences which gave bent to his genius in early life, and he there expressly declares that from one "thus nurtured" it were vain to expect "the classic poet's well-conn'd task." His long poems are not "epics" in the classic sense, like, for example, *Paradise Lost*; they are, in his own phrase, "romantic tales in verse." His distinctive merits are those of the born story-teller; his narrative flows with ease and rapidity; he has a keen eye for the picturesque; and in moments of special dramatic interest he is sometimes very great. He is at his best in scenes of stirring action (*e.g.*, Deloraine's night ride to Melrose in the *Lay*; the speeding of the Fiery Cross in *The Lady of the Lake*), and particularly in his battle-pieces (*e.g.*, the battle of Flodden Field in *Marmion*; FitzJames' duel with Roderick Dhu in *The Lady of the Lake*). His descriptions (as of Melrose Abbey by night in the *Lay*, of Edinburgh seen from Blackford Hill in *Marmion*, and of the country round Loch Katrine in *The Lady of the Lake*) are also remarkable for their pictorial power, though at times rather clogged by archaeological detail. But while excellent as stories Scott's verse romances are generally wanting in the higher qualities of poetry. Carried away by his fatal facility, he frequently sinks into the mere improvisatore and becomes diffuse and commonplace; his style is often slovenly, and is on the whole lacking in distinction; there is little that is final or memorable about his phrasing; his treatment of life is superficial and conventional; he brings no spiritual insight to bear upon his themes, and only the most obvious moral reflections suggest themselves to him by the way. We cannot, therefore, class him among the really great poets. But as a story-teller in verse he keeps his place unchallenged.

A few minor poets remain to be considered in this chapter. These we will take in their chronological order.

Samuel Rogers (1763–1855), the banker-poet, whose famous literary breakfasts figure conspicuously in the memoirs of his time, has to be included in our survey on account rather of the position which he occupied in the contemporary world of letters than of the actual interest of his own work. His first volume, *An Ode to Superstition, with Some Other Poems,* appeared in 1786—the year also of Burns's first volume. This was followed in 1792 by *The Pleasures of Memory,* a feeble production in classic couplets, which however Byron described as " one of the most beautiful didactic poems in the language " ; in 1798 by *An Epistle to a Friend* ; in 1814 by *Jacqueline,* a tale in verse ; in 1819 by *Human Life,* which Rogers himself regarded as his masterpiece ; and in 1822 by his guide-book poem—a sort of dilettante *Childe Harold—Italy.* This, though in blank verse, still shows by the artificial elegance of its diction that, despite the changes which had meanwhile come over English poetry, the author had never outgrown the influences of the eighteenth century. It contains what to-day is perhaps the best known of all his writings, the story of Ginevra. Rogers was, in Hazlitt's mordant phrase, " a very ladylike poet." His verse is graceful and correct ; but its poetic value is almost nought.

James Hogg (1770–1835) was born at Ettrick, Selkirkshire, and spent his boyhood mainly in tending his father's sheep. His education, such as it was, was almost entirely self-obtained, but his imagination was early stirred by the tales which his mother told him of " kings, giants, knights, fairies,

kelpies, brownies," etc.   His first attempts at verse were
in the form of songs and ballads for the lasses of his
neighbourhood.   Later he wrote out some old ballads
from his mother's dictation and sent them to Scott,
who included them in the third volume of his *Minstrelsy*.
This led to a friendship with Scott, through whose help
he published *The Mountain Bard* (1803).   This was followed by *The Forest Minstrel* (1810), *The Queen's Wake*
(1813)—his most important work—and many other
volumes of verse and prose.   He was long a picturesque
figure in Edinburgh literary society, and as such is
described by Lockhart in his *Peter's Letters to his Kinsfolk* (see *post*, p. 78) and by John Wilson, who took him,
not altogether to his satisfaction, as the painter's model
for the Shepherd in *Noctes Ambrosianae* (see *post*, p. 75).
He is after Burns—though a long way after—the greatest
of the Scottish peasant poets.   His inspiration came
direct from the legend-lore of his native soil, and he may
thus be regarded as an independent representative of
the movement which produced Scott's *Minstrelsy*.   His
finest work is to be found in his songs (*When the Kye
come Hame, The Village of Balmawhapple, The Boy's
Song*, etc.) and his ballads (e.g., *The Witch of Fife*).   In
some of his longer poems he was much influenced by
Scott, but the charming fairy tale, *Kilmeny* in *The
Queen's Wake*, deserves mention as a thing apart.

We come next to a poet of strikingly different
quality.   Walter Savage Landor (1775–1864) was born at
Landor.   Warwick, and having been expelled from Rugby
for insubordination and rusticated from Oxford,
where his eccentricities had earned for him the nickname
of "the mad Jacobin," retired to South Wales, where he
wrote his first important poem, *Gebir* (1798).   The raw
material for this was provided by the story of the legend-

ary founder of Gibraltar ; but though the subject was as
fantastic as that of one of Southey's Oriental epics, it
was treated with the utmost severity and concision of
classic art. Other small volumes of verse appeared in
1802 and 1804. On his father's death in 1805, Landor,
now a wealthy man, lived for a time in Bath. Three
years later, with a band of volunteers raised at his own
expense, he joined Blake's expedition in aid of the
Spanish rising against Napoleon. An indirect result of
this practical sympathy with the patriotic struggle in the
Peninsula was the drama *Count Julian* (1812), which,
like Southey's almost contemporary epic, deals with the
heroic story of Roderick the Goth. In the meantime
Landor had bought Llanthony Abbey, Monmouthshire
(1809), and had married (1811). But he quarrelled with
his neighbours and presently with his wife, and sought a
new home in Italy, where he remained till 1835. The
publication of the first instalment of his *Imaginary
Conversations* (1831) showed that he had now found a
new field in prose (see *post*, pp. 86–88). But though prose
was henceforth to be his most serious occupation, he
continued to write verse till the very end of his long
life. He settled again in Bath in 1835, but returned
to Italy in 1859, and there his closing years were
passed.

In his attitude towards life Landor is often described
as a pagan, and all his sympathies were indeed with what
was best and most heroic in the moral ideals of Greece
and Rome. Even his politics were inspired by antiquity,
for while an ardent republican he was essentially an
aristocrat, and his hatred of kings was balanced by an
equal hatred of the mob. These points are of importance to the student of his writings, the classic quality
of which has its roots in character, and is not merely,

like the so-called classicism of the eighteenth century, a product of academic taste.

It is this fundamental classic quality which gives Landor his distinctive place among the poets of his age. At a time when romantic freedom and spontaneity were often allowed to degenerate into licence and extravagance, he sought with patient and laborious care to realise his ideal of a style pruned of all redundancies, sculpturesque in its naked beauty, and as " compendious and exclusive " as that of Pindar himself. The result was precisely what he had from the first foreseen and been willing to accept : he has always been the poet of a chosen few—to speak frankly, of a coterie. His admirers find in his verse an almost perfect reproduction of the spirit and manner of the Greeks ; but the great body of lovers of literature, rightly feeling that even the perfect reproduction of antique modes is after all not the main business of the modern writer, naturally turn from work which, with all its technical excellence, impresses them as cold, artificial, and a little factitious, to poetry which is really alive with the life of its own time. The beauty of some of his narrative poems (e.g., *Chrysaor*, *The Hamadryad*), of his epigrams (e.g., *Of Himself*), and of his occasional lyrics (e.g., *Rose Aylmer*), must not, however, be forgotten.

Thomas Campbell (1777–1844) was born in Glasgow, and having distinguished himself at the University of **Campbell.** his native city, went to Edinburgh with the intention of taking up the law ; but he soon turned his attention to literature instead. After a visit to the Continent (1800–1801), he married (1803), and settled down in London to writing for the magazines and book-making. *Gertrude of Wyoming*, the best of his longer tales in verse, appeared in 1809. His later experiments in the same field—*Theodric* (1824) and *The Pilgrim of Glencoe* (1842)—added nothing to his reputation.

The first and most important of Campbell's more ambitious efforts, *The Pleasures of Hope* (1799), is a didactic poem of considerable force and brilliancy, but though charged in places with the revolutionary spirit, it belongs entirely to the eighteenth century in conception, in form, and in the rhetorical qualities of its style. *Gertrude of Wyoming*, a sentimental tale of Pennsylvania, in Spenserian stanzas, shows on the other hand the influence of the new taste. But notwithstanding the fame of his first work, Campbell's best title to remembrance is provided by his shorter poems. Some of his ballads (e.g., *Lord Ullin's Daughter*, *The Exile of Erin*, *Lochiel's Warning*, *Glenara*, *The Soldier's Dream*) have much dramatic power ; *The Last Man* reaches genuine sublimity ; while three great war-poems—*Hohenlinden* (inspired by a visit to the battlefield), *Ye Mariners of England*, and the *Battle of the Baltic*—are among the best things of their kind in our literature.

Scotland, as we can now see, is well represented in the poetry of the Age of the Revolution. Only one **Moore.** Irish poet of the same period is important enough to call for notice here—the " Bard of Erin." Thomas (always known as Tom) Moore (1779–1852) was born in Dublin and educated at the University there. Then he migrated to London to study law, carrying with him a translation of Anacreon which, published in 1800, achieved a success beyond its deserts. This he followed up with a book of light verse, chiefly amatory, under the pen-name of Thomas Little (chosen with reference to his diminutive stature), and with a volume of *Odes and Epistles* (1806). The next year he began his *Irish Melodies*, the issue of which, in ten parts, was not completed till 1834. Meanwhile, ambitious to rival Scott and Byron with work on a larger scale, he produced (1817) *Lalla Rookh : an Oriental Romance*, the glitter and sentiment of which captivated a public already enamoured of the East. The amusing satire, *The Fudge Family in Paris*, on the stock subject of the Briton abroad, appeared in the following year. His last long poem, *The Loves of the Angels* (1823), on a theme which about the same time Byron used for his *Heaven and Earth*, suffers sadly from comparison with *Lalla Rookh*. The most substantial work of Moore's remaining years was in prose, and includes a romance of some merit, *The Epicurean* (1827), and a *Life of Byron*, which deserves a place not far below Lockhart's *Scott*.

Immensely popular during his lifetime, Moore's poetry has not worn well, and the brilliancy which dazzled contemporaries of *Lalla Rookh* now seems tawdry and meretricious. As a political satirist (e.g., *The Twopenny Post Bag*) he was undeniably clever, but his wit has faded with the personalities which once gave it point. It is as a song-writer that Moore now survives, and as a song-writer almost entirely by virtue of his *Irish Melodies*. Himself an accomplished musician and singer, he wrote his lyrics either to music or for music, and they were intended, as he himself was careful to explain, " rather to be sung than read." Judged simply as songs, they are often admirable. As pure poetry, on the other hand, they cannot be ranked very high. While they have, it is true, a good deal of grace and at times a vein of real tenderness, they are as a whole cloying in their mere prettiness, their emotional value is small, and their sentiment thin and conventional. Despite their popular inspiration, indicated by their title, they are indeed just drawing-room lyrics, and though Moore was at pains to excuse their " national zeal," he need hardly have taken the trouble to do so, for even this is toned down in deference to the susceptibilities of the English public for which they were written. He was, as we otherwise know, a genuine patriot, but we should scarcely guess this from the *Melodies*, and as a national poet he cannot for a moment be mentioned in the same breath with Robert Burns.

CHAPTER III

THE YOUNGER POETS

ONE of the central facts for the student of literature—the fact, namely, that every writer necessarily responds to the conditions of his age in accordance with the peculiar qualities of his own nature and genius—is strikingly exemplified by the case of our three chief poets of the younger revolutionary group. Byron, Shelley, and Keats alike grew into manhood in time to feel the full influence of the great conservative reaction already described, and saw the same forces at work about them. Yet nothing could be more marked than the contrast between each and each in the character and temper of their poetry.

Scion of a wild, unruly stock, and only child of a profligate father and a neurotic mother, George Gordon Byron was born in 1788 ; succeeded to the title and family estates at the age of ten ; entered **Byron.** Harrow in 1801 ; and in 1805 passed thence to Cambridge, where by fits and starts he read omnivorously and lapsed into dissipation. A small volume of immature verse, *Hours of Idleness* (1807), was roughly handled by the *Edinburgh* in one of its " slashing " articles, and Byron replied with a satire, *English Bards and Scotch Reviewers* (1809), in which, in equally slashing style, he attacked not only the critics, but also the poets of the day. The next year he left England, and after an extended tour in Southern Europe and the East, returned in July 1811, bringing with him as a record of his journey the first two cantos of *Childe Harold's Pilgrimage* (1812). Intrinsic merit had much to do with the instant popularity of this poem, but even more perhaps the timeliness of the subject ; for Englishmen just then were deeply moved by the great Napoleonic drama which was being enacted on the Continent, and Byron's vivid descriptions, done on the spot, of places familiar by name to every reader, and his wonderful power of expressing in rapid and sonorous verse the feelings which the scenes naturally evoked, gave to the work an interest of actuality such as Scott's romantic tales did not possess. At the same time the character of the nominal hero, Childe Harold himself, who, despite his youth, has already drained the cup of pleasure to the dregs of bitterness, fell in with the romantic mood of a generation which found something essentially poetic in such a picture of disenchantment and melancholy.

But great as was the success of *Childe Harold*, it was surpassed by that of the metrical tales which followed it with astonishing rapidity during the next few years—*The Giaour* and *The Bride of Abydos* in 1813 ; *The Corsair* and *Lara* in 1814 ; *The Siege of Corinth* and *Parisina* in 1816. Popular taste had been well prepared for romances in verse by the vogue of Scott's ; but Byron opened a new field with these melodramatic Oriental stories of passion and crime beside which even *Marmion* seemed tame and *The Lady of the Lake* a little schoolgirlish and conventional. With these poems he took the public by storm ; Scott himself being among the first to recognise that the new favourite had beaten him " out of the ring." We cannot to-day share the enthusiasm of the early readers of such poems ;

yet while *The Giaour* and its successors impress us now as theatrical and often flashy, we must still admit that they contain occasional passages of real power and beauty.

It was while Byron was at the height of his fame that a decisive change occurred with dramatic suddenness in the current of his life. In 1815 he married Anne Isabella Milbanke. Within a twelvemonth he and his wife parted, never to meet again. The separation was the signal for an outburst of scandal and a complete revulsion in general feeling, and the public which had idolised the poet now loaded him with abuse. Filled with bitterness and smarting under a sense of personal wrong, he left England, as it proved for ever.

His first destination was Geneva, whither he was attracted by the presence of Shelley, whose writings he greatly admired, but whom he had not yet met. His route lay across Belgium and up the Rhine, and his impressions of the journey and of his sojourn in Switzerland in Shelley's stimulating society are recounted in the third canto of *Childe Harold* (1816). *The Prisoner of Chillon,* the most restrained and powerful of his narrative poems, also belongs to this time, together with the first two acts of *Manfred* (completed and published in 1817), which is interesting chiefly on account of its fine pictures of Alpine scenery. In November 1816 he went to Venice, where he lived till December 1819. Here he wrote the superb fourth canto of *Childe Harold* (1817), in which the shadowy figure of the nominal hero finally disappears and Byron himself dominates the stage ; the brilliant carnival poem *Beppo* (1817), and, in the same vein of social satire and in the same verse form (the Italian eight-line stanza), the first four cantos of *Don Juan*. At

Ravenna (December 1819 – November 1821) and at Pisa (November 1821 – September 1822) his poetic activity continued unabated. *The Prophecy of Dante* (1819) was inspired by his sympathy with the cause of Italian independence. In *Cain* (1821), his most thoughtful work, he boldly grappled with the problem of evil and of God's dealings with men as interpreted by the traditional theology. In *The Vision of Judgment* (1822) he made an absolutely crushing reply to Southey's unfortunate poem of the same title. Of his attempts at regular drama during this period—*Marino Faliero* (1820), *Sardanapalus* (1821), *The Two Foscari* (1821), *Werner* (1822)—it is enough to note that they mark his failure in a field in which, considering the fundamentally undramatic character of his genius, he could not be expected to succeed. Nor is it necessary to say anything more of his *Heaven and Earth* (1821) and *The Deformed Transformed* (1821) than that they are experiments of little value in the line of *Manfred* and *Cain*. But the successive cantos of *Don Juan*, which meanwhile pursued its tortuous course, continued to exhibit his qualities, both poetic and satiric, at their highest.

With the close of his stay at Pisa, Byron's career as a poet practically ends. By this time he was beginning to weary of poetry and to crave some fresh outlet for his powers, and his enthusiasm for national freedom prompted him to espouse the cause of the Greeks, then in revolt against the Turks. In July 1823 he took the field, and in April 1824 died of fever at Missolonghi. Three months before he had taken farewell of life in his last poem, the noble stanzas which bear date and title *January 22 : On this Day I complete my 36th Year*.

Byron's character was a mass of inconsistencies, and its contradictions reappear in his attitude towards both life and literature.   An aristocrat to his finger-tips, proud of his caste and tenacious of his privileges as a peer of the realm, he was yet a poet of liberty and of revolt against the whole established order.   In theory a fanatical supporter of Pope and the classic school, he did more than any other man, as he himself admitted, to complete the overthrow of the old poetic dynasty and secure the popular triumph of romanticism.

Great in quantity, his work is also apparently very varied, for he wrote in many styles—lyrics, descriptive poems, narrative poems (serious and serio-comic), tragedies, dramatic poems, satires.   But this variety is only superficial.   The outstanding feature of his poetry is its essential sameness.   His genius was not broad and catholic.   It was narrow and intense.   The egotism of his personal character is the ground-tone of his writings.   He does not, like the true creative artist, merge himself in the outer world.   He draws the world down into himself.   He can express his own emotions with almost unrivalled power.   But that power fails the moment he attempts to transcend the limits of what he himself had known and felt.   Hence the monotonous repetition of one and the same type in the long succession of Byronic heroes.   Hence, too, the pervading influence throughout his poetry of that spirit of disillusion, gloom, misanthropy, which we now designate by the word Byronism.   A rebel against society, and not only against society but also against the very conditions of human life, Byron is our one supreme exponent of the destructive forces of the Revolution.   Of its constructive energy, its social ardour, its utopianism, there is no trace in his work. He had a real passion for liberty.   But liberty for him was synonymous with pure individualism; it meant at bottom the right of each man to live as a law unto himself. He is from first to last the great iconoclast. He struck fiercely at the old order ; but he had no new faith, no new idealism, to offer in place of the idol-worship he helped to destroy. Thus he leaves us face to face with negation. *Vanitas vanitatum* was the text and epitome of all his criticism of life.

On the formal side the defects of Byron's poetry are very apparent. He wrote fast and carelessly under the impulse of the moment ; his facility was amazing, but his taste was poor ; he had neither the patience nor the capacity for self-criticism, and the polish which he admired in the Augustans was wholly beyond his reach. " I never recast anything," he once declared : " I am like the tiger ; if I miss the first spring, I go grumbling back to my jungle." His work is therefore wanting in the finer qualities of art ; he seldom keeps for long together at level flight ; and even his best passages are often marred by lapses into noisy declamation or downright commonplace. But if his technical shortcomings are numerous, his personal force is at times irresistible. When once his blood is fairly up, his verse sweeps on with a rush which carries everything before it, and his dash and vigour make us forget the minor imperfections of his style. Even disparaging criticism admits the vividness of his descriptions. As a poet of nature he has his secure place in our literature. Characteristically enough, he has no eye for the quiet beauties of a domestic landscape. But he can render the might and mystery of ocean, mountain, and tempest with a power which has never been surpassed.

Byron's immense European vogue and influence during his lifetime—and his name is written large on hundreds of pages of Continental literature—were in the main the result of the striking correspondence between his own spirit and the spirit of a generation which, carried away by the reaction which had followed the apparent failure of the Revolution, had lost hope for the future and faith in God and man. Egotist as he was, therefore, it happened that while he was writing for himself he also became the mouthpiece and interpreter of his time. And thus in turn the declension of his popularity, in England at least, which began soon after his death, was due more to the passing of the Byronic mood than to changes (great as they were) in literary taste. Yet unsatisfactory as his gospel of mere negation seems to us to-day, we must not forget how much his poetry did to keep the spirit of liberty alive among the European peoples in the dark days for democracy which were ushered in by the Holy Alliance and Waterloo.

The son of a wealthy, narrow-minded country gentleman, Percy Bysshe Shelley was born at Field
Shelley. Place, near Horsham, Sussex, on 4th August 1792. He was sent to Eton in 1804, and there his shyness and his many eccentricities of behaviour, which included a single-handed revolt against the abominable fagging system, earned for him the nickname of " mad Shelley." (For a noteworthy reference to his experiences at school, see the *Dedication* to *The Revolt of Islam.*) He read widely in the classics, from whose pages he fed his appetite for beauty, and in the eighteenth-century philosophers, who filled his mind at once with religious doubts and with glorious visions of the future progress of the human race. At the same time, under the influence of Mrs. Radcliffe and M. G. Lewis, whose novels he devoured with avidity, he scribbled two crude romances, *Zastrozzi* and *St. Irvyne,*

or the Rosicrucian, both of which were published in
1810. In the same year he went up to Oxford, whence,
however, he was expelled in the following March for
issuing a pamphlet entitled *The Necessity of Atheism*.
Shortly after this he met in London a schoolgirl of
sixteen, named Harriet Westbrook, whom he was led
to regard as the victim of domestic tyranny; his
chivalrous nature was aroused by her troubles, and,
in an unfortunate hour for both, he married her (August
1811). This hasty step completed his alienation from his
family, and he found himself adrift in the world. For
some time he led a wandering life, occupied mainly
with various ill-considered schemes of political reform;
and then in 1813 he definitely began work as a poet by
the printing, for private circulation only, of *Queen Mab*,
which he described as " a Philosophical Poem," and
introduced with Voltaire's famous phrase, " Écrasez
l'Infâme," by way of motto. Though owing something
of its orientalism to Southey's *Thabala*, the irregular
blank verse of which he took as his model, the poetry
of the poem is Shelley's own. Its stated philosophy,
on the other hand, is in the main that of Godwin's
Enquiry into Political Justice, which even in his Eton
days had been his law and his gospel. Following his
master, whose cold abstractions he translates into
impassioned verse, he denounces all existing institutions,—kings, governments, priests, church, property,
marriage,—and strikes fiercely at Christianity itself.
Yet reckless and violent as it is (" villainous trash,"
Shelley afterwards called it), the poem is redeemed
by occasional passages of genuine poetry, and by that
exalted faith in love as the one thing needful for the
salvation of the world, which was always the basis of
the poet's faith. We must be careful, however, not to

4

judge Shelley by this boyish production. When in 1821 *Queen Mab* was surreptitiously published, he wrote a letter to *The Examiner* regretting its appearance, " not so much from literary vanity, as because I fear it is better fitted to injure than to serve the sacred cause of freedom."

Before *Queen Mab* was finished, Shelley had made the personal acquaintance of Godwin, and a friendship soon sprang up between him and Godwin's daughter Mary, a girl of seventeen, in whom he found a kindred soul. That friendship ripened into love, and in July 1814 he eloped with her to the Continent. After six weeks in France and Switzerland the runaways returned to England, and the following summer Shelley wrote his first great poem, *Alastor, or the Spirit of Solitude*, an idealised rendering of his own quest for absolute beauty, but at the same time an object-lesson to those who live in selfish isolation from mankind. The next year he and Mary settled near Geneva, and there in November the news reached them that poor Harriet had ended her life by suicide. Into the details of the tangled story of Shelley's first marriage we cannot now enter. It will be enough to say that, though his apologists have done their utmost to throw the entire responsibility for its tragic failure upon the young wife, Shelley certainly cannot be exonerated from blame. The way now clear, he lost no time in legitimising his relations with Mary, and they were formally married on 30th December 1816. This second union was altogether a happy one. In Mary he found intellectual companionship, and a comfort and support amid many troubles arising from quarrels with his family, lawsuits about his property and his children, and his own fragile health.

The summer of 1817, spent at Great Marlow, is

chiefly memorable for the production of a long narrative
poem in Spenserian stanzas, first entitled *Laon and
Cythna*, but published early next year as *The Revolt of
Islam*. Confused and almost unintelligible as a story,
this poem has great interest as an expression of Shelley's
hope for the world. In the preface, which is a document
of great importance on both the personal and the historic side, he defines his position and states the grounds
of his faith, drawing a sharp distinction between the
French Revolution itself, as an event, and the large
general movement of liberation of which it was only a
phase or manifestation, and declaring his belief that
the reaction against it had already spent its force, and
that all the signs of the time pointed to a " renewal of
public hope." " In that belief," he adds, " I have composed the following poem." *The Revolt of Islam* is
indeed the proclamation of Shelley's indomitable
revolutionary faith, and its keynote is the saving power
of love—the love which in it " is celebrated everywhere
as the sole law which should govern the moral world."
That love is embodied in the central figure Laon ; and
here an instructive comparison is at once suggested
between Shelley's typical hero and the typical heroes of
Byron. The latter are self-engrossed egotists at war
with society. Laon, on the contrary, is a noble-minded
enthusiast who willingly becomes a martyr for the
cause of man.

Shortly after the publication of *The Revolt*, Shelley
left England for Italy, his home for the brief remainder
of his life. At Lucca he finished an unimportant
" eclogue " of modern life, *Rosalind and Helen* (1818) ;
at Venice, where he spent part of the autumn of the
same year with Byron, he wrote a delightful poem in
the conversational style, *Julian and Maddalo*—Maddalo

being an idealised portrait of Byron, Julian of the poet himself. This was followed in the spring of 1819 by the magnificent lyric drama *Prometheus Unbound*, in which he re-fashioned the old Greek myth of the fire-bringer in such wise that it became in his hands an allegory of humanity in its age-long conflict with despotism and final triumph over evil. To the same year belong a five-act tragedy, *The Cenci* (the plot of which is really too horrible for the modern stage, but which contains scenes of very great power), and the most important of Shelley's poems dealing directly with English political affairs, *The Mask of Anarchy*, written on the occasion of the massacre at Manchester, and, as Mrs. Shelley notes, " in a more popular tone than usual."

Early in 1820 the Shelleys settled in Pisa, where they had many friends, and where the poet's genius continued to expand. Some of his finest lyrics were the work of this year, together with the charming *Letter to Maria Gisborne*, in whose house at Leghorn part of the summer was spent. About this time Shelley became much interested in a young Italian girl, Emilia Viviani, whose beauty and sorrows made a deep appeal to his ardent sympathies ; his idealising imagination quickly transfigured her into a type of the absolute per-fection of womanhood ; and his spiritual passion found expression in the vague but lovely verses of *Epipsychidion* (1821)—a poem which he himself declared to be intended only " for the esoteric few," and which is indeed too obscure and too unreal for general enjoyment. It has unfortunately to be added that, not for the first time in his life, Shelley was soon disillusioned regarding the object of his worship, whom he found to be a very commonplace young woman after all.

In February and March 1821 he was chiefly occupied with his *Defence of Poetry*, the most important of his prose writings, and a work of great value for the light which it throws upon his own high conception of his art. Then in April he learned of the death of Keats in Rome, two months before. He and Keats had met at Hampstead through the kindly offices of their common friend, Leigh Hunt, and letters had afterwards passed between them ; but nothing approaching intimacy had followed. Shelley, however, had a sincere admiration of his young contemporary's genius, and when he heard, as the baseless report then ran, that he had been killed by the brutal severity of his reviewers, he was stirred to indignation, and *Adonais*, one of our greatest elegies, was the result. Considering the circumstances, it is inevitable that this superb poem should be wanting in the warm human emotion which we find, for example, in Tennyson's *In Memoriam*. Keats's death is in fact the occasion, not so much of personal sorrow, as of righteous anger and rapturous meditations over life and death. Magnificent throughout, *Adonais* rises in the closing stanzas to perhaps the highest point which Shelley ever reached. Two things about the poem are specially interesting : Shelley's pathetic description of himself in stanzas 31–33, and the insight which it gives us at the end into his religious ideas. He had chosen in *Queen Mab* to announce himself as an atheist, though even then he had been careful to explain in a note that while denying the existence of " a creative Deity " he held fast to " the hypothesis of a pervading Spirit co-eternal with the universe." Though it is impossible to reduce the impassioned utterances of *Adonais* to a formal creed, they prove beyond the shadow of a doubt that whatever might be his philosophic position, he believed implicitly in the triumph of the spiritual over the material and of life over death.

Political enthusiasm inspired one more poem during 1821—the lyrical drama *Hellas*, bred of his intense sympathy with the Greek struggle for freedom. Published in November, this was Shelley's last important completed work. In the following spring he and his wife moved to Spezzia. On 8th July, while returning from a visit to Leigh Hunt at Leghorn, his little boat was caught by a sudden squall, and he was drowned.

By the common consent of the critics, Shelley's place is with our greatest English poets. Yet without dissenting from this view, the ordinary lover of poetry may still justly complain of the unsubstantial quality of his work as a whole. This defect was perceived by Mrs. Shelley who, with reference to the brilliant fantasy, *The Witch of Atlas*, expressed her regret that her husband lived so habitually amid mere abstractions and so rarely "addressed the common feelings of men." But despite her efforts to turn his attention to more concrete themes, he kept to his chosen way, and the "human interest and passion" which she desiderated for his poetry are precisely the elements which it lacks. In the world of his imagination we move for the most part among shadowy shapes which come and go through scenes which, though exquisitely beautiful, are still as unreal as dreamland.

His genius was fundamentally lyrical, and it is in his pure lyrics—in such things of ethereal loveliness as *The Cloud*, *The Skylark*, the *Stanzas written in Dejection at Naples*, the *Hymn to Intellectual Beauty*, the *Ode to the West Wind*—and in the longer poems which are entirely lyrical in impulse and character like *Adonais*—that he most definitely challenges comparison with the greatest singers of all time. Such lyrical poetry largely represents the personal side of Shelley's inspiration. Of the other side, the humanitarian, the record is given in such works as *Queen Mab*, *The Revolt of Islam*, and *Prometheus Unbound*, which overflow with his enthusiasm for liberty, his love of man, and his "passion for reforming the world." The change of tone which we note as we pass from the personal to the humanitarian poetry is very significant. The personal poetry is often profoundly melancholy. But the melancholy disappears the moment Shelley ceases to think of his own little life and assumes the rôle of leader of men and prophet of the Golden Age to come. His own attitude towards the political movement has already been defined. But it is well to lay stress upon the fact that, alone among the English poets of his time, he continued to preach the gospel of revolutionary faith and hope.

Younger by seven years than Byron and by three years than Shelley, John Keats was born on or about **Keats.** 31st October 1795, in Moorfields, London, where his father was manager of a livery-stable. The boy received his entire education, which was good so far as it went, if it did not go far, at a private school at Enfield. In 1810 he was apprenticed to a surgeon at Edmonton, and though in 1814 his indentures were cancelled, he continued his professional studies, and having passed his examination at Apothecaries' Hall, was in March 1816 appointed dresser at Guy's Hospital. In the meantime, however, his mind had taken an irresistible turn towards literature. Two incidents in particular belonging to this period count as factors in the development of his genius. His first acquaintance with *The Faerie Queene*, made in his eighteenth year, stimulated his own poetic faculty, which hitherto had lain dormant ;

while a little later the discovery of the *Iliad* and the *Odyssey* in Chapman's translation opened up to him that great wonderland of legend—the "wide expanse . . . that deep-browed Homer rules as his demesne "— which thus far he had known at second hand only through his careful study of the *Æneid*.

Both Spenser and Homer were brought to his notice by his old schoolfellow Cowden Clarke. It was that same friend who in the spring of 1816 also introduced him to Leigh Hunt, with whom he soon became intimate, and to whom he dedicated his first book of verse (1817). This little volume, with its many immaturities of thought and style, was obviously the work of a very young man, who as yet had learned little of the principles of his art, and we need not perhaps be surprised that it fell dead from the press. But there were things of promise in it—like the lines beginning " I stood tiptoe upon a little hill," and here and there phrases which revealed a true poet's imaginative insight and power of felicitous expression. Nothing daunted by this first failure, Keats now stirred himself to a more ambitious effort, and in the spring of 1818 produced the long narrative poem *Endymion,* in which, in four books of upwards of one thousand lines each, the old Greek myth of the shepherd-prince's love for the moon-goddess Diana is fashioned into a vague parable of the soul's quest for ideal beauty. Keats was himself fully aware that in this poem he had undertaken a task which was for the moment beyond his powers, and in his preface he spoke disparagingly of it as " a feverish attempt rather than a deed accomplished." Its defects are indeed very obvious. As a story it is rambling and confused, broken up by episodes and overloaded with digressions ; its descriptions are choked

with detail ; its style is diffuse and florid. Yet with
all its faults *Endymion,* while certainly not a great
poem, is at least, as Shelley said, " full of some of the
highest and the finest gleams of poetry " ; and in
reading it we come from time to time upon passages
(like the famous opening of Book I.) so instinct with
imagination and so rich in beauty of phrase that, as
even Jeffrey admitted, they may almost be used " as
a test to ascertain whether anyone has in him a native
relish for poetry and a genuine sensibility to its intrinsic
charm."

Unfortunately, contemporary critics were blind to
these redeeming qualities, and seizing only upon defects,
they made *Endymion* the subject of the most vulgar
and virulent abuse. In dealing with Shelley's *Adonais*
I have already referred to the report, which presently
became current, that the gross attacks of *Blackwood*
and the *Quarterly* were directly responsible for the
illness which ended in Keats's premature death. Such
reports were, as I have said, baseless. Keats's own
letters of the time prove that he was in fact but little
disturbed by the vituperation of his assailants. Far
more accurately than these he had himself taken the
measure of his work. He knew that *Endymion* was
" slipshod " ; he realised that it had been written
" without judgment " ; he treated it only as an experiment and a means of self-discipline. In writing it he
felt that he was preparing himself " for verses fit to
live " ; having printed it, he was anxious only to
" forget it and proceed."

How rapidly his mind and taste were now maturing
we can see at once when we turn to his third and last
volume, *Hyperion and Other Poems,* published in July
1820 : the volume which contains his really great

contributions to English literature. The title poem, dealing with the overthrow of the Saturnian dynasty, though incomplete, is, as Leigh Hunt said, a " noble fragment," and its Miltonic blank verse has a majesty suggestive of the " large utterance of the early gods " ; *The Eve of St. Agnes* and *Isabella* are romantic narratives full of sensuous beauty and charm ; while *Lamia*, the story of a young Corinthian's love for a serpent-woman, shows how much the poet had gained in the mastery of the couplet since the writing of *Endymion*. But while these longer poems are all things of note, it is in the shorter poems in the volume that Keats's most perfect work is to be found. The ballad of *La Belle Dame sans Merci* and the three great odes— *To a Nightingale, On a Grecian Urn,* and *On Melancholy* —are masterpieces of their kind.

For some time before the publication of this volume Keats had been failing in health, and when it appeared he was seriously ill with consumption. In September 1820 he resolved as a last hope to try what Italy would do for him. He reached Rome in November, and there he died on 23rd February following, having not yet completed his twenty-sixth year.

Keats's place is among " the inheritors of unfulfilled renown," and in reading his poetry we must always make allowance for the fact that it is to a large extent tentative and incomplete. But taking it as it stands, we can perhaps best appreciate its essential qualities by comparing it with the work of Byron and of Shelley. Byron, as we have seen, was our one great exponent of the destructive forces of the Revolution, Shelley our one great apostle of continued faith and hope. Keats was neither iconoclast nor utopian. He knew nothing of Byron's stormy spirit of revolt ; he had no sympathy with Shelley's humanitarianism and "passion for reforming the world." His own attitude towards the movements and conflicts of his time was one of artistic detachment. He did not fight his age ; he did not denounce it ; he did not preach to it, nor did he seek to inspire or guide it. He simply effected an imaginative escape out of it, not like Shelley into a future land of promise, but into the past of Greek mythology or mediaeval romance.

This brings us at once to his own idea of poetry and its functions. "Every great poet is a teacher," said Wordsworth ; "I wish either to be considered as a teacher or as nothing." We recall the statement here that we may note Keats's emphatic repudiation of such didacticism : "We hate poetry that has a palpable design upon us," he declared. Poetry in his view should be "unobtrusive." It should not be the vehicle of philosophy, of religion, of social and political theories. It should be simply the incarnation of beauty. "A thing of beauty is a joy for ever"—in that famous opening line of *Endymion* he strikes the keynote of all his work. "I have loved," he writes in one of his later letters, "the principle of beauty in all things" ; and again : "With a great poet the sense of beauty overcomes every other consideration, or rather, obliterates all consideration." He even reproved Shelley for his preoccupation with propagandist purposes : "You will, I am sure, forgive me for sincerely remarking that you might curb your magnanimity, and be more of an artist, and load every rift of your subject with ore." Such passages define both the end and the limit of his own effort. It was to the service of beauty in various forms and manifestations—beauty of nature, of romantic legend, of classic story—that his brief life was consecrated.

His treatment of nature is at one with his general treatment of life. Sensuous love of the sensuous beauty of nature—a love of nature just for its own sake and without ulterior considerations—is its outstanding feature. No modern poet has been nearer than he was to the simple " poetry of earth," which for him was " never dead." But there was nothing mystical about his feeling for it ; nothing of the religious quality which we find in Wordsworth and Shelley. In his interpretation nature is never symbolical ; it is never fraught with spiritual messages or moral meanings.

Historically Keats is specially important for two reasons. In the first place, he is the most romantic of the romantic poets in the sense that he is the one in whose work there is the least leaven of the eighteenth century. This is shown particularly in his form and style. Classic scholars have noted with surprise the essentially Hellenic spirit of this London-born son of a livery-stable keeper. His " natural affinity with the Greek mind," as Prof. Jebb called it, is indeed one of those mysteries of heredity of which literary history is full. Yet Greek as he was in temper, there was nothing classic about his art, which was indeed ultra-romantic in its luxuriance, its total want of temperance and restraint. It must be remembered that he never learned to read a sentence in the language which would have been for him the tongue of tongues, and that he knew Homer only through Chapman's vigorous but thoroughly Elizabethan translation.

Secondly, his work marks a temporary rupture between poetry and the forces of contemporary life. Broadly viewed, it represents the exhaustion of the impulses bred by the social and humanitarian movements of the Revolution. For this reason, though he died before any of his great contemporaries, he seems more than any other poet of his time to stand at the end of his epoch. For the re-quickening of English poetry new impulses and inspirations were required, and these, as we shall see later, came with the beginning of the Victorian Age.

The later revolutionary age was one of great poetic activity, and only a few of its minor poets can be mentioned here. Of those whom we select from the mass, some are chosen because of the intrinsic value of their work ; others because, as exponents of current taste, they have a certain interest in literary history.

It is natural to turn first to one who stood in close personal relationship with all the three great poets who **Leigh Hunt.** have been considered in this chapter, James Henry Leigh Hunt (1784–1859). Dependent as he was upon his pen—which was the pen of a very ready writer—Leigh Hunt naturally gave the greater part of his energies to prose (see next chapter). His most considerable work in verse—*The Story of Rimini* (1816)— is historically important because it was the first poem in which the long-standing tradition of the classic couplet was defied, and an attempt made (as he himself pointed out in his *Autobiography*) to revive the freer manner of Dryden and the " variety of his cadences, at least as far as they broke up the monotony of Pope." In this he was followed by both Shelley and Keats, under whose influence the romantic or " loose," as contrasted with the classic or " closed," couplet was restored to English poetry. Hunt himself afterwards declared that his attempt to enlarge upon a subject which had been treated with " exquisite sufficiency " by Dante in one of the most famous episodes of the *Inferno*, was an act of bad taste, and critics now agree that what makes the *Story* interesting is not its amplified rendering of tragic passion, but the occasional beauty of its digressions and descriptions. But beyond this initial fault of conception, the poem suffers from the defects which are generally characteristic of the writer's narrative verse—want of dignity and strength and a tendency to lapse into triviality and mere prettiness. His genius was really too volatile for sustained work, and the best of his poetry is therefore to be sought in his shorter pieces—in the admirable *Abou Ben Adhem* ; in *The Panther* ; in the charming lyric, " Jenny kiss'd me " (" Jenny " being Mrs. Carlyle) ; and in some of his sonnets—notably two which he wrote in friendly competition, in the one case with Keats and Shelley, in the other with Keats—*The Nile* and *The Grasshopper and the Cricket*. It may be added that he had a natural turn for translation. Some of his transcripts from the Italian poets are excellent.

Another poet who had a certain connection with Keats, for he married the sister of Keats's most intimate **Hood.** friend, John Hamilton Reynolds, is Thomas Hood (1799–1845), who began his literary career with the publication in *The London Magazine* of *Lycus the Centaur, The Two Peacocks of Bedfont*, an *Ode to Autumn*, and other poems, in all of which the influence of Keats is very marked. In 1825, with the help of Reynolds, he produced a little volume of light verse entitled *Odes and Addresses to Great People*, the success of which practically determined his career. The public which had been indifferent to his appeal as a poet welcomed him with loud applause in his new rôle of fun-maker, and accepting what seemed to be his destiny, he devoted himself in the main to the business of fun-making for the rest of his life. While the serious poetry which he still wrote occasionally shows us how much literature lost in consequence, no blame attaches to Hood personally for such sacrifice of his genius to lower aims. It was with him a matter of hard necessity. He had married in 1824 ; he had to provide for a growing family ; and his pen was his only means of support. He had therefore to produce what would pay, and as a result the larger part of his voluminous work belongs to the class of hack-writing. Unhappily, he was early attacked by consumption, and henceforth was continually handicapped by the steady encroachments of disease. For more than twenty years he kept up the struggle with a cheerful courage which calls for our warmest admiration, and remained active to the end.

It is probable that Hood's pre-eminence as a comic poet of unrivalled resources and the most accomplished punster in the language has been mainly responsible for the comparative neglect of his poetic claims. This is much to be regretted, because he was a true poet if not exactly a great one. One supreme merit at least must be conceded to him : the individual quality in his best work is very strong, and he did certain things in his own way which no one else has ever done so well. Some of his ballads and lyrics, like the superb *Dream of Eugene Aram*, the exquisite *Death Bed*, *Fair Ines*, " I remember, I remember," *The Song of the Shirt*, and *The Bridge of Sighs*, deserve the highest praise ; his *Melancholy* easily keeps its place among our finest odes, and his *Silence* among our most perfect sonnets ; his *Plea of the Midsummer Night Fairies* is full of airy grace and delicate fancy ; *The Haunted House* is wrought with splendidly sustained imaginative power ; while *Miss Kilmansegg and her Precious Leg* is a masterpiece in a very difficult form of poetry, in which the special combination

of qualities in his genius particularly fitted him to excel—
the gruesome grotesque. His best work bears only a
very small proportion to his total output ; but judged
by his best he is entitled to a higher rank among our
poets than is usually accorded to him.

Winthrop Mackworth Praed (1802–1839), whom it is
natural to associate with Hood, owes his place in the

Praed. history of English literature to his excellence
as a writer of what are known as *vers de société*,
and in such things as *The Season, A Letter of Advice*, and
The Belle of the Ball-room he shows a lightness of touch,
a wit, and a grace which have never been surpassed.
Though a certain amount of sentiment blends with
his vivacity, he keeps almost entirely to the surface of
life, and, unlike Hood, rarely strikes a deeper note of
passion or earnestness. But there is genuine tenderness as well as humour in his character-study of *The
Vicar*, while in *The Red Fisherman* he for once rivalled
Hood in Hood's peculiar vein of the gruesome grotesque.

A poet of very different quality from either of the
foregoing stands next on our list. Thomas Lovell

Beddoes. Beddoes (1803–1849) was the son of a well-
known physician and of Maria Edgeworth's
sister Anna. While still an undergraduate at Oxford
he published a volume of verse, *The Improvisatore* (1821),
of which he afterwards succeeded in destroying all but
some half-dozen copies, and a drama, *The Bride's Tragedy*
(1822). After this, though he continued to write,
nothing of his appeared in print during his lifetime.   In
1825 he went to Göttingen to study medicine, and in 1832
took his degree at Würzburg.   Dabbling in revolutionary
politics, he was obliged to fly first from Bavaria and
later from Zurich, where he had set up in practice.
Then for a time he wandered about the Continent, falling

deeper and deeper into dejection, and ultimately in a fit of melancholy committed suicide at Basel. Beddoes' genius was morbid, sombre, and fantastic ; he was, in his own phrase, " a creeper into worm-holes." He was much influenced by Shelley and by German romantic literature, but most of all by the Elizabethan dramatists, and especially by such writers as Webster and Cyril Tourneur, in whose lurid pages he found his most congenial inspiration. Such inspiration is shown in *The Bride's Tragedy*, and even more clearly in *Death's Jest Book*, a sort of dramatic nightmare, regarded by admirers as his best and most characteristic work. As a dramatist he has no claim to distinction, for he possessed neither constructive power nor power of characterisation. But a few of his lyrics (e.g., *Dream Pedlary, Love in Idleness*, and the songs and dirges in *Death's Jest Book*) have great imagination and beauty, and if the praise which some recent critics have lavished upon them is a little extravagant, it is not altogether without justification.

Before closing this chapter we must find space for two women-poets who enjoyed considerable popularity during their lifetime, though little is now left of their fame.

Mrs. Hemans. The daughter of a Liverpool merchant, Felicia Browne, afterwards Mrs. Hemans (1793–1835), published her first volume of verse when she was only fifteen. She was a very fluent writer, and her works include a tragedy, *The Vespers of Palermo*, which failed on the stage ; two other plays ; narrative poems of an extremely romantic and sentimental kind (e.g., *The Abencerrage, A Tale of the Secret Tribunal, The Forest Sanctuary*), and a very large body of minor verse. The bulk of her production, however, is now quite forgotten, though a few of her shorter pieces (like

5

the still familiar *Casabianca*) survive in anthologies for children. Her verse in general is thin at its best, and when not at its best, feeble and insipid ; but the sweetness of some of her lyrics deserves a word of recognition. As the charm has long since faded from her writings it may be worth while to recall the fact that Jeffrey, Byron, Wilson, Scott, and Lytton were among her admirers, and that Wordsworth included her among the friends whose loss he deplored in his *Extempore Effusion on the Death of James Hogg.*

Letitia Elizabeth Landon (1802–1838), who wrote under the initials L.E.L., while still young published **L.E.L.** three novels and several volumes of verse, including *The Improvatrice* (1824), *The Troubadour* (1825), and *The Golden Violet* (1826), and died under mysterious circumstances at Cape Coast Castle soon after her marriage to the Governor, George Maclean. It is said that with the possible exception of Moore she was the most popular of all English versewriters between Byron's death and the rise of Tennyson ; but to-day it is evident that such popularity must be explained by reference to her success in catering for contemporary taste rather than by the actual merit of her work. Wilson praised her for her originality, but it is difficult now to see the point of his judgment, for her subjects are of the romantic class which had vogue at the time, while her style is full of echoes from Scott, Byron, and Moore, and is totally devoid of personal distinction. She has been described as " a feminine Byron," and the phrase to some extent indicates the particular quality in her writing which helped her most to catch the ear of the public ; but her feminism is much more pronounced than her Byronism, which is indeed of a very weak as well as inoffensive kind. Her verse is easy and musical ; but the melancholy in which she freely indulges is conventional, and her emotion in general either unreal or commonplace. In her case, even more than in that of Mrs. Hemans, sentiment too often runs into sentimentalism and downright gush. As to-day we turn over her pages and note how little there is in them of the stuff of genuine literature, our feeling in regard to her temporary popularity is one of surprise.

CHAPTER IV

GENERAL PROSE

In considering in the mass the general prose literature of the Age of the Revolution, we must first emphasise the profound influence exerted upon it by the establishment of the modern review and magazine. The periodical essay had flourished greatly during the eighteenth century, but it had followed in the main the lines of the *Spectator* ; that is, it had been, not a joint-stock undertaking, but the enterprise of individual writers working independently, and with only occasional and uncertain help from outside. It is true that the new form of periodical had made its appearance in Cave's *Gentleman's Magazine* as early as 1731, in *The Scots Magazine* in 1739, in *The Monthly Review* in 1749, and in *The Critical Review* in 1756. But these ventures had been supported chiefly by the pens of ill-paid hacks ; something of the taint of Grub Street was upon them ; their circulation was limited and their reputation very small. It was not till the beginning of the nineteenth century that review and magazine emerged as things of hitherto unsuspected power in the literary world.

The distinction of priority belongs to *The Edinburgh Review*, which was founded in 1802 by Francis Jeffrey, Sydney Smith, Francis Horner, and Henry (afterwards Lord) Brougham, and of which Jeffrey was for many years the leading spirit. At the outset the *Edinburgh* was not aggressively political, but it soon came to figure as the great organ of the Whig party, and this led in 1809 to the establishment in London by John Murray, at Scott's instigation, of *The Quarterly Review* as a Tory rival and counterblast. The first editor of the *Quarterly* was the surly and dictatorial William Gifford, who remained in charge till 1826, when, after a brief interval, he was succeeded by Scott's son-in-law, Lockhart. Next came two important magazines, the range of interest and appeal in which, as the title implied, was meant to be wider than those of the review properly so called : *Blackwood's Edinburgh Magazine* in 1817, and, as a Southern competitor, *The London Magazine* in 1820. The inception of a third magazine, *Fraser's*, which dates from 1830, just falls within our present period. Meanwhile the regular newspaper and journal underwent expansion, and in the hands of editors like Leigh Hunt came to partake more and more of the character of the magazine.

The direct influence on literature of this immense development of periodicals in one and another form will be readily understood. A fresh and profitable channel was provided for authors by vocation, and at the same time a powerful impulse was given to the occasional essay. Hence nearly all the writers to be dealt with in this chapter found the chief outlet for their energies in this new field, and became in consequence essayists rather than makers of books. The fragmentary and discursive character of much of their production is thus explained. Moreover, the development of periodicals brought with it an enormous development of criticism, and especially of the criticism of current literature. This was of course the main business of the reviews, which set up indeed to be the final

arbiters of taste ; but criticism also filled a large place
in the magazines and journals of the time. More than
ever before, therefore, criticism now became a recognised and popular branch of the literary profession.

One other point of outstanding interest in the prose
literature of the age of Wordsworth must also be noted
in the changes which it underwent in style.   Eighteenth-
century prose had been graceful and urbane in the hands
of Addison and Goldsmith ; plain and vigorous in those
of Swift ; formal and weighty in those of Johnson ; in
those of Hume clear and polished ; in those of Gibbon
stately and grandiose.   It had been on the whole an
excellent instrument for all the purposes to which it had
been put.   But it had been characterised by the defects
as well as by the qualities of its century.   It had in
general wanted warmth and colour, and thus while it
had enabled its writers to say with admirable effect all
that they had to say, it could never have become
an adequate medium for strong passion or high imagination.   When, therefore, the romantic movement
brought strong passion and high imagination once more
into literature, a transformation of the manner of prose-
writing was inevitable.   The new wine had to shape
for itself new bottles.   As for more than a hundred
years before this poetry had been prosaic, now in
turn prose tended to become poetical.   The eighteenth-
century tradition of order and regularity was largely
abandoned and a new prose arose—a prose of ampler
range, richer harmonies, more varied and more intricate effects.

This change had to some extent been heralded by
the oratorical prose of Burke.   But its real beginning
coincides with the culmination of the romantic revival
in the early years of the nineteenth century.   It was

thus the natural analogue of the change which meanwhile came over the manner and style of poetry. And as in the case of poetry so in that of prose : the change was not in one direction only but in many directions. Romanticism, as we have seen, stood for the repudiation of convention and rule and for the right of the individual to express his own individuality without let or hindrance in his own individual way. Hence the personal note is strong in the new romantic prose, and variety is one of its most marked characteristics.

In dealing with the writers who come within the scope of this chapter we will take first those who were chiefly associated with the two great Edinburgh periodicals ; then the London men who were mainly if not entirely magazinists and miscellanists ; and lastly, such writers as do not fall naturally under one or other of these two heads.

Francis Jeffrey was born in Edinburgh in 1773, was educated at the High School (where he had Scott as a schoolfellow) and at the Universities of Glasgow **Jeffrey.** and Oxford, and was called to the Scottish Bar in 1794. He was editor of *The Edinburgh Review* from its foundation (conjointly with Sydney Smith for the first three numbers) till 1829, when he became Dean of the Faculty of Advocates. He entered Parliament in 1830 ; was raised to the Bench in 1834 ; and died in 1850.

Jeffrey himself regarded his *Treatise on Beauty*, long since forgotten, as the corner-stone of his fame, which, however, now rests entirely upon the essays, some two hundred in number, which he contributed to his review. As a critic he is honest and acute, but at the same time narrow, inflexible, and superficial. His main concern is always with manner and style. To matter and thought he gives little attention. Nor does he ever attempt to consider impartially the aims and principles of the writers whom he discusses, or to cultivate that faculty without which the highest criticism is impossible— the faculty of provisional sympathy. For this reason he never gets at the centre of his subject ; he is always an outsider, whose own prepossessions have for him the force of undeviating law. Theoretically, he took his stand with the conservatives. " Poetry," he once affirmed, " has this much in common with religion, that its standards were fixed long ago by certain inspired writers, whose authority it is no longer lawful to call in question." But in practice he was far from adhering to this extreme position. He made it one charge against the rising school of poetry in his time that its system " would teach us to undervalue that vigilance and labour which sustained the loftiness of Milton and gave energy and direction to the pointed and fine propriety of Pope." Yet his view of Pope corresponded with that of the romanticists : " Pope is a satirist, and a moralist, and a wit, and a critic, and a fine writer, much more than he is a poet " ; and he had a cordial word of praise for Cowper because he " threw off the whole trammels of French criticism and artificial refinement." He was therefore not opposed to innovation as such, but only to innovation which, as in the case of Wordsworth, whom he pursued with relentless animosity, ran counter to his limited judgment and tastes. His outrageous dogmatism and frequent brutality, which gained for him the nickname of " Judge Jeffrey " (in reference to the " bloody judge " of the seventeenth century), are characteristics which he shared with many other critics of the time. We must give him credit for the downright good sense by which his opinions were often marked. Few probably would to-day demur to his views of Joanna Baillie's tragedies (so injudiciously praised by Scott and Wilson), or to his strictures on *Marmion* ; while even in regard to Wordsworth he was not always so hopelessly wrong as our present bias in Wordsworth's favour might lead us to suppose. But mere good sense is of small help in the appreciation of the finer qualities of poetry, and to these, save when they were embodied in forms already familiar, he was deaf and blind. Wordsworth's obvious faults he could perceive clearly enough ; Wordsworth's essential greatness and significance were entirely beyond his ken.

As one of the founders of the *Edinburgh*, to which first and last he contributed some sixty-five articles, the Rev. **Sydney Smith.** Sydney Smith calls for passing notice, though his actual literary importance is very small. Born in 1771 and ordained in 1794, he early made his mark both as a preacher and as a wit, while his earnest efforts in behalf of many reforms gave him an even wider and more substantial reputation. He spent much of his life as a village parson, but was at the same time a familiar figure in London literary society. He died in 1845. A man of positive intellect and sound common sense, Sydney Smith had little feeling for pure literature, and his occasional essays in criticism possess no value. He was, on the other hand, a brilliant and effective writer on the ballot, the game laws, prison abuses, and other questions of his day, his zeal for Catholic emancipation inspiring the most famous of his books, the *Letters of Peter Plymley* (1807–1808). His controversial writings are full of wit and vivacity, but they deal for the most part with issues which are now dead, and they have in consequence lost much of their flavour.

John Wilson was born in 1785, and was educated at Glasgow and Oxford, where he won fame both as a scholar and as an athlete. For a time he lived in the Lake Country in intimate association with Wordsworth and his circle. Then, having in 1818 lost the whole of his private fortune, he settled in Edinburgh and was presently called to the Bar. From 1817 onward he was one of the mainstays of *Blackwood's Magazine*, and in 1820 was appointed Professor of Moral Philosophy in the University of Edinburgh. He died in 1854. Wilson was a man of magnificent physique, a lover of nature and an ardent sportsman (his love of sport embracing cock-fighting and the prize ring) ; and his mind was as robust as his constitution. His literary output was very large and very miscellaneous, but the more ambitious parts of it are the least characteristic. His poems (*The Isle of Palms*, 1812 ; *The City of the Plague*, 1816) are mediocre examples of the verse-romance popularised by Scott and Byron ; his prose tales (*Lights and Shadows of Scottish Life*, 1822 ; *The Trials of Margaret Lyndsay*, 1823) occupy only a minor place in the Scottish fiction of the time. Essentially a magazinist, he found his true channel in *Blackwood*, for which he wrote continually on all sorts of subjects, from 1817 till 1852. His name is chiefly associated, however, with a series of seventy papers (of which thirty-nine were from his pen) entitled *Noctes Ambrosianae*, which appeared at irregular intervals in *Blackwood* between 1822 and 1835. These *Noctes*, called " Ambrosianae " from Ambrose's Tavern, which forms the scene of the convivial meetings recorded in them, are dialogues dealing with eating, drinking, poetry, sport, men, women, and things in general ; their interlocutors including, among many others, Wilson himself (under his pen-name of Christopher North), Hogg, the Ettrick Shepherd, and a certain Tickler, commonly identified with the writer's uncle, Robert Syme. They gave Wilson ample opportunity for the play of the boisterous high spirits which were his substitute for genuine humour, and they contain plenty of good things ; but their interest was mainly local and temporary, and to-day, though they are still remembered, they are probably not much read, at any rate by Southerners, who find an additional difficulty in their broad Scotch dialect. Wilson's criticism in general has little value ; his sympathies were wide and generous, but his taste was very uncertain ; and his judgments were largely dictated by caprice. In his style, which is luxuriant and highly coloured, he discarded entirely the traditions of the eighteenth century ; he may indeed be regarded as one of the first exponents of the new romantic prose : an honour which, however, he shares with the writer who comes next on our list.

While Wilson's importance in our literature is now mainly historical, the author of *The Confessions of an* **De** *English Opium Eater* has a substantial claim **Quincey.** to be considered one of the really living figures among the prose writers of his generation. The son of a Manchester linen merchant, Thomas Quincey (the " de " was a later addition of his own) was born in the same year as Wilson—1785. At seventeen he ran away from school, and drifting to London, lived for some months as a homeless wanderer, and underwent the strange experiences so graphically described (with how much imaginative colouring it would be difficult now to determine) in the *Confessions*. At Oxford, where he remained from 1803 to 1807, he first resorted

to opium as a palliative for pain.   An ardent admiration
for Coleridge prompted him to seek out that vagrant
philosopher, through whom in turn he became ac-
quainted with Wordsworth and Southey, and in
1809, with his settlement at Grasmere, he became
himself one of the " Lake " group.   For some years he
contributed to *Blackwood* and the *Quarterly*, but the
publication of the *Confessions* in *The London Magazine*
in 1821 was the beginning of his fame.   He left Cumberland in 1828, and the rest of his life was spent mainly
in or near Edinburgh, where he died in 1859.

De Quincey had little capacity for sustained effort,
and of his two attempts at regular book-making—*The
Logic of Political Economy* (which does not properly
belong to literature) and *Klosterheim*, a romantic novel
—neither can be accounted a success.   He was fundamentally a magazinist and essayist, and the seventeen
volumes of his collected works are almost entirely
composed of papers, encyclopaedic in the range of
their subject-matter, reprinted from the periodicals in
which they originally appeared.   Wide as was his
reading and acute as was his mind, however, he wrote
a great deal on subjects with which he was not qualified
to deal, and despite his parade of scholarship, which
often savours of pedantry, and his logical subtlety,
which frequently degenerates into the captious and
trivial, his speculations in philosophy have no higher
value than is to be expected in the work of a brilliant
amateur.   Nor is his literary criticism of much greater
importance, for his temper was fitful and his judgment
untrustworthy.   Among his special gifts must be
reckoned his power of narrative (e.g., *Joan of Arc, The
Spanish Nun, The Revolt of the Tartars*) ; his imaginative power (as in his many visions) ; his sublimity (*e.g.,*

his *English Mail-Coach* and *Suspiria de Profundis*) ; and his mastery of a grim kind of humour, the most famous example of which is the wonderful essay on *Murder considered as One of the Fine Arts*. Judged by his best, he remains as a stylist unsurpassed and seldom equalled in what he himself called " impassioned prose " —the prose of gorgeous colour and intricate harmonies. But he made the capital mistake of regarding this kind of prose as intrinsically superior to any other, thus ignoring the fundamental principle that style can be evaluated only in relation to matter ; and though he can often be grand, he could never be simple. His defects are many and at times so aggressive as to inter- fere seriously with our pleasure in reading him. His love of erudite display and his mania for minute analysis are often irritating ; his habit of endless digression is a sore tax on our patience ; his taste is faulty ; his style, when not sustained by imaginative energy, becomes fearfully diffuse, involved, and inflated. His collected works contain a vast amount of perishable matter, but his few really great things are in their way unique.

John Gibson Lockhart was born near Wishaw in 1794 ; was educated at Glasgow and Oxford ; was called to the Bar in 1816, and next year formed a connection with *Blackwood's Magazine*. In 1820 he married Scott's daughter Sophia, and in 1825 moved to London on his appointment to the editorship of the *Quarterly*, a position which he filled till within a few months of his death in 1854. His principal title to fame, and a very substantial one, is his *Life of Scott* (1837–38). His *Life of Burns* (1828), though excellent, is now mainly remembered as the occasion of Carlyle's noble essay. His clever satire on Edinburgh society,

Lockhart.

Peter's Letters to his Kinsfolk, is full of the caustic wit
for which he early became famous and which made him
a power on the Tory side of politics. He also wrote
among many other things four novels : *Valerius* (1821),
a romance of the times of Trajan ; *Adam Blair* (1822), a
story of a Scottish minister's sin and repentance ; *Reg-
inald Dalton* (1823), a tale of Oxford life ; and *Matthew
Wald* (1824), a study of madness. His criticism, for
which we have to turn chiefly to his numerous review
articles, shows that, like many other men in that age
of transition, he was partly of the old and partly of the
new. His personal associations with Scott had doubtless much to do with the romantic taste which found
expression in his spirited *Ancient Spanish Ballads* ; but
the natural bias of his mind, strengthened by political
animosities, made him vehemently hostile to romanticism as represented by Shelley and Keats. His nickname, "the Scorpion," points to his gift of sarcasm,
which he often used with deadly effect. In his plain
and unadorned style he had nothing in common with the
romantics.

It is fitting that we should give to Charles Lamb the
place of honour among the London men, to whom we
Lamb.   now turn, because no writer of his own or indeed of any other time belonged more completely to the metropolis than he did : "the streets of
London," as Hazlitt said, were "his fairy land." The
son of a clerk to one of the Benchers, he was born in
1775 in the Temple, and there he passed the first seven
years of his life. At Christ's Hospital, where he remained another seven years, he laid the foundations of
his lasting friendship with Coleridge. In 1789 he
obtained a small clerkship in the South Sea House, and
in 1792 was transferred to the East India House, in the

service of which he continued till 1825. The best part of his life was thus spent in daily drudgery, but this, like his narrow means, he accepted with a cheerful spirit. His courage was, however, more severely tried in other ways. Family responsibilities early weighed heavily upon him, but even these were slight in comparison with the terrible tragedy which affected the whole of his career. One day in 1796, his sister Mary was suddenly seized with acute mania and killed her invalid mother with a knife which she snatched from the dinner-table. She was acquitted of the charge of murder on the ground of temporary insanity, and presently recovered her reason, but henceforth she was always subject to recurring mental attacks. The care of this beloved and afflicted sister now became the principal concern of Lamb's life ; without a murmur, he renounced all personal interests, even the thought of marriage, that he might devote himself entirely to her ; and year by year the two lived together, with this black cloud always hanging over them, in what he himself called "a sort of double-singleness." The greatness of his sacrifice is indicated here and there in his essays, as in the beautiful *Dream Children* ; but Lamb never complained, and his patience and quiet fortitude are the more sublime because he never adopted the heroic pose. All through his anxieties, his friendships and his books were his main sources of consolation. He was pensioned by the India Company in 1825, and died at Edmonton in 1834.

Lamb's work outside the essay is of relatively slight importance. His small output of verse contains some meritorious sonnets and, among the autobiographical poems, one of singular beauty—the well-known *Old Familiar Faces*. His one noteworthy experiment in the serious drama, *John Woodvil : a Tragedy* (1802), is interesting chiefly as evidence of his loving study of the Elizabethans. His "romance in miniature," *Rosamund Gray* (1798), is an artless production of the kind popularised by Mackenzie's *Julie de Roubigné* and Mrs. Inchbald's *Simple Story*; but the idyllic charm of its opening chapters is utterly spoilt by the crude melodrama of the close. The *Tales from Shakespeare* (done in conjunction with his sister, 1807), while they keep their place among children's classics, have no other claim to distinction. It was in the essay and in the essay alone that Lamb found his true field, and his famous collection, *The Essays of Elia* (1823–33),[1] is marked by a combination of qualities which renders it unique and inimitable. The matter of these essays is almost entirely personal ; they are made up of reminiscences, sketches of friends, confidences, meditations on the sights and sounds of the city streets, fantasies, informal disquisitions on literature and the stage : in all of which, as Ainger has said, it is "the man Charles Lamb that constitutes the enduring charm of his written words." The whole of his character, in all its curious complexity, is indeed revealed in these intimate pages : the depth and tenacity of his affections (e.g., *Mackery End*); his whimsical humour (*A Dissertation on Roast Pig*); his tenderness (*Dream Children*); his prejudices (*Imperfect Sympathies*); the sadness which lay only just beneath the surface of his fun, and which, while it continually gave a subtly pathetic undertone even to his merrymaking, prompted him at times to sombre musings over life and death (*New Year's Eve*). Like his matter and manner, his style is all his own ; its old-world flavour and its quaint

[1] The pseudonym which he has made immortal was taken from the name of an Italian clerk in the South Sea House when he was a boy there, thirty years before.

archaisms ("hypochondry" for "hypochondria," "visnomy" for "physiognomy," and so on) point to the powerful influence of his favourite seventeenth-century authors ; but it is never imitative.

As a critic Lamb has a prominent place among the leading exponents of that side of romanticism which was fed by reviving interest in the great writers of the period before the Restoration. His *Specimens of the English Dramatic Poets contemporary with Shakespeare* (1808), with the original and sympathetic, if often rather fanciful, comments with which they were interspersed, did much to stimulate a taste for the Elizabethan and Jacobean playwrights, and thus at once to extend and to supplement the growing enthusiasm for Shakespeare. His limitations were very marked. He cared nothing, for instance, for the Waverley Novels or for the poetry of Byron and Shelley ; and his opinions were occasionally whimsical : as when he supported the paradox, which we may be sure would have greatly astonished the dramatist himself, that Shakespeare's plays suffer from representation on the stage. But within the scope of his own special interests he is a wonderfully suggestive critic

William Hazlitt was born in 1778. The son of a Unitarian minister, he began life in his father's calling, **Hazlitt.** but soon abandoned all thought of a clerical career. For years he struggled hard to make a living as a portrait painter, and it was with much regret that failure at length compelled him to give up the brush. Under the encouragement of Coleridge, whose acquaintance he made in 1798, he wrote his first book—*An Essay on the Principles of Human Action* (1805), the fruit of his early studies in philosophy. He established himself in London in 1812 ; became a writer for the newspapers

6

and reviews ; and later found a congenial field on the lecture platform. His last three years were devoted to a *Life of Napoleon*, of whom, despite his republicanism, he was an ardent champion. He died in 1830.

Apart from his relatively unimportant writings on art and his various excursions, now no longer interesting, into political journalism, Hazlitt's work falls naturally into two classes—the miscellaneous and the critical. To the former class belong his three volumes of collected essays, *The Round Table* (1817), *Table Talk* (1821), and *The Plain Speaker* (1826) ; to the latter, *The Characters of Shakespeare's Plays* (1817), the three courses of lectures on *The English Poets* (1818), the *English Comic Writers* (1819), and *The Dramatic Literature of the Age of Elizabeth* (1821), and the series of portraits of contemporary notabilities entitled *The Spirit of the Age* (1825).

As a miscellaneous essayist he easily ranks with the best in English literature. His range was very wide ; for he is excellent alike in narrative and description, in light gossip and in serious discussion ; while his style presents a rare combination of vigour and grace. But admirable as was his work in the general essay, it was even more admirable in literary criticism. He was indeed on the whole the best equipped, the best balanced, and the most satisfactory critic of his generation. It is true that his intense prejudices, personal and political, sometimes interfered with his judgment, especially in the case of contemporaries. But otherwise he was wonderfully catholic in his sympathies and was quick to recognise and welcome excellence wherever he found it. Such catholicity, which enabled him to do justice alike to the Age of Elizabeth and to the Age of Anne, and to see the merits of Wordsworth without being blind to those of Pope, was of particular value at a time when literary controversy ran high and few critics were large-minded enough to transcend the limits of their own chosen creed (see, *e.g.*, his essay *On Criticism* in *Table Talk*). He is always stimulating and suggestive ; his insight is often penetrative ; and his power of compact and summary statement is another arresting feature of his style.

We have already dealt with Leigh Hunt as a poet. We have here to consider him as a prose writer. A **Leigh** journalist by taste and necessity (he had till **Hunt.** almost the last to make his living by his pen), he edited many periodicals, and in addition wrote continually in other papers and magazines of the day. Many of his separately published volumes—his *Men, Women and Books* (1847), *Jar of Honey from Mount Hybla* (1848), *Table Talk* (1851), his two series of selections from the poets with running comments, *Imagination and Fancy* (1844) and *Wit and Humour* (1846), and his *Stories from the Italian Poets* (1847)—are only journalism in another form. He also produced editions of Sheridan and the Restoration dramatists, and among more substantial undertakings, an historical romance of the times of Charles II.—*Sir Ralph Esher* (1832) ; two delightful books on London—*The Town* (1848) and *The Old Court Suburb* (1855) ; *The Religion of the Heart* (1853), vague in theology, but optimistic, kindly, and devout ; and a rambling *Autobiography*, which Carlyle, who was by no means easy to satisfy in such a matter, pronounced " a pious, ingenious, altogether worthy and human book." His essays are, in his own words, " purely miscellaneous, depending for [their] subject and treatment on the suggestion of the moment." Often slight in theme and careless in style, and generally discursive, garrulous, and egotistical, they owe their charm mainly to the pervasive presence of the writer's sunny nature, his quaint wit and fancy, his tenderness, and his love for all pretty and pleasant things. They make good reading for the idle hour, when the intellectual muscles need relaxation, and the literary perfume which they exhale is not the less delightful for being that of an older world. As a critic Hunt possessed neither the subtle insight of Lamb, nor the depth of Coleridge, nor the mental strength of Hazlitt, but he deserves a place not far below these. His love of literature was genuine and the range of his sympathies very wide, and while he cared little about critical principles, he had a capital faculty not only for seeing what was good, but also for helping his readers to see it as well. In this way he did useful work in spreading a taste for literature among the general public.

It remains for us to speak of two writers of importance who can be classed neither with the Edinburgh nor with the London group—Cobbett and Landor.

A man of boundless energy and restless temper, William Cobbett, like Defoe, whom in many ways he **Cobbett.** resembled, lived a life full of variety and adventure. Born in 1762, he sprang straight from the soil, and as the son of a Surrey farmer in very humble circumstances received little education beyond what he obtained for himself. His first calling was that of ploughboy ; then he became a solicitor's clerk in London ; after which he joined the Army and saw service in Nova Scotia. Obtaining an honourable discharge, he settled in the United States in 1792, and established a newspaper called *Peter Porcupine's Gazette*. But his outspoken criticisms of American institutions and people got him into trouble ; he was twice prose-

cuted for libel ; and on the second occasion in 180c
fled to England to escape payment of the fine imposed.
Encouraged by the Government, he now started his
Weekly Political Register. Thus far he had been a Tory
among the Tories ; but in 1804 his opinions underwent
a complete change, and he soon became an uncompromising Radical. Having suffered two years' imprisonment for a violent attack upon flogging in the Army,
and having further got into money difficulties, he once
more went to America (1817), and spent some time
farming on Long Island. He was back in England in
1819, and threw himself with characteristic impetuosity
into the agitation which ultimately led to the Reform
Bill of 1832. He sat in the new House of Commons
as member for Oldham till his death in 1835.

Cobbett was incomparably the greatest power in the
journalism of his time, and wielded an influence so
enormous that Southey called him " the evangelist of the
populace." With his political writings, however, we
have here nothing to do, nor are we concerned with
the coarseness and truculence which he frequently
imported into his controversies. The most important
thing about him for us is his remarkable style. Whatever the value of his subject-matter, he was a master
of simple, racy, clear, vernacular English, and his
writing is always refreshingly free from literary convention and the taint of bookishness. He thus belongs
to the sturdy stock of Bunyan and Defoe, beside whom
we may confidently place him without fear that he will
suffer by the comparison. According to his own theory,
too much attention to mere form is the common mistake
of men of letters ; the first word that comes to hand is in
nine cases out of ten the best word for one's purpose.
Yet he was not a careless writer ; his searching criticism,

in his *English Grammar*, of the Royal Speech in Parliament, shows his keen feeling for the proper use of words. Among his more prominent works may be mentioned his *Advice to Young Men*, full of egotism, homely wisdom, and shrewd common sense, and his *Rural Rides*, in which his character is most completely revealed—English to the backbone, a lover of the country and of country life, a hater of shams and " gentility," and a fervent admirer of the good old English yeomanry, and of the sports, beef, and beer which had made them what they were. His *English Grammar*, too, is an entertaining book, because, unlike grammars in general, it bears the impress of personality on almost every page.

The present juxtaposition of the names of Cobbett and Landor is only accidental, but it will serve a purpose in **Landor.** helping us to realise the extreme contrast between the two men: the one a master of the colloquial and vernacular style ; the other of an artificial kind of prose as far as possible removed from every suggestion of colloquialism or vernacularity. " Poetry," said Landor himself, " was always my amusement ; prose my study and business " ; and it is generally admitted that his prose writings are the more valuable part of his work.   Of these the most important in bulk and interest are the *Imaginary Conversations*, a series of dialogues between notable people, the composition of which extended over some thirty years, and which number nearly a hundred and fifty.   They cover a very wide field, and many of the great, and many too of the minor, figures of history, ancient and modern, stand out in high relief in his " rich and ample page."   Yet with all their range and variety they fall naturally into two classes—the dramatic and the reflective or philosophical.   In the dramatic *Conversations*, which are generally brief,

Landor's method broadly resembles that of Browning in his dramatic monologues ; he takes a situation which is specially adapted for the revelation of character and concentrates his attention upon the psychology of his speakers. These dialogues often show great power ; but their figures have a statuesque rigidity of outline ; there is no movement in them ; their situations do not develop even psychologically ; and all the characters declaim in Landor's measured prose. In the reflective *Conversations,* which are often of considerable length and are generally extremely discursive, Landor indirectly gives us his personal philosophy, or, as his own Cicero puts it, delivers his opinions " in the voice of others " ; as in the dialogue of Epicurus with two of his girl-disciples, and in the discourse of Marcus Tullius Cicero with his brother Quinctus. There is nothing systematic about this philosophy, and it is nowhere set forth methodically or in detail. But though Landor was not a great thinker, he was, as Lowell admirably said, " a man of great thoughts," and many passages may be culled from his pages which are memorable no less for their truth and nobility than for their beauty of expression. Landor's aristocratic temper and deep republican sympathies, his instinctive leanings towards classic modes of thought and feeling, his love of the heroic, and his scorn of the mean and petty, are everywhere in evidence. His other principal prose works have the same dramatic character as the *Conversations,* and are indeed Conversations in an extended or modified form. *The Pentameron* (1837) is a series of five " interviews " between Boccaccio and Petrarch, whose talk runs almost entirely upon literature ; *The Citation and Examination of William Shakespeare* (1834) reproduces the trial of Shakespeare before Sir Thomas Lucy for deer-stealing ; *Pericles and Aspasia* (1836) tells a tale of ancient Athens, the medium of letters being in this case substituted for that of dialogue. As pure stylist, Landor has been regarded by some critics as the greatest of his age ; but this claim is made on grounds which we cannot here accept. His prose has indeed both the merits and the defects which we have already noted in his verse. It has great beauty of a stately kind, and in perfection of phrase it is often remarkable. But it is still highly artificial prose, and its too obvious artifice frequently impairs its charm. Fine as it is within its limits, it is stiff, formal, and wanting in ease, variety, and the supreme virtue of naturalness.

CHAPTER V

THE NOVEL

In the closing decades of the eighteenth century the novel had to a large extent forfeited the critical esteem which Richardson and Fielding had won for it. Its popularity was still on the increase, and the output was enormous; but with rare exceptions those who now catered in it for public amusement were at best writers of mediocre ability, whose works have long since been forgotten even by name. A few novels were, however, still produced which have a certain place in the history of literature, and if we examine these in the mass we find that they fall into three well-defined classes. To begin with, there was the romance, which frankly rejecting all canons of plausibility, depended for its interest upon sheer sensationalism and the free use of the mysterious and the terrible. This form of fiction had its origin in Walpole's *Castle of Otranto* (1765), and was now cultivated with immense success by Mrs. Anne Radcliffe (e.g., *The Mysteries of Udolpho*, 1794) and Matthew Gregory Lewis (*Ambrosio, or the Monk*, 1795). In striking contrast with this there was, secondly, the novel of manners or realistic story of social and domestic life, especially of fashionable life. This continued to offer an attractive and fertile field to a host of women writers, one of whom, Maria Edgeworth, whose work takes us over the border into the nineteenth century, will be

considered later in this chapter. Then, thirdly, a natural
product of an age of theory and speculation, there was
the doctrinaire novel, in which, as in the writings of
Robert Bage (*Man as he is*, 1792 ; *Hermsprong, or Man
as he is not*, 1796), of Thomas Holcroft (*Anna St. Ives*,
1792 ; *Hugh Trevor*, 1794), and notably of William
Godwin (*Caleb Williams*, 1794, etc.), the machinery of
fiction was used for the propagation of revolutionary
ideas.

Of these three classes that which promised best in the
years immediately preceding the rise of Scott was the
realistic novel of contemporary life, which had indeed
already been enriched by two of Jane Austen's contributions to it. With the general reaction against the
Revolution the doctrinaire novel lost much of its vogue.
In the field of romance the lead of Mrs. Radcliffe and
" Monk " Lewis was successfully followed by Charles
Robert Maturin in *The Fatal Revenge* (1807), and six
years later than *Waverley*, *Melmoth the Wanderer*, the
most powerful production of the sensational school.
By this time, however, the romantic novel had taken a
fresh turn in the romance of history. The principal
practitioner in this line was Jane Porter, of whose works
(*Thaddeus of Warsaw*, 1803 ; *The Scottish Chiefs*, 1810)
it is sufficient to say that they are true neither to the
specific facts of history nor to the large and permanent
facts of human life. Yet they have a faint interest in
showing how little had been achieved in the imaginative
recreation of the past before Scott triumphantly proved
how an historical novel might be written.

Such in brief was the state of English prose fiction
when the publication of *Waverley* opened an entirely
new chapter in the story of its development.

Though Scott did not appear as a novelist till he had

established his fame as a poet with half a dozen romances
in verse, the idea of writing a novel had long been in
his mind. It had occurred to him, he tells
Scott.
us, before the time of the *Lay*, when he had
nourished " the ambitious desire of composing a tale of
chivalry, which was to be in the style of *The Castle of
Otranto*, with plenty of Border characters and supernatural incident " : in fact, a sort of *Lay*, though in prose.
Accident turned him to verse instead, and his success
naturally led him to put the design aside. Some time
after this he wrote a conclusion for Joseph Strutt's
unfinished antiquarian *Queenhoo Hall*, and while doing
so, satisfied himself that the Middle Ages did not offer
as good material for prose fiction as he had supposed—
a curious discovery for the future author of *Ivanhoe*
—and that " a romance founded on a Highland story,
and more modern events, would have a better chance
of popularity than a tale of chivalry." This view was
strengthened by the immense sale of *The Lady of the
Lake*. Upon this, he " threw together " the first
chapters of *Waverley*, but being still preoccupied with his
verse romances, he did not persevere with his experiment. Then, or a little later, he was much impressed
by Maria Edgeworth's early stories, with their detailed
pictures of the Irish people, and it struck him that what
she had done so well for Ireland he might do for Scotland.
Under this new inspiration he returned again to the idea
of a prose tale, though now his thoughts ran in the
direction of a novel of contemporary manners. Already
he was beginning to realise that the vein he had opened
up in the *Lay* and had worked so successfully in *Marmion*
and *The Lady of the Lake* was getting exhausted, and the
sudden rise of Byron forced upon him the necessity
of seeking a fresh outlet for his genius. Just then,

when he was hunting in a drawer for some fishing tackle, he came by lucky chance upon the draft of the first chapters of *Waverley*, and " took the fancy of finishing " the story, which he did with such extraordinary rapidity that the remaining two-thirds of it were written in three weeks. *Waverley* was published in 1814, and though Scott was not prepared even now to quit the poetic field, the success of his new venture indicated that henceforth his creative work was to be in prose.

Scott thus approached the novel from two sides : first from the side of romance, and then from the side of realism. This fact is important because it points to the blending of the romantic and the realistic in the best of his own work. Another detail worth noting is, that though he was himself unconscious of it at the time, he had in his later verse-romances been gravitating towards the novel. The *Lay* was simply an offshoot from and an elaboration of the old ballad type. *Rokeby*, in which he himself said that the interest was made to centre for the first time not in incident but in character, is to all intents and purposes a Waverley novel hampered by the limitations of verse.

Scott's choice of subject in his first novel, and the method of treatment which that subject entailed, may be said to have determined his conception of the historical novel as a novel of manners set in an historical framework. As a youth he had been much in the Highlands at a time when to visit the Highlands was to step out of the present into the past ; he had met " folks of the old leaven," and had talked with people who remembered the " affair " of '45 ; and his avowed purpose in writing *Waverley* was " to preserve," in the form of a fictitious narrative, " some idea of the ancient manners " of which he had " witnessed the almost

total extinction." *Waverley* is thus a picture of life
and character painted from direct observation, though
the plot itself is provided by the last Jacobite rising a
quarter of a century before his birth. In this first
attempt to revive (or, as he puts it, " to preserve ")
the past, Scott therefore combines two kinds of interest
never before united—the interest of a romantic episode
of history and the interest of a faithful study of the
social background. In his next two novels, however,—
Guy Mannering (1815) and *The Antiquary* (1816),—the
historical element is entirely absent ; and though in each
case there is plenty of romantic incident (the former,
indeed, shows the influence of the sensational school),
both books owe their vitality to their richly humorous
handling of the homely details of Scottish life. In
both these stories, moreover, he advanced towards the
present instead of receding farther into the past, the
central date of the one being 1765 and of the other 1795.
Then at the end of 1816 came *The Black Dwarf* and *Old
Mortality* ; and with these we mark Scott's first experiment in revivifying the past, not of reminiscence
and oral tradition, as in *Waverley*, but of books. The
former, the action of which is placed in the opening
years of the eighteenth century, is a failure ; the latter,
with its masterly study of the Scottish Covenanters of
the seventeenth century, ranks among the greatest of
Scott's novels. These were followed in 1818 by *Rob
Roy*, in which a tale of private adventure is loosely
connected with the Jacobite commotion of 1715, and
The Heart of Midlothian, an outstanding masterpiece
(*temp.* 1736), specially memorable on account of its
heroine, the noble Jeanie Deans. *The Bride of Lammermoor* (1819), a tragic love-story of great power (*temp.*
1695), and the far slighter *Legend of Montrose* (1819 ;

temp. 1645), bring Scott's first period as a novelist to a close.

Thus far, as will be seen, he had produced nine novels, and in these he had kept to Scotland and had gone no farther back in time than the middle of the seventeenth century. He now began to feel the need of breaking fresh ground, and this he did in *Ivanhoe* (1820), the first of his novels the scene of which is laid outside Scotland, and also the first in which he explored the distant past (*temp.* 1194). The immense success of this new experiment naturally prompted him to range more freely over history. His next three novels—the uninteresting *Monastery* (1820), its far better sequel *The Abbot* (1820), and the still better *Kenilworth* (1821)—all deal with the third quarter of the sixteenth century. In *The Pirate* (1821 ; *temp.* 1700) he made good use of the materials gathered during a trip to the Orkney and Shetland Islands. Then in *The Fortunes of Nigel* (1822) he turned to the early years of the reign of James I., and in James himself painted his finest piece of historical portraiture. *Peveril of the Peak* (*temp.* 1678), the longest and heaviest of all his novels, followed in 1823.

In the same year Scott made yet another new departure in *Quentin Durward*, for in this tale of the adventures of a young Scottish archer in France in the days of Louis XI. he carried his scene of action for the first time to the Continent. In *St. Ronan's Well* (1823) he returned abruptly to Scotland, and made his solitary experiment in the field of nineteenth-century life. *Red-gauntlet* (1824) deals incidentally with the afterwash of the Jacobite rising described in *Waverley*, while in time of action it is almost contemporary with *Guy Mannering*. its immediate successors, *The Betrothed* and *The Talisman* (both 1825), take us back like *Ivanhoe* to the period of the Third Crusade ; while *Woodstock*, which followed in 1826, is a tale of the period of the great Civil War. In *The Surgeon's Daughter* (1827) we are again in the later eighteenth century ; in *The Fair Maid of Perth* (1828) in the beginning of the fifteenth ; in *Anne of Geierstein* (1829) in the days of Charles the Bold, whose reappearance forms a connecting link between this book and *Quentin Durward*. In the meantime, it will be remembered, Scott's fortunes had collapsed, and though thus far there was little sign of nervous strain in his work, his two remaining novels, published together in 1831, give melancholy evidence of failing powers. The first of these, *Count Robert of Paris*, deals with Constantinople at the end of the eleventh century, and thus is the earliest in period of the whole series. The other, *Castle Dangerous* (*temp.* 1306), falls in historic time between *Ivanhoe* and *The Fair Maid of Perth*, and, as it happens, is Scott's only excursion into the fourteenth century. To complete this summary of his work in prose fiction four short stories have to be added : *The Death of the Laird's Jock* (*temp.* 1600) ; *My Aunt Margaret's Mirror* (*temp.* 1702) ; *The Tapestried Chamber* (*temp.* 1782) ; and *The Two Drovers* (*temp.* 1795).

Several points are suggested by or arise out of this survey. In the first place we note Scott's enormous historic range : his novels, from *Count Robert* at one end to *St. Ronan's Well* at the other, extending over some eight centuries—that is, from the time of the First Crusade to that of the Napoleonic power. Secondly, if we consider the order in which they were produced, an important fact comes to light. Scott did not begin with subjects remote from him in place or time. He began with subjects which lay near at hand, and of which he had personal knowledge, and though after his third novel he began to seek a wider field, he still kept for some years to Scotland and to a period no farther back than the middle of the seventeenth century. It was only when this ground was pretty well exhausted that he felt it necessary to open up fresh sources of interest in the history of other lands and more distant times. Finally, the fact must be emphasised that he is distinctly at his best in novels which, like *Guy Mannering*, *The Antiquary*, *Old Mortality*, *The Heart of Midlothian*, *The Bride of Lammermoor*, fall within his original geographical and historical limits. It is true, of course, that these novels represent his genius at its freshest. But beyond this it is evident that he lost something of his grip on life and character when he left his familiar field. In the Scotland of the seventeenth and eighteenth centuries he was perfectly at home, as he was at home in no other place and in no other time.

Scott's creative power was extraordinary, and he had an astonishing faculty for rapid work. But his facility in composition had its inevitable drawbacks. If he wrote easily he also wrote carelessly, and his technique suffered in consequence. In construction, as he himself frankly admitted, he is singularly weak. Yet such weakness was not due wholly to indifference. It was in large measure the result of his preoccupation with his characters, for whom he felt "the force of paternal affection," and whose expansion under his hands was often fatal to proportion and the orderly evolution of his design. This point is important, because it shows that while Scott's novels are emphatically novels of action, his real interest was always in the men and women who carry on the action. As a delineator of character his method was of course very different from that of our modern psychological novelists, with their minuteness of analysis and meticulous attention to light and shade. He painted with a big brush and in large bold outlines only ; the subtleties and complexities of character were beyond his reach ; and when, as in a few instances, he sought to master them, the resulting failure showed his limitations. But within these limitations his characterisation is marked by wonderful vitality. It is specially noteworthy, as indicative of the realistic quality of his genius, that he scored his greatest successes with the homely figures of his own country-side—his Scottish lawyers, peasants, farmers, and old-fashioned retainers—who gave him his most ample opportunity for the play of his broad and genial humour and his power of rich and racy dialogue. At the other end of the scale his historic personages also demand attention. These may not always be absolutely true to fact ; but Louis XI., James I., the Young Pretender, and Queen Elizabeth are certainly fine pieces of imaginative re-creation.

This brings us to his treatment of history. It is usual to speak loosely of the Waverley Novels as one and all historical ; but we must distinguish between those which, like *Guy Mannering*, *The Antiquary*, and *The Bride of Lammermoor*, have only an historical setting and a certain amount of "local colour," and those which, like *Waverley*, *Quentin Durward*, *Kenilworth*, *Woodstock*, introduce historical events and people. It is of course mainly by reference to the latter class that the value of his work as history is to be determined, and on this point we can scarcely admit his claim, as historical novelist, to a seat " on the bench of the historians of his time and country." It is not only that his anachronisms and faults of detail are numerous and often glaring ; far more important than this is the fact that the general impression which he leaves of the spirit of a given epoch frequently (as in the notorious case of *Ivanhoe*) needs much rectification. His great achievement was in making the past real and vivid to the imagination. In this way, as Macaulay said, he supplements the plain narrative of the historian by a series of pictures composed of materials which the mere historian was accustomed to throw aside till Scott taught him their value. For this reason his influence upon the historians themselves was very marked.

Even more important was his influence on prose fiction. He definitely raised the novel to a plane of equality with other kinds of imaginative literature. The historical novel, as we understand it, was his creation. At the same time, by his detailed descriptions of manners, customs, and social settings, he gave, as the case of Balzac shows us, a strong impulse to writers whose sphere and methods were very different from his own. That his novels have maintained the place which they occupied in the estimation of his own generation cannot be alleged. Modern criticism fastens upon his shortcomings—the frequent clumsiness of his workmanship, his want of psychological insight, his inability to penetrate beneath the outward panorama to the spiritual forces of the ages he describes. But the inherent and lasting greatness of his work must not be overlooked. All deductions made, he still ranks among our masters of prose fiction.

The contrast is striking between Scott and his chief contemporary in the novel. The author of *Waverley* **Jane** keeps us in the highway of life. With Jane **Austen.** Austen we are concerned only with the narrow interests of provincial society and the doings of "three or four families in a country village." Her deliberate and painstaking art—"the most wonderful," Scott himself declared, he "ever knew"—is also marked by precisely those qualities of delicacy and fineness of touch in which his own was conspicuously deficient.

Jane Austen was born in 1775 at Steventon, Hampshire, of which place her father was rector. Till she was twenty-five she lived at Steventon, the monotonous routine of existence in a secluded country parsonage being broken only by occasional visits to Bath, then a fashionable resort. In 1801 her father resigned his living, and after eight years spent mainly at Bath and Southampton, Jane settled with her mother and sister at Chawton, Hampshire. There she remained till 1816, when, already in failing health, she moved to Winchester, where she died in the following year.

Jane Austen began to write when she was very young, and three of her novels—*Pride and Prejudice, Sense and Sensibility*, and *Northanger Abbey*—were ready for the press before she had completed her twenty-sixth year. It was not, however, till 1811 that with the publication of *Sense and Sensibility* she made her first appearance in print. *Pride and Prejudice* followed in 1812, *Mansfield Park* in 1814, and *Emma* in 1815. The year after her death *Northanger Abbey* at last saw the light as a companion piece to the recently finished *Persuasion*. These six novels, together with a few fragments, make up the short tale of her productions.

It was a first principle with Jane Austen to write only of what had come within the scope of her own observation, and as her world of experience was extremely circumscribed, so also was the range of her books. All her novels are compounded of the same kind of materials ; they are " scenes of provincial life " in the narrowest acceptation of the term : they deal with the common-place doings of village and country town ; their actions centre in the parsonage and the homes of the local gentry ; the clergymen, the squire, the gossips of the neighbour-hood, the matchmaking mothers, their marriageable daughters, and the possible or impossible lovers of these, are the characters which for the most part occupy her thoroughly genteel stage. It is a very leisurely life to which she introduces us, and we might expect to find it a very dull one, but it is out of these unpromising elements that, with the help of her satiric humour and never-failing irony, she weaves her admirable social comedy. Romantic adventures and strong emotions have little place in the world which she portrays, and life's deeper problems are deliberately ignored by her. It is significant that though clergymen figure so prominently in her novels it is in their social capacity only ; no religious or ethical interest is ever suggested.

Her strongest point is her characterisation, which is noteworthy for its subtlety and firmness of touch. True to her uncompromisingly realistic principles, she rarely indulges in exaggeration or caricature, but depends for her effects upon her skilful handling of human nature in its most customary forms. She is also eminently successful in tracing the interactions of her characters, as in the fine study of the changing relations of Elizabeth Bennet and Darcy in *Pride and Prejudice*. Her method approximates to that of the dramatist in the large use that she makes of dialogue for the exposition of character.

In a final estimate of her work due weight must be given to the limitations which have been indicated. Her world was very small and she kept entirely to the petty interests which lay on its surface. Thus Charlotte Brontë was thoroughly justified in speaking of her novels

as " tame and domestic," and George Eliot in empha-
sising her want of moral depth.   At the same time the
fullest praise must be accorded to the perfection of her
art.   Her books lack the essential elements which make
greatness in literature, but as a miniature painter she
has never been excelled.

Among Scott's other contemporaries in fiction priority
must be given to an Irishwoman already mentioned as
Other   having had a certain influence on his own work.
Novelists : Maria Edgeworth (1767–1849) was the daughter
Maria
Edge-   of Richard Lovell Edgeworth, a clever, ec-
worth.   centric Irishman of innumerable whims and
crotchets, who was much affected by revolutionary ideas,
and especially by the new notions about educational reform which were in the air at the time.   Her first books—
The Parent's Assistant (1796) and *Practical Education*
(1798)—show the strength of her father's influence upon
her : the latter, indeed, being written in collaboration
with him.   She opened her true career with *Castle
Rackrent* (1800), which at once lifted her far above the
crowd of fashionable novelists whose works then deluged
the market.   She continued to write fiction till 1834 ;
but her fame really rests upon three Irish tales—the
one just named, *The Absentee* (1812), and *Ormond* (1817)—
which, though old-fashioned in style, retain their freshness as vivid pictures of aspects of life and character
which she herself knew well.   She never outgrew the
didactic bias which had been given to her by her father,
and like all her other writings, these are to some extent
overweighted by a too obvious moral purpose.   But she
had the gift of story-telling ; wit, humour, and pathos ;
and no little skill in characterisation and dialogue.

In her hands the Irish novel was merely a novel of
manners ; in the hands of writers like Sydney Owenson,

afterwards Lady Morgan (e.g., *The Wild Irish Girl*, 1805), Gerald Griffin (e.g., *The Collegians*, 1828), and
Other Irish Novelists. the brothers John and Michael Banim (e.g., *The Croppy*, 1828), it became melodramatic and patriotic. The finest fruit of this national inspiration is to be found in William Carleton's *Traits and Stories of the Irish Peasantry* (1830–32), in " the fun, frolic, and folly " of which, as John Wilson said, " there is no want of poetry, pathos, and passion."

The vogue of *Waverley* and its immediate successors incidentally created a public for novels of Scottish life,
Scottish Novelists. even on lines very different from those which Scott himself followed. Two representatives of the new Scottish school have a claim to special distinction—Galt and Miss Ferrier.

John Galt (1779–1839), a very voluminous and very unequal writer, is now remembered chiefly for his
Galt. *Ayrshire Legatees* (1820), which is composed of letters from a Scottish family visiting London, and his *Annals of the Parish* (1821), the rambling chronicle of a small isolated western village from 1760 to 1810, supposed to be written by its minister, the Rev. Micah Balwhidder, and happily blending humour and pathos in the persons and incidents described. Another book of the same character, *The Provost* (1822), is almost as good. Galt's other novels, with the possible exception of *Sir Andrew Wylie* (1822) and *The Entail* (1823), may be disregarded. His several attempts to emulate Scott in the historical romance were complete failures.

Susan Edmondstone Ferrier (1782–1854) was the daughter of an Edinburgh lawyer who for a time was one of Scott's colleagues in the Court of Session. Though a personal friend of Scott, she went her own way

entirely uninfluenced by him. Her three novels—
Marriage (1818), *The Inheritance* (1824), and *Destiny*

Susan   (1831)—all deal with old-fashioned Edinburgh
Ferrier.   and country-house society, and cleverly depict
national idiosyncrasies without the slightest background
of romance. Some of her characters, like Mrs. MacShake
and the three maiden aunts in *Marriage*, are portrayed
with genuine humour.

In England, though novel-writing went on with great
activity, little of importance was produced till towards

English   the close of Scott's life a new generation arose
Novelists. of whose labours we shall have to take account
in a later chapter. Now and then a work of real merit
appeared, like Mrs. Shelley's *Frankenstein* (1818), a
belated example of the sensational school, the five series
of sketches entitled *Our Village* (1824–32) by Mary
Russell Mitford, and the inimitable Persian tale of
adventure, *Hajji Baba of Ispahan* (1824), by James
Justinian Morier. But the general average was low.

Perhaps the most popular novelist of the moment
was Theodore Hook (1788–1841), who for some years

Hook.   amused a large public with a number of loosely
constructed stories full of farcical humour and
practical joking (e.g., *Sayings and Doings*, 1824–28;
Maxwell, 1830; *Gilbert Gurney*, 1836; *Jack Brag*,
1837). These still possess a slight interest both as
pictures of life among the middle classes and fashionable
society, and as examples of the humorous novel just
before Dickens; but they have no literary merit, and
most of the laughter has long since gone out of them.

The writings of Thomas Love Peacock (1785–1866),
on the contrary, though never widely popular, retain
their fine flavour for the critical few. Peacock began as
a poet, but he found his true line in prose fiction with

Headlong Hall in 1816. This was followed by *Melincourt* in 1817, *Nightmare Abbey* in 1818, *Maid Marian* in 1822, and *Crotchet Castle*—the best of all his novels—in 1831. Then, after an interval of nearly thirty years, during which his literary activity was confined to the magazines, he produced *Gryll Grange*, his last book, in 1860. His novels have no interest merely as novels, for his scenes and dialogues are strung on the thinnest thread of story, and his characters are little more than embodiments of abstract qualities and representatives of conflicting points of view. He was first and last a satirist, and he used the form of fiction as the vehicle of satire even, as he told his friend Shelley, when, as in *Maid Marian*, he turned back into the romantic past. As he was a man of many and strong antipathies the range of his satire is fairly extensive : modern talk about progress and reform, the pet ideas of the political economists, reviews and reviewers, and everything Scottish and American being among the chief objects of his attack. Pungency of wit and vivacity of dialogue are his main characteristics, but the poet in Peacock was never killed by the rather cynical humorist, and the lyrics scattered through his pages are among their most attractive features. In the history of English prose fiction he stands entirely alone. He owed nothing to his English predecessors, his affinities being rather with the French philosophical story-writers of the eighteenth century ; and he exercised no influence upon those who followed him.

PART II

THE VICTORIAN AGE

THE EARLIER PERIOD (1830–1872)

CHAPTER I

INTRODUCTORY

WE take 1830 as the initial date of a new era in English history because the decade opened by it was so distinctly a time of beginnings in many things. When Victoria ascended the throne in 1837, most of the movements which were to give its specific character to the first half-century of her reign were already gaining power. Turn where we will, signs of change are evident. Five years before, the passing of the Reform Bill had definitely shown that the strong Conservative reaction which, following hard upon the French Revolution, had arrested progress for nearly a generation, had at length spent its force. A fresh chapter in the annals of English politics commences at this point. Lyell's *Principles of Geology* (1830–33), with its emphasis upon the uniformity of nature's processes, at the same time marked an epoch in science. The year which saw the publication of the closing volume of this great work is also notable for the issue of the first of the *Tracts for the Times*—the real inauguration of that religious revival, known as the Tractarian or Oxford Movement, which both directly and through the opposition which it aroused exercised an immense and long-continued influence on English thought. Meanwhile the mechanical agencies which were to contribute so much towards the transformation of society during the Victorian era were fast coming into operation : for the first important railway was opened in 1830 ; the electric telegraph was first put to public service in 1837 ; in 1838 the transmission of mails by railways began ; in the same year the first train ran into London, and steam communication was established between England and the United States. And concurrently with these new impulses in politics, in science, in religion, and in practical life, came the rise of a new literature. As the great writers of the romantic period fell off one by one, another race arose to take their place. The "thirties" were the seed-time of Victorian verse and prose. Tennyson's *Poems, chiefly Lyrical*, appeared in 1830 ; Browning's *Pauline* in 1833 ; Carlyle's *Sartor Resartus* in 1833–34 ; Dickens's *Sketches by Boz* in 1834–36 ; Thackeray's *Yellowplush Papers* in 1837. Men who in 1840 looked back over the preceding ten years must have realised that in that short space of time a new world had grown up about them.

Hence the sanguine temper, the sense of elation, the feeling of expectancy which now succeeded to the gloom and apathy of the later revolutionary age. Belief in progress revived, nourished by the thought of all that science, industry, and peaceful commerce would presently accomplish for "the relief of man's estate," and the spirit of optimism spread far and wide. This change in the national mood at once found expression in the new literature, the general note of which for some years to come was faith in the present and hope for the future.

There was, it is true, ample cause for the disquietude and alarm felt by a few here and there for whom the signs of the times were by no means so encouraging as they seemed to most of their contemporaries. The

Reform Act, while it broke the political monopoly of the land-owning oligarchy, gave great dissatisfaction to the working classes, who saw too late that they had in no way benefited by it. The consequence was renewed agitation for the extension of the franchise, culminating in the Chartist movement (1836–49), which for the first twelve years of the Queen's reign kept the whole country in a state of continuous upheaval. This movement was much strengthened by the industrial depression which in large measure resulted from the failure of the Government to revise the now outworn system of finance in accordance with the demands of changed economic conditions. Year after year work grew scarcer, food dearer, and the roar of " a hungry people " louder and more menacing. Chartism was, however, admittedly at bottom " a knife-and-fork question "; with the gradual improvement which followed the repeal of the Corn Laws in 1846, it died away, and it was not till 1867 that the second Reform Act registered the steady political advance of democracy. But meanwhile the widespread unrest had been fruitful in other ways. Attention was turned to social problems and especially to the sufferings of the poor, and a wave of humanitarianism swept over the country. Parliament undertook the correction of many abuses— in the criminal code, in the factory system, in the relations of capital and labour. Even more significant was the movement called Christian Socialism, which, under the leadership of Frederick Denison Maurice and Charles Kingsley, came into prominence toward the end of the "forties." Such humanitarianism was one of the strongest formative influences in our earlier Victorian literature, which is everywhere full of social interests and zeal for reform.

Another very important aspect of democratic progress during the Victorian Age was the spread of popular education. The first education grant, made in 1834, paltry as it was, was at least evidence that the national conscience had at last been stirred regarding this subject. The founding of the Working Men's College, just twenty years later, may be mentioned as another landmark in our educational history. The work done in the national schools was lamentably poor, it is true, but it still counted for something in the intellectual life of the masses, and meanwhile it was powerfully reinforced by the activity of the printing press. The Society for the Diffusion of Useful Knowledge had begun its issue of inexpensive books as early as 1827 ; *The Penny Magazine* and *Chambers's Edinburgh Journal*, both devoted to the task of disseminating information among the people, had appeared almost together in 1832 ; and other enterprises of the same kind quickly followed. But it is especially from the abolition of those two "taxes on knowledge," the Stamp Duty in 1855 and the Paper Duty in 1861, that we may date that enormous increase in the number and circulation of newspapers, magazines, encyclopaedias, and cheap publications of all descriptions, which was so marked a feature of the Later Victorian Age. That the consequent immense extension of the reading public had a profound effect on literature is of course obvious, but this is too large and intricate a subject to be considered here. The only point that we need now to emphasise is, that the whole educational movement of the time, inside the schools and even more without, co-operated with contemporary movements in politics and with the far-reaching influence of railway, telegraph, and steamship in creating the modern spirit by destroying provincialism, broadening the popular horizon, breaking down the barriers of the old social system, spreading knowledge and sympathy as between man and man, section and section, and nation and nation, and assuring to each individual, whatever his position, an opportunity such as his forefathers had never enjoyed of realising and expressing what was in him. All these results are reflected in Victorian literature, which, taken in the mass, is in its range, diversity, and comprehensiveness essentially democratic.

Meanwhile the progress of science was as remarkable as that of democracy. It is a commonplace of history that the fifty years following the passing of the first Reform Bill added far more to our positive knowledge of the universe and to our mastery over the forces of nature than the whole preceding eighteen centuries of the Christian era. On the practical side the application of science to life wrought a complete change in the material conditions of civilisation and in the general habits of the people. From this point of view science may be regarded as the most powerful ally of democracy. The change which it produced in thought was no less complete. If the men of the Victorian Age lived in an entirely different world from that of their grandfathers, their attitude towards the universe and its ultimate problems was also entirely different. Of the greatest of modern scientific generalisations, for instance, the doctrine of evolution,—specially associated with the names of Darwin, Wallace, and Herbert Spencer,—it is not too much to say that within a few years it had absolutely revolutionised all current ideas about nature, man, and society. This rapid and triumphant advance of science along many lines deeply affected the whole intellectual life of the time. It helped to foster a markedly utilitarian and materialistic temper. It encouraged reason at the expense of imagination and the feelings. It stimulated the spirit of curiosity, inquiry, analysis, criticism, and speculation. Above all, it precipitated a vast upheaval in thought. New theories came into conflict with old dogmas ; the pillars of orthodoxy were rudely shaken ; fierce battles were fought over the first articles of the traditional faith. Hence the religious and spiritual unrest of the central years of Victoria's reign ; hence the efforts, on the one side to overthrow, on the other to reconstruct ; hence, too, the return of the mood of doubt and the pessimism which coloured so much of the literature presently to be considered.

Before we turn to the details of that literature, however, there is one more general aspect of it to be noted, without due recognition of which this brief introductory survey would be quite incomplete. It is a guiding principle in historical interpretation that every strong movement sets up a counter-movement. Moreover, as John Stuart Mill pointed out, in any epoch of change some of the greatest men are likely to be found among the leaders of reaction. For these reasons we should expect to find, as in fact we shall find, that much that is most distinctive and interesting in Victorian literature is inspired by hostility to the dominating influences of democracy and science. Especially is this true of the large and noble body of verse and prose which is directed against the rationalistic and materialistic temper of the age and the main purpose of which is to proclaim the supremacy of spiritual things. We are here, of course, principally concerned with this idealistic protest as it is expressed, in ways as various as the personalities of the writers, through the medium of general literature. The great Oxford Movement within the Church itself must not, however, be ignored, on account of its bearings outside the sphere of theology. That movement originated, as Newman himself afterwards explained, in antagonism both to liberalism in religion and to the dry old rationalism of English Protestant thought. But the most significant thing about it for us is that, viewed in a large historical perspective, it is to be interpreted as an outburst of romanticism on ecclesiastical soil. It was indeed essentially romantic, broadly because of the pre-eminence which it gave to emotion and imagination in matters of faith and ritual, and in a narrower sense because its revival of the Catholic spirit implied a return to the mood and temper of the Middle Ages. A similar interest attaches to another " renaissance of wonder and mystery," fundamentally akin in origin though more than a decade later in appearance, and this time in the domain of art—the movement initiated by the Pre-Raphaelite Brotherhood. This too, though many other considerations entered into its programme, was at bottom a protest against both the puritan and the materialistic view of life and in favour of the imaginative and the emotional, and like the religious reaction it was strongly impregnated with mediaevalism.

The romantic spirit being thus active in religion and art, it was of course inevitable that it should also become a vital force in literature, and what is known as the second great romantic revival—that of the mid-Victorian period—was the result. This revival was in fact closely connected in its inception with Pre-Raphaelitism, as we shall see later. For the moment we have only to notice that it had this much in common with the general idealistic movement, that it was bred of a spirit of

8

opposition to the materialistic tendencies of the age. But unlike the idealists, the romanticists attacked materialism from the aesthetic rather than from the religious or moral point of view. Their quarrel was not so much with the godlessness of modern civilisation as with its appalling ugliness. From this ugliness they sought, like the romanticists of the earlier part of the century, to effect an imaginative escape into the past. Mediaevalism thus became once more a powerful factor in literature. To this extent the romantic movement was reactionary. Yet even here the strong social interests of the time made their influence felt. For in the end the romantic spirit combined with the spirit of reform, and its protest against materialism, without ceasing to be aesthetic, assumed a practical character.

CHAPTER II

THE GREATER POETS

By the beginning of the period on which we now enter, the great romantic tide was ebbing fast. Some twenty-five years of brilliant and varied activity were followed by a lull. Keats, Shelley, and Byron were dead ; Coleridge had turned his flagging powers into other channels ; Wordsworth, though he had many years before him—years during which he was to win his way gradually to public recognition—was no longer an original force in literature. A number of minor poets meanwhile filled the gap, of some of whom we have already spoken, while others will be mentioned later. But at the moment there was no one writing verse in England with strength of genius sufficient either to revive the failing romantic tradition or to initiate a fresh movement on his own account. The way was therefore clear for a great new poet ; and two great new poets appeared almost simultaneously in Tennyson and Browning.

Alfred Tennyson was born on 6th August 1809 in the rectory at Somersby, Lincolnshire. In 1827 he colla-
Tennyson. borated with one of his brothers, Charles,[1] in
a little volume of very slight promise, *Poems by Two Brothers* ; the next year went up to Cambridge ;

[1] Afterwards known as the writer of some excellent sonnets. Another brother, Frederick, was also a poet of some distinction (*Days and Hours*, 1854 ; *The Isles of Greece*, 1890 ; *Daphne and Other Poems*, 1891).

and in 1829 gained the Vice-Chancellor's medal with a poem on *Timbuctoo*. His first independent volume, *Poems, chiefly Lyrical*, appeared while he was still an undergraduate, in 1830 ; his second, *Poems*, soon after he left the University in 1832. Criticism now began to take stock of him, and while he was warmly welcomed in some quarters, as by Leigh Hunt in *The Tatler*, he was made the object of attack by Wilson in *Blackwood* and by Lockhart in the *Quarterly*. That he profited by the rough handling of both these critics is evident, but always sensitive, he suffered much under it, and it was doubtless one cause of the long silence which followed. Another and deeper reason for that silence is however to be found in an event which exerted a profound influence over his life—the death in September 1833 of his dear friend Arthur Henry Hallam.

When at length he once more appeared before the public with the *Poems* of 1842, it was to be generally acknowledged as, in Wordsworth's phrase, " decidedly the first of our living poets." Hitherto his work had been sadly deficient in intellectual foundation. Such foundation was now provided ; for the stir of new ideas in the world at large, the inspiration of which he began to feel, the death of Hallam, which had thrown him back upon the great problems of life and destiny, and his personal relations with Carlyle, which helped to stimulate his awakening philosophical and social interests, had all contributed to the enrichment of his mind and the expansion of his thought. On the side of style, moreover, the new volumes showed an equal advance, for the puerilities and affectations of 1830 and 1832, save in a few poems here and there, disappeared, and simplicity and strength were united with beauty.

The social influence which had now come into his work was the impulse directly behind his first long poem, *The Princess* (1847). He had become much interested in what he believed to be one of the great questions of the day—that of the higher education of women and their place in our fast-changing modern society. This question he handles under the guise of a fantastic story, half serious, half sportive. As a contribution to the problem stated, his curious " Medley," with its obvious want of breadth and its rather conventional insistence upon the eternal dualism of sex, will probably seem unsatisfactory to most readers of to-day. As a poem, on the other hand, it is rich in the writer's characteristic excellences ; its pictorial power is remarkable ; its blank verse is of great beauty ; while its lyrics are among the most exquisite that he ever wrote.

In 1850 Tennyson married Emily Sellwood and was appointed poet-laureate in succession to Wordsworth. That year is further notable for the publication of *In Memoriam*, a monody on Hallam which had long been growing slowly to completion beneath his hands. In genesis a song of mourning, this superb poem (or more correctly, series of poems) is also a record of Tennyson's spiritual struggles in the dark days which had followed Hallam's death and a declaration of his crowning faith in God and immortality. While as an elegy it ranks with the greatest in our literature, it therefore stands apart, since it is not only an elegy, but also a piece of spiritual autobiography.

In Tennyson's next volume, *Maud and Other Poems* (1855), the inspiration of the hour was even more clear than in *The Princess* or *In Memoriam*. It was the time of the Crimean War, and the poet, always patriotic to insularity, was carried away by the popular frenzy to the extent of using the great European conflict as a central motive in his lyrical monodrama of love and madness. *Maud* is marred by its foolish praise of war as a supposed cure for the evils of peace, and otherwise as a whole it is far from perfect. But in places it has genuine dramatic power, and it contains many passages of supreme beauty. Among the poems published with it were. *The Charge of the Light Brigade* (the subject of which has made it popular beyond its deserts) and, by far the best of Tennyson's official productions, the stately *Ode on the Death of the Duke of Wellington*.

For many years before this Tennyson had been brooding over the legend-cycle of King Arthur and the Round Table, but thus far had done nothing with it beyond a few lyrics and the fine epic fragment, *Morte d'Arthur*, in the volume of 1842. To this subject he now turned in earnest, and he continued to be occupied with it from 1859, when the first four *Idylls of the King* appeared, till 1885, when the publication of *Balin* and *Balan* brought the series to a close. Taken collectively, these poems, twelve in number, constitute Tennyson's largest and most ambitious work. Though, as the title suggests, they are wanting in that unity of design and composition which is essential to a great epic poem, they are none the less built up about a common theme, and each, while in a sense an independent "picture," marks a stage in the progress of the tragic story of the downfall of Arthur's kingdom which runs through them all. That story is further developed as a parable of human life and civilisation, Arthur being presented as the undying Ideal, and the temporary ruin of his work as the result of the co-operation of two opposed yet closely connected powers of evil—sensuality (always for Tennyson the deadliest enemy of the soul of man) and the morbid perversion of religion. In this way, though not without some sacrifice of their simple human interest and romantic beauty, the old-world legends are made the vehicles of a new-world moral meaning.

A volume containing the ever-popular *Enoch Arden* and some other poems, largely of the same general character (1864), represents Tennyson's only other noteworthy work in pure poetry while the *Idylls* were still in hand. But meanwhile he had broken fresh ground in the regular drama—a bold experiment for a man of sixty-six. His three principal plays—*Queen Mary* (1875), *Harold* (1876), and *Becket* (1884)—deal with great crises in the history of the English people, and are therefore illustrative of his fervent patriotism. Though closely fashioned upon the Shakespearean model, they suffer inevitably from the mere literary man's practical ignorance of the stage ; yet comparison of the immature *Queen Mary* with the really strong and effective *Becket* shows that by study and effort he was at length able in a measure to overcome even this serious disadvantage. His other dramas, all unimportant, might, read by themselves, be taken to indicate failure of power with advancing years. But as his remaining volumes of verse prove, his genius continued almost unimpaired to the end. There is little lack of vigour in the *Ballads* of 1880, or in *Locksley Hall Sixty Years After* (1886), while *The Ancient Sage* (1885) and *Akbar's Dream* (1892) are alike in their ripeness of thought and in the beauty of their style contributions of the highest value to the religious poetry of the century.

During all these years of quiet industry Tennyson had led a very peaceful and uneventful life. The death of his second son, Lionel, in 1886, was the one great sorrow of his old age. Otherwise he was completely happy in his home, as he was in his friendships and his fortunes. In 1884 he was raised to the peerage. He died on 6th October 1892.

In outlook and sympathy Tennyson was a typical English gentleman of his generation, and like other English gentlemen he was unable to divest himself of the prejudices or to transcend the limitations of his class. Yet despite the fact that his attitude towards life was always that of an aristocratic outsider, he was unquestionably the most thoroughly representative poet of his age. His poems, indeed, mirror the changes which came over the temper of English society from the opening of his long career to its close. The sanguine spirit of his early writings, with their overflowing faith in science, commerce, and progress; the religious struggles of his middle manhood, registered in *In Memoriam*; the excitement which fills the pages of *Maud*; the gloomy forebodings of the *Epilogue* to the *Idylls of the King* and the second *Locksley Hall*; even the chastened hopefulness of *The Dawn*, *The Dreamer*, and *The Making of Man*: these are not expressions of personal feelings only; they are reflections also of successive moods of the generation into which he had been born. This sensitiveness to the shifting currents of thought and feeling in the world about him was undoubtedly a large factor in his popularity. But it points at the same time to the underlying weakness of his genius. He was always rather the follower and interpreter of his age than its pathfinder and prophet.

It was for this reason that in his social and political poetry he was satisfied to be the exponent of the most cautious school of contemporary liberalism. His early belief in progress he never quite lost, for to the end he held that if " the old order changeth, yielding place to new," it is because " God fulfils Himself in many ways." But a strongly conservative element lay at the foundation of his thought. He was always the poet of law and order even more than of progress ; he dreaded revolution, rash rupture with the past, " raw haste, half-sister to delay " ; he clung stubbornly to English traditions and institutions, and when it seemed to him that these were threatened, alarm drove him into the reactionary camp. At the same time his interest in common people and things shows that, notwithstanding his profound distrust of democracy, he was indirectly influenced by the expanding democratic sympathies of his day. Such poems as *Dora* and *Enoch Arden* were, it is true, written against the grain, and when we compare them with the corresponding work of Wordsworth we can see that there is something rather factitious about them.[1] But the fact that they were written at all is highly significant, and their presence in the body of his verse contributes, as much as that of *The Princess* or *In Memoriam*, to its representative character.

As a religious poet Tennyson was closely identified with that development of liberal theology which much affected the cultured thought of the Victorian era and found organised expression in the Broad Church Movement. At once sceptical and mystical, deeply impressed by the impotence of the human mind before the eternal enigma of things, keenly alive to the destructive influences of modern science and speculation, yet here too, passionately anxious to " conserve the hopes of man," he was peculiarly fitted to become the poetic interpreter of his century's spiritual unrest, and its

[1] We must in fairness, however, except the dialect poems (*The Northern Farmer, The Spinster's Sweet-Arts*, etc.), which are as genuine and as excellent as the Dorsetshire poems of William Barnes (see *post,* pp. 155, 156).

" two voices " of faith and doubt are perpetually heard in his work. But vague as was otherwise his religious teaching, he held firmly to his belief in God and immortality, and these will be found to provide the cornerstones of his entire philosophy of life. While, however, he always asserted these spiritual verities against the scientific materialism which he abhorred, he accepted from contemporary science its greatest generalisation, the doctrine of evolution, which he had already embodied in his poetry before Darwin's *Origin of Species*, and which remained to the last a steadying element in his thought.

In his poetry of nature Tennyson was once more emphatically the child of his age. He knew nature as intimately as Wordsworth, and he far excelled Wordsworth in pictorial power. But where Wordsworth had looked on nature with the eye of the poet and the mystic only, Tennyson saw it with the eye of the scientist as well—" red in tooth and claw," " one with rapine," and full of terrible facts and unanswered riddles well calculated to stir the brooding mind to " evil dreams." It was this constant sense of the cosmic struggle which made it impossible for him to seek in nature for the oracles of God, though the doctrine of evolution encouraged him to believe that nature shared with man in the large general tendency of the ages towards that " one far-off divine event " in which he trusted as the ultimate consummation of all things.

Tennyson took the highest view of poetry and its functions ; not " art for art's sake " but " art for man's sake " was the central principle of his poetic creed. None the less he was always immensely concerned about the formal perfection of his work. As pure artist he is indeed one of the greatest in our literature. His style at times suffers from a general want of robustness and from that tendency to over-refinement which became the common habit of his many imitators; but at its best it is marked by a wonderful combination of ornateness with simplicity, while one of its outstanding merits is its absolute lucidity. His ear was almost faultless; his lyrical measures are of exquisite beauty; while in blank verse he is incontestably our greatest master after Milton.

Tennyson's friend and one great poetic rival, Robert Browning, was the son of a clerk in the Bank of England, **Browning.** who was also a scholar and a book-lover, and was born at Camberwell on 7th May 1812. Left free to follow his own devices, he early began to devote himself to poetry, music, and art. His chief favourite among English poets was Shelley, and Shelley's influence is very marked in his first volume, *Pauline*, a study of spiritual development vague as a whole but beautiful in parts (1833). After this he travelled in Russia and Italy. *Paracelsus*, a highly imaginative interpretation of the life and character of the sixteenth-century physicist, appeared in 1835; the drama *Strafford* (written for Macready, who produced it at Covent Garden) in 1837; *Sordello*, the psychological history of an obscure troubadour mentioned by Dante, in 1840; and between 1841 and 1846 the eight parts of a series entitled *Bells and Pomegranates*, containing *Pippa Passes* (the first of Browning's poems to make anything like a popular appeal), several plays, and a collection of *Dramatic Romances and Lyrics*. Throughout this series his wonderful psychological insight and special power of unravelling the complexities of motive and passion were fully revealed, while at the same time it was pretty clearly shown that, great as was his dramatic genius, his real field was not the stage. In 1846 he married Elizabeth Barrett, then more widely known as a poet than himself, and, for the sake of her health, took her at once to Italy. Fifteen years of perfect happiness followed, during which he published two closely connected religious poems, *Christmas Eve* and *Easter Day* (1850), and two volumes of *Men and Women* (1855), containing much of his finest work in his true line—that of dramatic poetry. Three years after Mrs. Browning's death in 1861 appeared a smaller but equally remarkable collection of the same kind, *Dramatis Personae*. Then came in four volumes in 1868–69 *The Ring and the Book*, a gigantic and rather shapeless poem of more than 20,000 lines of blank verse, in which the sordid and repulsive story of a sixteenth-century Roman murder-case provides the foundation for a series of character-studies, extraordinarily penetrative and brilliant, though at times wearisome through prolixity and repetition. Broadly speaking, though there are some important exceptions to be allowed for, the publication of this immense work may be said to divide Browning's career into two periods : an earlier period of steady growth and fine accomplishment, and a later period of obvious poetic decay. In the writings which followed one another in too rapid succession during the last twenty years of his life there is indeed little that adds in any way to his fame and much that very seriously detracts from it. Here and there in them, however, we come upon flashes of the old power, as in *Dramatic Idylls* (1879–80), and occasional poems, as in *Asolando* (1889), in which the lyric note is still clear and strong.

After his wife's death Browning made his home in London, though he still spent much time in visits to the Continent. In November 1889 he joined his son, an artist, in Venice, and there he died on 12th December of that year.

While as thinker and artist Tennyson always leaned towards the conventional, Browning's unconventionality in matter and manner is one of his most conspicuous characteristics. This unconventionality explains both the difficulty which he long experienced in gaining the ear of the public and his subsequent enormous popularity with readers who, already growing weary of the dominant Tennysonian tradition, welcomed him for the freshness of his thought and style. But his independence was attended by dangers to which he fell a prey. Though never a careless writer (as is often erroneously supposed), he was too impetuous and impatient to think much about the refinements of art, and his work—especially his later work—is frequently damaged by the faults which are common in over-hasty production, as well as by others into which he was tempted by the exuberance of his genius and his love of the startling and unusual. His well-marked peculiarities—his prolixity, discursiveness, tricks of style, grotesque rimes, abuse of highly special learning, frequent obscurity — are not admirable in themselves, though there have not been wanting injudicious " Browning-ites " who have tried to prove them so ; but they were the defects of his qualities, and need not interfere with our recognition of the strength, beauty, and enduring poetic value of what is best in the enormous bulk of his writings.

Browning's genius was fundamentally dramatic ; his one absorbing interest was human life ; and so wide was his range and so catholic were his sympathies that nothing in its tragedy or comedy seemed to come amiss to him. For this reason he has been called " the poet of man." But the phrase is misleading. Tennyson was far more the poet of man than Browning was. Browning was the poet not of man—of humanity in the mass—but of men and women as individuals ; and the more individual they were—the more strongly marked and exceptional their idiosyncrasies and experiences—the better he liked them. Hence his fondness for whatever was curious, out-of-the-way, even abnormal in the " typical souls " whom he took for his study—a fondness which often led him into some strange by-ways and crannies of life (e.g., *Johannes Agricola in Meditation, Porphyria's Lover, Mr. Sludge the Medium*). Moreover, in dealing with such " typical souls " he concerned himself almost entirely with their inner life—with moral and spiritual forces and conflicts. Such complete subordination of action to pure psychological interest goes far to explain both his failure in the regular drama and his supreme success in the art-form which he made specially his own and in which his dramatic genius was allowed full play unclogged by the requirements of stage machinery—the dramatic monologue. Splendid examples of his work in this form will be found in his *Dramatic Romances, Men and Women,* and *Dramatis Personae* ; while, except for the introduction and conclusion, this is the form adopted in *The Ring and the Book.* Even in the monologue the limitations of Browning's dramatic genius are often apparent : most of his characters—even his Caliban, even his Pompilia—share his peculiar mental habits, and one and all they talk in his unmistakable dialect. But these defects are of little account against his extraordinary psychological insight and analytical power.

Browning was very anxious that his readers should understand that his poetry was throughout " dramatic in principle," and in fact it is very seldom that in the whole mass of his writings he speaks avowedly for himself. Yet, despite his insistence upon his artistic objectivity, he continually uses the dramatic form for the indirect conveyance of his own ideas. His moral judgment in respect of the problems raised in his studies of character is generally obvious. Often his ideas are expressed sympathetically, as, *e.g.*, amid much that is purely dramatic, in *A Death in the Desert, A Grammarian's Funeral*, the Pope's monologue in *The Ring and the Book*, and even more simply in *Rabbi Ben Ezra*. Often again he skilfully makes some unwilling witness—a Cleon or a Karshish—bear negative testimony to the truths he is most anxious to enforce. A definite philosophy of life is indeed expounded everywhere in Browning's poetry, and as this philosophy is made up of a few central principles, repeated and re-illustrated again and again, under all sorts of different forms, it is easy to understand its import and bearings.

Its foundations are firmly laid in the poet's unflinching religious faith. To begin with, he postulates two transcendental certainties, which he regards as absolute and axiomatic—God and the soul (see, in particular, *La Saisiaz*, a poem inspired by the death of his friend, Miss Anne Egerton Smith). God we may conceive under three aspects—as infinite power, as infinite wisdom, and as infinite love ; but the soul is satisfied only with the assurance of God as love, and it finds the God of love mainly through the exercise of its own God-given faculty of love ; for, while knowledge helps us little in the quest for God, " love finds Him by first leap." But while this sense of the intimate relation of man to God bulks large in Browning's teaching, an even larger part is played in it by the thought of the immortality of the soul. Life as we know it is full of failure, sorrow, and sin ; those who, like Cleon, seek only a secular solution of the problem, must, like him, be everlastingly baffled by it ; but the mystery is cleared when with Abt Vogler we realise that the " broken arcs " of earth will presently be united in heaven's " perfect round." Here we reach the rational basis of Browning's robust optimism. His strange and almost perverse fondness for exploring the most sordid and ugly phases of human life, though in part due to temperamental bias, was in part also the result of his philosophical preoccupation with evil. He loves to face the most appalling facts of experience that thereby he may the better vindicate the strength of his own convictions (see, e.g., *Apparent Failure*). Evil for him is a factor in the development of the soul ; it is one of many agencies in our education. For this life is only " probation," and " the earth no goal, but starting-point of man " ; and not only suffering, struggle, failure, but even sin itself is seen to have its spiritual value when looked at in the light of eternity. Yet, though Browning holds fast to this probationary view of life, he is not led by it into any ascetic denial of life or gospel of other-worldliness. He in fact repudiates asceticism and all its implications. This is because he refuses to recognise the traditional antithesis between the " natural " and the " divine " ; since all is of God, the natural is itself divine. Idealist as he is, he therefore finds the spiritual in the material, not outside of it. This life is a tabernacle life ; yet it should be lived out to the full, not shirked. Whatever Heaven may have in store for us, we can best prepare ourselves for its larger opportunities by making the most of the educational discipline which the present world affords.

Browning's strenuous and militant ethical teaching

is in complete harmony with these religious ideas. Everywhere he shows his sympathy with the adventurous spirit and his hatred of cowards and trimmers of all kinds (see, e.g., *The Statue and the Bust*). His emphasis is always thrown upon individuality, and whatever stirs the soul out of its sluggishness and apathy—difficulties, dangers, obstacles, temptations, doubts, rebuffs—is regarded by him as beneficial. So concerned is he indeed for the freedom of the soul, that he lays his greatest stress upon impulse and spontaneity, and, treating sins of passion leniently, reserves his strongest condemnation for cold calculation and worldly prudence. At this point it may doubtless be urged that, while Tennyson's criticism of life tends towards timidity and compromise, Browning's on the other hand makes for unrestraint. But there is at least something extremely bracing about his hearty repudiation of all merely conventional standards, as there is in his perpetual insistence on the thought that we are to test life not by achievement, but by aspiration, effort, aim. Here his view of conduct connects itself very closely with his view of art. In life, as in art, perfection means a low ideal, while imperfection is itself a sign of vitality and a promise of growth ; in art, as in life, the highest spirituality should be combined with the fullest and frankest enjoyment of the beauty of the natural world.

Browning was very much a man of his time in his intellectual alertness, his eclecticism, his universal curiosity, and the analytical turn of his genius. But otherwise he did not so much represent as challenge his age. He challenged its philosophic negations, its scientific materialism, its religious uncertainties. He challenged its halting temper, its melancholy, its pessimism. " Hope hard in the subtle thing that's

9

spirit " was the note of his message to his generation. The men and women of the mid-Victorian age were very much troubled about their souls, and many of them were asking doubtfully whether life was quite worth living after all. To them he brought a gospel of invincible religious faith and energising moral power, answering their misgivings in the words of his own Pippa :

" God's in His heaven—all's right with the world."

I have said that at the time of their marriage Mrs. Browning was more widely known as a poet than her husband. She was also some years his senior, **Mrs. Browning.** for she was born at Coxhoe Hall, Durham, on 6th March 1806. Exceedingly precocious, she is said to have been able to read Homer in Greek when she was ten, though her *Battle of Marathon*, written when she was only fourteen, is far more suggestive of Pope's version of the *Iliad* than of the original. An *Essay on Mind* (1826) is likewise both in matter and style curiously reminiscent of the eighteenth century. Between these two publications a serious accident to her spine laid the foundations of the invalidism which, later confirmed by the shock caused by her only brother's tragic death by drowning, compelled her for many years to pass her life between bed and sofa. Thus thrown upon her own resources, she devoted herself with increased ardour to study and composition. On her mother's death in 1828 the family settled in London, but though she now saw more society, the quiet routine of her existence was otherwise little changed. In 1838 she published *The Seraphim and Other Poems*, a volume which is important, not on account of the intrinsic value of the title-piece, which is indeed far from great, but because it included some things of promise, like *The Romaunt of Margret*, and a few of real achievement, like the tender and touching *Cowper's Grave*. This was followed in 1844 by two volumes entitled simply *Poems*, a new edition of which, with many additions, among them the splendid *Sonnets from the Portuguese*, appeared in 1850. These *Sonnets* had been inspired by her love for Robert Browning, whose wife in the meantime (1846) she had become. Of Browning's influence upon her own work it is impossible to speak with certainty ; but it seems to have told in two directions : on the one hand, in broadening her intellectual horizon ; on the other, in increasing her carelessness, already too pronounced, in respect of form. Her intense sympathy with her adopted country in its struggle for freedom was soon evinced by a volume of political verse, *Casa Guidi Windows* (1851). Then came her most ambitious poem, *Aurora Leigh* (1857), setting forth her " highest convictions on Life and Art " in nine books of fluent blank verse. Though she had decided leanings towards romanticism (see, e.g., *Rhyme of the Duchess May*, *The Lay of the Brown Rosary*), she still held strongly to the view that modern poetry should deal boldly with the living issues of modern life (see *Aurora Leigh*, v. 139–221). Already, in *Lady Geraldine's Court-ship* (1844), she had tried to write a "romance of the age " ; but the rather conventional sentimentality of this work had ruined it completely as an experiment in realistic poetry. *Aurora Leigh*, which save for its form is in fact a modern sociological novel, is a much more resolute effort in the same direction, and it is successful to this extent, that as a novel, notwithstanding its prolixity, it is thoroughly interesting, though its social teachings are nebulous and its characterisation poor. Another contribution to the Italian cause, *Poems before*

Congress, appeared in 1860. She died on 20th June of the following year.

Mrs. Browning was a woman of noble impulses and pure ideals. Chronic invalidism often breeds selfishness ; in her case, as her fine humanitarian spirit shows, it rather inspired sympathy with the suffering and the sorrowing (e.g., *Aurora Leigh, The Cry of the Children*). Yet it left an unfortunate mark otherwise in a certain hectic quality—a want of health and robustness—which are too often apparent in her writings. The contrast between wife and husband at this point is very remarkable.

While the total bulk of her poetry is very large, comparatively little of it is likely to survive on its own merits. Fearful diffuseness is one of her most conspicuous defects ; there is scarcely one of her longer poems which would not have gained immensely by compression. But she has many other faults besides mere volubility : among them, emotionalism so overwrought as to be at times hysterical ; extravagances of thought and expression ; irritating mannerisms ; outrageous abuse of diction and rime ; strange perversions of taste and even occasional lapses into downright vulgarity, to be accounted for only on the supposition that they were due to a delicate woman's determination to escape from the limitations of her delicacy and to be strong at all costs. In no sense a thinker, she also made a profound mistake in attempting in some of her more pretentious writings to handle subjects which really lay beyond her scope. Yet with all her failings, she was a woman of real genius ; her sincerity is unmistakable ; her passion and pathos are often true and deep ; while her verse has not infrequently a melody and charm which are entirely her own. Her one really great contribution to literature is unquestionably the series of love-poems already referred to, and called by a title intended to veil their intensely personal character from the public eye—*Sonnets from the Portuguese.* As a sincere record of a woman's passion these sonnets are all but unique. At the same time, they show how much the writer gained in strength by the concentration necessitated by the sonnet form.

Next in order of date to Tennyson and Browning, and perhaps also of importance, comes Matthew Arnold, who **Matthew Arnold.** was born at Laleham, Middlesex, on 24th December 1822. He was the eldest son of Thomas Arnold, the famous schoolmaster, and spent most of his boyhood under his father's care at Rugby. Thence in 1841 he went up to Oxford, where he won the Newdigate Prize with a poem on *Cromwell,* took a second class in classics, and in 1845 was elected to a fellowship of Oriel. The powerful influence of the University upon him is clearly shown in the academic bias which characterises his work both as critic and as poet. In another way also it was very pronounced. During his undergraduate days Oxford was deeply stirred by the Tractarian Movement. To Arnold's highly sensitive nature this movement made a strong appeal, and he was specially impressed by the preaching of Newman. But the excitement was temporary, and the revulsion of thought which followed it carried him into scepticism. Yet to the last he maintained that the Oxford revival had been productive of good in mitigating to some extent the crudeness of English middle-class liberalism and the popular evangelical religion—a view which throws much light upon one side of his intellectual character.

It was not till 1849—two years after he had left

Oxford to become private secretary to Lord Lansdowne —that Arnold published his first volume, *The Strayed Reveller and Other Poems*, containing in such things as the title-piece, *Mycerinus, The Forsaken Merman, Resignation,* and the *Sonnets To a Friend, Quiet Work,* and *Shakespeare,* some of the best verse that he ever wrote. A second volume, *Empedocles on Etna and Other Poems,* appeared in 1852 ; in 1853 a collection comprising so much of his previous books as he wished to preserve together with a number of new poems, one of which was the epic " episode " *Sohrab and Rustum* ; and in 1855 *Poems : Second Series,* the principal feature of which was another long narrative in blank verse, *Balder Dead.* In the meantime, early in 1851, Arnold had been appointed Inspector of Schools, and had married. For a long time his duties were so taxing that they left him little leisure for the pursuit of literature, and when, later on, he began once more to write he turned chiefly to prose (see *post,* Chap. IV.). But he did not give up verse entirely. In 1857 he was appointed Professor of Poetry at Oxford, and in support of the thesis set out in his inaugural lecture—the supreme claims of classicism—published in 1858 a lifeless and dreary imitation of Greek tragedy entitled *Merope.* This melancholy mistake was, however, redeemed by the *New Poems* of 1867. After this he produced very little verse. On several occasions he was sent by the English Government to inquire into the state of education on the Continent, and his official reports are regarded as documents of great value. In 1883 and again in 1886 he lectured in the United States. He died (suddenly, as his father had done before him) in April 1888.

In his theory of poetry Arnold was a confirmed classicist. Holding those exaggerated views regarding the supremacy of antique literature which are common with men deeply imbued with the traditional academic culture, he looked back to the Greeks for inspiration and guidance, and from them he learned, first, that the only really great poetry is impersonal poetry—for which reason a poet who aspires to greatness should devote himself to epic and drama ; and secondly, that in order to get as far away from himself as possible a poet should abandon his own time and choose his subjects out of the past. It was in accordance with these principles of objective art that his own more ambitious poems were written. One of these has already been dismissed as a total failure. Of the remaining four, *Sohrab and Rustum*, a stately and impressive poem, though too obviously reminiscent of Homer, is the finest, and *Empedocles on Etna* really the most interesting, not indeed as a drama, but because there is so much of Arnold himself in the characterisation of the central figure, and so much lyric beauty in the songs of Callicles. *Balder Dead*, like *Sohrab and Rustum*, a " Homeric echo," is not equal to this, and *Tristram and Iseult*, in which, like Tennyson, Morris, and Swinburne, Arnold drew upon the Arthurian story, proves his inability to deal effectively with strong passion and a romantic theme. Of these poems in general it may be said that they are carefully fashioned and finished and have much beauty in parts, but that they are a little stiff, formal, and academic—products of intellectual effort rather than creative power. Arnold's theory in fact broke down in his own practice under the irresistible influence of his intensely introspective nature. The really vital part of his poetry—the part by virtue of which he keeps his distinctive place in literature—is the personal part of it ; the part in which, fortunately ignoring all theory, he simply obeyed the promptings of his genius.

The dominant thought of this personal poetry is the thought of change. Arnold realises that he has fallen upon an era of transition. He sees the Time-Spirit everywhere at work ; the social systems and the religious creeds in which men had lived at peace with themselves in the past are obsolete or obsolescent ; for the moment everything is in the melting-pot. Thus he finds himself " wandering between two worlds, one dead, the other powerless to be born " ; touched at times by wistful regret for the things which are doomed to destruction ; determined none the less to keep his face resolutely towards the dawn, yet doubtful as to what the new day may bring forth. As we should expect in the work of a poet at once so subjective and so sincere, Arnold's mood varies ; now he sinks into dejection so deep as to be almost hopeless (e.g., *Dover Beach, Obermann*), now again he ascends the mount of vision and has a glimpse of the promised land (e.g., *The Future, Obermann Once More*). But on the whole, his ground-tone is that of pensive sadness and melancholy. Such poetry is necessarily depressing, but it never becomes enervating because of the presence in it always of a fine stoical moral spirit. As a poet of nature he belongs to the lineage of Wordsworth, though his feeling for nature is far more urban (e.g., *Lines written in Kensington Gardens*), and he goes to nature not so much for spiritual revelation as for relief from the tumult and distractions of the everyday world. It is highly characteristic of his poetic temper that certain aspects of nature reappear continually in his verse ; he loves particularly the quiet of the high Alpine pasture lands, twilight, calm night, and the moon's " pensive light." Equally characteristic is the fact that he is " at his best in the mood of lament." His elegiac poems (e.g., *Thyrsis, Rugby Chapel*) are amongst the finest in our literature ; but it is significant that even his most personal elegies, like the two just named and his tender lament over his favourite dog (*Geist's Grave*), are steeped in the philosophic spirit ; while the critical element which is uppermost in several of them (e.g., *Memorial Verses*, 1850 ; *Heine's Grave*, the *Obermann* poems, *Stanzas from the Grande Chartreuse*) is doubly interesting as showing the bias of his mind and as a sign that in a bookish age criticism will invade even poetry.

As an artist Arnold has been justly praised for his restraint, his lucidity, and the chasteness and purity of his style. On the other hand, his range was very narrow ; there is little in his verse of the " liquid diction and fluid movement " which he himself so much admired ; while his ear was very defective, as we often feel even when he is working in established forms, but even more when he experiments in irregular unrimed metres (e.g., *Haworth Churchyard, Heine's Grave*). Too intellectual, too melancholy, and superficially too cold for the majority of lovers of poetry, he has never been widely popular ; but he has always had his " audience fit though few," particularly among thoughtful readers of classic tastes.

From Matthew Arnold, at once classicist and poetic interpreter of the intellectual complexities of modern life, we now turn to a group of writers who stand in every respect in sharpest contrast with him—those of the new romantic school. Foremost among these both in age and influence was Rossetti.

Charles Gabriel Dante Rossetti (always known in the form which he early adopted as Dante Gabriel Rossetti) was born in London on 12th May 1828. Though English by birth he was Italian by blood, his father Gabriele (himself a poet and a Dante scholar) being a refugee from Naples, and his mother, Frances Polidori,

Rossetti. the daughter of a Tuscan though by an English wife. Literary tastes were strong in the family, for Dante Gabriel's only brother, William Michael, became a critic of some note, and of his two sisters, the elder, Maria Francesca, achieved distinction as a writer on Dante, while the younger, Christina, attained a high place among Victorian poets. After six years at King's College, Rossetti at fifteen left school to take up the study of art. In 1848 he joined three friends—Millais and Holman Hunt, the painters, and Woolner the sculptor —in forming an association which they called the Pre-Raphaelite Brotherhood, other young enthusiasts among their acquaintance being brought a little later into the cause. Their purpose was nothing less than the reform of English art, then hampered by academic conventions and steeped in the spirit of domestic materialism. At the outset they had no thought of any mediaeval revival, their object, according to the statement of their short-lived organ, *The Germ*, being merely " to encourage and enforce our entire adherence to the simplicity of nature." But Ruskin, who had indoctrinated them with this idea of a " return to nature," had also filled them with admiration for " the earnestness of the men of the thirteenth and fourteenth centuries," whom he had held up as examples of the sincerity, the truthfulness, and the fine religious quality which modern art had lost. It was this admiration which led them to choose the name Pre-Raphaelite as the best indication of their aims ; by it they announced, as Ruskin himself explained in their behalf, their emphatic repudiation of the Renaissance and all its works. What followed was in the circumstances inevitable. The young Brothers, instead of being satisfied to absorb only the spirit of the early Italian masters, straightway began to imitate them, reproducing their themes, their style, their mystical and symbolical tendencies, even their quaint mannerisms ; and in the end the P.R.B. became a neo-mediaeval school. Of its broad significance from this point of view as part of a general movement in thought at the time we have already spoken, and it is not our business here to pursue its fortunes further in the history of art, though it is necessary to add that in the stronger men the healthy naturalistic impulse soon conquered the antiquarianism. The one fact now to be emphasised is that though, like his chief associates, Rossetti quickly broke away from the trammels of the original programme, —though, for instance, he gave up the practice of specifically sacred art,—the essential mediaevalism of the Brotherhood remained a fundamental feature of his own work because it was deeply ingrained in his genius and character.

For a number of years, while steadily gaining reputation as a painter, Rossetti was scarcely known as a poet beyond his immediate friends, though in 1861 he showed his extraordinary skill as a translator in a volume entitled *The Early Italian Poets* (afterwards republished as *Dante and his Circle*). The year before he had married Eleanor Elizabeth Siddal, whose tragic death from an overdose of laudanum in 1862 was a blow from which he never completely recovered. He was at the time preparing for the press a collection of original verse ; in a moment of passionate grief he placed the manuscript in his wife's coffin, and it was buried with her. It was, however, later exhumed, and his first volume of *Poems*, largely composed of matter thus rescued from destruction, appeared in 1870. Though on the whole well received, these poems were made the subject of a slashing criticism by Robert Buchanan in a magazine article, reissued as a pamphlet, entitled *The Fleshly School of Poetry*, in which, together with Swinburne, the author was denounced for the immorality of his writings. . The effect of this indictment was disastrous. Rossetti was already in poor health and in a morbid mental condition. His nervous state was now increased by continual brooding over Buchanan's attack,[1] and, other causes aiding, he fell into extreme depression, became the victim of obstinate insomnia, and in an evil hour resorted to chloral, which of course only intensified his troubles. His last years were clouded with gloom and spent very much in seclusion. He died on 9th April 1882.

The first point to emphasise in the study of Rossetti is that his Italian blood was a determining factor of the utmost importance in his work, which throughout, in theme, character, and tone, is not Northern and Protestant but Southern and Catholic. But it is not enough to think of him as an Italian poet transplanted to English soil. We must recognise him also as a kind of "throw back," in whom the essential qualities of his remote ancestors were curiously revived. Entirely unmodern in his tastes and feelings, and caring nothing for the things which specially interested the world around him, he was, in Mr. Hall Caine's terse phrase, "an anachronism in these days." It was only accident of birth that made him a denizen of Victorian London, with its fog and grime, its hideous houses, its commercial materialism, its talk of science, progress, and "the march of mind"

[1] He replied in *The Stealthy School of Criticism*. It may be added that Buchanan afterwards withdrew his charges, so far as Rossetti was concerned, and made such amends as lay in his power by dedicating to him his romance *God and the Man*.

—all of which things he detested. His real home—
the home of his imagination and sympathies—was the
Florence of Dante's time.

Hence in reading his poetry we feel that we are
leaving the modern world almost entirely behind us. A
handful of political sonnets and the powerful Browning-
esque dramatic monologue, *A Last Confession,* serve indeed to remind us that he was the son of a refugee
patriot, while there are a few among his poems, like *The
Burden of Nineveh* and the realistic *Jenny,* which in
different ways bear the unmistakable stamp of their
age. But on the whole his imaginative escape from
his own century is almost complete, and his identifi-
cation with mediaeval modes of thought and feeling so
absolute that in his poems as in his pictures we
seem to breathe the very atmosphere of the *Vita Nuova,*
the *Paradiso,* and the early Catholic painters. He is
in fact, as a Catholic critic has said of him, " a mediaeval
artist, heart and soul."   As interpretations of the essential spirit of the Middle Ages—their claustral temper,
their worship of womanhood, their passionate devotion
to the Virgin, their combined sensuousness and mysticism—such poems as *World's Worth, Ave,* and *The
Blessed Damozel* stand unique and unapproachable in
our literature.

This extraordinary power of entering into the
mediaeval spirit was not, however, the result of
religious conviction.   It was the result only of intense imaginative and emotional sympathy. Rossetti
was not a Roman Catholic or an Anglican Catholic ;
in the matter of creed he was not a Christian at all.
In his religious views, so far as these were ever
formulated by him, he was, as his brother testifies,
"a decided sceptic," and now and then his scepticism

finds utterance in his poetry (e.g., *The Sea-Limits, The Cloud Confines, Soothsay*, the Italian *Barcarola*). But that poetry in the mass was the expression, not of his intellectual doubts and speculations, but of his imagination, and in his imagination he lived wholly in the world of mediaeval Catholicism, sharing its sentiments and partaking of its general attitude towards life, though with the dogmatic foundations of its faith he had no concern. Thus he provides a singularly interesting example of a phenomenon by no means rare in literature—that of the survival of ancestral forces under changed forms of expression.[1] Though himself an agnostic, his genius was yet moulded and coloured by the Catholic ideals of the stock from which he sprang, and these ideals are indeed the main inspiration behind his poetry and painting. Only with him they were no longer matters of intellectual conviction. They were matters simply of emotional intuition and sympathy. What were with his forefathers motives of life reappear in his work as motives of art.

Regarded more generally, Rossetti claims special attention as a balladist and as a sonnet-writer. In his ballads he is particularly successful when dealing with situations of great tragic intensity (e.g., *Eden Bower, Sister Helen, The White Ship*). In his sonnets he ranks easily with the two or three supreme English masters of the true Italian form on the strength of the fine sequence, *The House of Life*.

The salient characteristics of Rossetti's poetry as a whole are its wonderful sensuous beauty, its richness of imagery, its gorgeous though often overwrought style, and that quality of strangeness which Pater regarded as an essential feature of romantic art. His

[1] See Seeley's *Goethe after Sixty Years*.

technique is often marvellous—how mavellous we hardly realise perhaps until we come to analyse his original stanza forms with their heavy weight of rimes and intricate metrical effects. But there is nearly always something exotic, frequently a little morbid and unwholesome, about the beauty which he creates. There are times when in reading him we feel oppressed, as in the atmosphere of a room laden with rare but rather sickly perfumes, and yearn for a breath of the open air and for a note of naturalness and simplicity. Admirable as his art is, it is indeed more than a little suggestive of that decadence which is perhaps inevitable in poetry which is not fed by the healthy currents of normal life.

The youngest of Gabriele Rossetti's four children, Christina Georgina, was born in London in 1830, and was **Christina** thus two years Dante Gabriel's junior. She **Rossetti.** was educated entirely at home, where her religious nature early expanded under the influence of her mother, who was a devout member of the Anglican Church. When she was a mere child her verses began to be treasured in the household, and in her seventeenth year a small selection of her writings was printed by her grandfather Polidori at his private press. Three years later she contributed seven pieces to the Pre-Raphaelite *Germ.* Her first published volume, *Goblin Market*, with two designs by her brother, appeared in 1862 ; *The Prince's Progress and Other Poems*, also illustrated by Dante Gabriel, in 1866 ; *Sing-Song : A Nursery Rhyme Book*, in 1872 ; *A Pageant and Other Poems*, in 1881 ; a collective edition of her verse, in 1890 ; and after her death, a supplementary volume of *New Poems*, edited by William Michael Rossetti, in 1896. She also published prose stories of little importance and several devotional books, one of which, *Time Flies, a Reading Diary* (1885), contains some of her finest religious lyrics. Of fragile health and ascetic temper, she lived a very sequestered life, the greater part of her time being divided between the care of her mother (who herself lived till 1886) and exercises of piety. She died in 1894.

At one important point the contrast between Christina Rossetti and her more famous brother is extremely instructive, for the interest in dogmatic religion which he never felt was a controlling influence in her life, and is therefore naturally uppermost in her work, a considerable portion of which is indeed explicitly devotional. As a religious poet she had, with the possible exception of Newman, no serious rival among her contemporaries, and such poems as *Passing Away, Advent, Symbols, Anima Mundi, Paradise*, to name only a few, have all the emotional and technical qualities which are essential to perfection in a field of art in which anything like perfection is rarely attained. Her religious poetry as a whole, however, is not entirely healthy in tone, while at times it is marred by quaintness and subtleties which remind us of what is least admirable in the writings of those seventeenth-century poets, particularly Herbert and Crashaw, with whom she has often been compared.

Her more general verse is almost entirely lyrical in impulse and form, and at its best (as, *e.g.*, in *An Apple Gathering, Maude Clare, Maiden Song*, " When I am dead, my dearest," and some of her sonnets, notably the series entitled *Monna Innominata*), it has a singular beauty which it is easier to feel than to describe. Both in her style and in her metrical effects she sometimes recalls her brother, but her individual note is always unmistakable. That individual note is equally clear in her two experiments in sustained narrative. The first of these, *Goblin Market*, a wonderful achievement in fantastic art, is absolutely unique in conception and execution. *The Prince's Quest*, while not so strikingly original either in matter or in manner, still impresses us as a poem which only its author could have written.

Some comparison between Christina Rossetti and Mrs. Browning is inevitable. That Mrs. Browning had the advantage in various important respects is evident. Her genius was far greater in volume, in range, and in intellectual power ; it was enriched not only by deeper scholarship, but also by much wider experience ; her outlook and her sympathies were broader and more generous. Miss Rossetti suffered much from her claustral life and the limitations which it entailed ; we feel it in the general absence of a strong human interest from her writings, in the monotony of her emotional expression, and in her predominantly morbid tone. On the other hand, she certainly excelled her elder sister in pure imagination, in intensity of poetic vision, and very obviously in all the essentials of art. She had far more restraint ; was happily free from any tendency to hysterical over-emphasis or mere gush ; and was never guilty of those astonishing faults of taste which often disfigure Mrs. Browning's work.

While kinship of genius as well as of blood justify us in treating the two Rossettis in the foregoing close connection, it is not through Christina, but rather **William Morris.** through Morris, that the main line of Dante Gabriel's influence, and more broadly of the romanticism represented by him, is to be traced. William Morris came of a prosperous middle-class family, and was born at Walthamstow on 24th March 1834. At Marlborough he was touched by the High Church movement (as the sequel proved, on its aesthetic side), and when in 1853 he went to Oxford, it was with the intention of taking orders.   At the University his innate love of Gothic was strengthened by the study of Ruskin's then recently published *Stones of Venice*, of one chapter of which— the famous chapter on " The Nature of Gothic "—he afterwards wrote : " To some of us, when we first read it, now many years ago, it seemed to point out a new road on which the world should travel." On coming of age, he stepped into an income of £900 a year. About the same time he abandoned the idea of a clerical career, and in 1856 articled himself to George Edward Street, the architect, who was one of the great practical forces in the Gothic revival. His friendship with Rossetti turned his attention to painting, and he was one of the artists chosen by that master to help him with the frescoes in the Debating Hall of the Oxford Union. In 1859 he married Jane Burden, a woman of great beauty of the Pre-Raphaelite type, who had sat both to Rossetti and to him, and in 1861 he founded the firm of Morris & Co., Decorators, the aim of which was the regeneration of the household arts and crafts. Meanwhile in 1858 he had published his first volume, *The Defence of Guinevere and Other Poems* (the other poems including *King Arthur's Tomb, Shameful Death,* and *The Haystack in the Floods*), which announced the rise of a new romantic poet of very high promise. In order of date this was the first product in book-form of the Pre-Raphaelite impulse, and like Christina Rossetti's *Goblin Market*, four years later, it was marked by the mediaeval leanings and the stylistic mannerisms of the school. *The Life and Death of Jason,* a long narrative poem, classic in subject but entirely mediaeval in tone and colouring, appeared in 1866, and in 1868–70 the four volumes of *The Earthly Paradise*, the work with which Morris's name as a poet will always be chiefly associated. The prologue to this immense col-

lection of poems—itself a very fine story of adventure—
tells how " certain gentlemen and mariners of Norway "
set sail to find the Earthly Paradise, and after many
years of wandering came to a strange land inhabited by
descendants of the old Greek stock, and the body of the
work is composed of the twenty-four tales (twelve of
romantic and twelve of classic origin) with which the
new-comers and their hosts entertain one another and
beguile the time. Many of these tales, like *The Ring
given to Venus* and *The Man born to be King*, are admirable examples of story-telling, and all of them, whatever
their source, are steeped in mediaevalism. Yet notwithstanding his profound sympathy with the Middle Ages
and his obvious indebtedness to his acknowledged
master Chaucer, Morris failed to recapture the naïveté
of the childlike art which he so greatly loved. The
spirit of melancholy and of wistful yearning, as for
something beautiful which has been lost—the spirit of
the poet's own troubled era—broods over his pages,
touches even his old-world material with a quality
radically foreign to it, and finds full expression in the
charming lyrical interludes.

The Earthly Paradise was followed in 1873 by a
dramatic experiment which he called a " morality,"
Love is Enough, and then in 1877 came the last of
Morris's long narrative poems, *Sigurd the Volsung*, a
product of his growing enthusiasm for the Icelandic
sagas, and an epic tale of great vigour, written in swing-
ing anapaestic couplets which were admirably suited to
its subject and had the further attraction of freshness.
About the same time his energies took a new turn. As
his romantic poetry shows, he had always been dis-
satisfied with modern life. Thus far, however, like
Rossetti, he had simply sought an imaginative escape

out of it. Still acting on the aesthetic impulse—for, as
he once told an interviewer, his overwhelming sense of
the ugliness of commercialism and the capitalistic régime
was behind his revolt—he now entered the field of
practical politics as a leading advocate of socialism.
Thus his romanticism changed into utopianism ; that
land of heart's desire which had hitherto been for him
only a vague memory of bygone ages now became
a land of promise, remote indeed, but not therefore
unattainable. Such transformation of this " dreamer
of dreams," this " idle singer of an empty day," into
an ardent reformer is significant as an illustration of
the powerful sway of social interests during the Victorian
era ; but in his case propagandist zeal found a channel
mainly in practical activity, though two prose tales—
The Dream of John Ball (1888) and *News from Nowhere*
(1890)—and some of his later poems (e.g., *The Pilgrims
of Hope*) were written to expound his new ideas. Despite his preoccupation with practical affairs he still
found relief in purely imaginative work, as in *Poems by
the Way* (1891) ; and during the last years of his life he
produced a series of prose romances, full of the charm
of his earlier stories in verse and written in a curiously
archaic style, of which the most important are *The
House of the Wolfings* (1889) and *The Roots of the
Mountains* (1890). He had already translated much
from the Icelandic. His versions of the *Æneid* and
the *Odyssey*, neither really successful, have to be added
to the long list of his writings. He died in 1896.

After Rossetti, Morris is the principal representative
in English poetry of the second mediaeval revival. As
a story-teller pure and simple he has no superior among
our nineteenth-century poets, and the charm of his
leisurely narratives is greatly enhanced by the easy and

melodious flow of his verse and the beauty of his descriptions. But his tales are generally rather thin, for the note of deep passion is seldom sounded in them, and the men and women who move across his pages are for the most part very shadowy and unreal. His poems, to use his own distinction, appeal rather to the mood of idleness than to the strenuous mood ; they provide, as has been well said, fit reading for a sleepy summer afternoon, but their permanent hold upon us is very slight. None the less, such work deserves praise because it possesses in full measure qualities which are rare in modern literature.

We now come to the youngest of the greater Victorian poets and the only one among them who outlived the **Swin-** century. Algernon Charles Swinburne was **burne.** born in London on 5th April 1837, just two months before the Queen ascended the throne. After five years at Eton he entered Oxford in 1857, and during his three years of residence there became attached to Rossetti, Morris, and Burne-Jones, who were then engaged on their frescoes in the Hall of the Union. Rossetti's influence on him was very strong, and it was to him that he dedicated the two plays, *The Queen Mother* and *Rosamund*, which he published together in 1862. These were merely experimental ; but in their successor, the superb lyrical drama in Greek form, *Atalanta in Calydon* (1865), Swinburne at eight-and-twenty produced what is perhaps the very finest of all his works. To the same year belongs *Chastelard*, the first part of a trilogy on Mary of Scotland, continued by *Bothwell* in 1874 and completed by *Mary Stuart* in 1881. Meanwhile the publication in 1866 of a volume of miscellaneous verse entitled *Poems and Ballads* had taken the critics by surprise and aroused a storm of protest which did not subside for several years. The charge brought against the young poet was that in certain of these poems he had openly flouted Christian ideals and proclaimed a gospel of neo-paganism (e.g., the *Hymn to Proserpine*), and that in others (e.g., *Anactoria, Laus Veneris, Dolores, Faustine*) he had used his genius to pander to unworthy passion. This was the main contention of Robert Buchanan in his *Fleshly School of Poetry*, to which reference has already been made. The outcry was excessive, though it must still be admitted that the volume contained a few things at least which were fairly open to censure. But whatever exception might be taken to the unwholesome hot-house atmosphere of some of the poems, their splendour of diction and the marvellous freshness and beauty of their versification were recognised by all unbiased critics. These same technical qualities were equally apparent in *Songs before Sunrise* (1871), but otherwise this new volume, which was largely inspired by the poet's devotion to Italy and the cause of political freedom, offered in its more healthy and bracing tone a welcome contrast with its immediate predecessor. In *Erechtheus* (1876) Swinburne returned to the antique, but while this further experiment in classic tragedy is closer to the Attic model than *Atalanta* had been, it falls far short of that wonderful achievement in spontaneity and charm. Among Swinburne's numerous remaining volumes of verse, miscellaneous and dramatic, mention need here be made only of a second (1878) and third (1889) series of *Poems and Ballads*; a tragedy, *Marino Faliero* (1885), which is reckoned after *Mary Stuart* as his best work in regular dramatic form; and two Arthurian narrative poems, *Tristram of Lyonesse* (1882) and *The Tale of Balen* (1896). His prose work, which he began early and continued till nearly the end, will be considered in a later chapter. For the last thirty years of his life he lived with his friend Theodore Watts-Dunton, the well-known critic, at Putney, and there he died in 1909.

Many influences combine in Swinburne's poetry —in particular, those of the Greek dramatists, of the Elizabethan playwrights, of the pre-Raphaelites, and of the French poets, Victor Hugo (always the chief god of his idolatry), Gautier, and Baudelaire, and his work is in consequence extremely complex in texture and style. In a broad way he may be regarded as carrying on the pagan traditions of Keats and Landor, though his Hellenism is deeply impregnated with the romantic spirit. Despite his close personal relations with Rossetti, Morris, and Burne-Jones, the mediaevalism with which these men inspired him was only superficial and temporary; it prompted him to a few experiments, like the masque of *Queen Bersabe*, and to one or two poems of real note, like *Laus Veneris*; but he was too pronouncedly hostile to the mediaeval spirit for it to have any firm hold upon him. From first to last he persisted in his work in the drama, and his plays fill a considerable space in his collective writings; but while they have plenty of passion and fire, and at times show genuine skill in characterisation, they have the usual defects—lack of action, tendency to endless talk, general want of dramatic fibre and grip—of plays written without reference to the stage. In his narrative poems again the main interest is overlaid by lyrical digressions which, however beautiful in themselves, continually impede and confuse the story. It is indeed the pure lyrical impulse which predominated in Swinburne's genius, and as a lyrical poet of unparalleled power over the resources of the language and an extraordinary faculty of creating metrical effects, he will keep his place in our literature. But while thus defining his pre-eminence we also indicate his limitations. His greatness is as a maker of metrical music; with that music he delights us for a time; but it is surprising how little his poetry leaves with us when the magic of the mere melody is gone. His opulence of language and his astonishing facility in the manipulation of rime and rhythm were indeed constant snares to him. Like the consummate virtuoso, he rejoiced too much in mere dexterity. Verbal beauty was with him too often an end in itself, and his marvellous powers of expression were united to the most extreme tenuity of thought. For this reason he is not a poet who wears well; we read him at first with avidity, but presently tire of his " words, words, words." His metaphors and similes have a singularly nebulous quality; and in his poetry of nature (though he can give us wonderful impressions, as in his many poems of the sea) his descriptions with all their delusive richness and luxuriance are generally indefinite in detail and vague in their total effect. Moreover, even as a stylist his writing is often spoiled by over-indulgence in verbal tricks and the abuse of special devices, like alliteration and onomatopoeia, which, if not sparingly employed, easily degenerate into irritating mannerisms. But these perhaps may be accounted relatively insignificant weaknesses. Swinburne's radical defects are his want of balance, restraint, clearness of mental and moral vision, and the unsubstantial character of his work on the intellectual side.

CHAPTER III

OTHER POETS

THOUGH it is convenient for us to draw a line of distinction between "the greater" and the "other" poets of the Victorian Age, it must be remembered that there are enormous differences of value among those of the second class; some of them being fairly entitled to a place very close to that of their greater contemporaries, while some are minor poets in the narrowest acceptation of the term. As it would obviously be impossible to graduate them satisfactorily according to merit, while, owing to their extreme diversity, any systematic arrangement of them is equally out of the question, we will here adopt in the main the chronological order; departing from this only when it seems necessary for the sake of clearness or where for any reason several poets fall naturally into groups.

First in sequence comes a writer, who in date of birth belongs to the older generation, but who did not **Barham.** establish his reputation until the field had been well occupied by younger men. Richard Harris Barham was born in 1788, entered the Church in 1813, became a minor canon of St. Paul's in 1821, and died in 1845. Though he produced much other literary work, including a couple of novels, his fame rests entirely upon *The Ingoldsby Legends*, which, under the pen-name of Thomas Ingoldsby, he began to contribute to *Bentley's Miscellany* in 1837, and to which he continued to add to the end of his life. These *Legends* scored an instant success, and their popularity has been little affected by lapse of time and changes of taste. They contain tales in prose as well as in verse, but those in verse are not only the more numerous but also by far the more important. Barham was in his own special way a humorist of the first order ; his work overflows with fun and frolic ; and he knew too how to use the grimly tragic as an offset to his broad and sometimes rather boisterous comedy. His subjects were occasionally invented, but were more often taken from the by-ways of history or legend, and his quaint out-of-the-way learning, like his extraordinary facility in grotesque riming, was a distinct element in his general effect. Though a few of them are modern in theme, the *Legends* as a whole may be regarded as a burlesque offshoot from the mediaevalism of Scott and his followers, which was by this time beginning to run to seed. They have, however, another somewhat deeper, though closely connected, significance. At the time of their production the Anglican movement was making great headway in the Church. Barham, a staunch Protestant, was strongly opposed to all neo-Catholic tendencies, and many of the *Legends*, like the famous *Jackdaw of Rheims*, were written to satirise what he considered the childish superstitions of the ancient faith. Such poems can none the less be enjoyed to the full without any thought of their underlying polemical purpose.

No such permanent interest can be claimed for the work of Sir Henry Taylor, who for most readers of to-day

Taylor. is scarcely more than a name. In the course of a long, quiet, happy life (1800–86), forty-eight years of which were spent in the Colonial Office, Taylor was the personal friend of many of the most notable men of letters of his time, and his admirable *Autobiography* contains much that is interesting about some of his famous contemporaries of two generations. His poetic works include four tragedies—*Isaac Comnenus* (1827); *Philip van Artevelde* (1834)—usually accounted his masterpiece ; *Edwin the Fair* (1842) ; and *St. Clement's Eve* (1862); a romantic comedy—*A Sicilian Summer* (1850); and a volume of miscellaneous verse—*The Eve of the Conquest and Other Poems* (1847). Taylor was a man of strong intellect rather than of creative power. Though formed on the Elizabethan model, his plays have little dramatic life ; they are simply closet-dramas— the work of a thoughtful and cultured man, who, while a fair judge of character, was without any deep psychological insight. In style they are chaste and dignified. Their high moral and political ideals and sound, practical wisdom are of the kind otherwise expounded by the author in his collection of Baconian essays, *The Statesman* (1836). His *Notes from Books* (1849) contain some instructive criticism.

While we should of course regret the loss of Taylor's work, it cannot be said that such loss would be very serious. The case is different with that of his

Barnes.   exact contemporary, William Barnes (1800–86), a Dorsetshire clergyman and scholar, who occupies a distinct place in modern literature as the author of *Poems of Rural Life in the Dorset Dialect* (1844, 1859, and 1862). The peculiar value of these poems lies in their freshness and entire freedom from all suggestion of literary convention ; they are idyllic poems in the true, not in the academic, sense ; and they deal with the simple pathos and beauty, and at times with the quaint humours, of the little world which they portray without any trace of artificial arcadianism. Like Burns, Barnes was at his best only when writing in the "Doric." Indeed the dialect itself had so much to do with his success that nearly all the native charm of his "eclogues" disappeared when he made the unfortunate experiment of translating some of them into standard English.

The mediaevalism which appeared as burlesque in Barham found a serious exponent in another clergyman, **Hawker.** the eccentric Robert Stephen Hawker, who was born at Plymouth in 1803, went to Oxford in 1823, gained the Newdigate Prize for English verse in 1827 with a poem in the usual academic style on *Pompeii*, entered the Church, and in 1834 became vicar of Morwenstow, a small village on the wild north Cornish coast, nine miles from Bude. In that remote corner of the world, beloved of his rough parishioners, he spent his life under conditions which doubtless helped to strengthen his profound hatred of all modern tendencies in society and thought and the ingrained mysticism of his temper. He died in 1875, having been received into the Roman communion within a few hours of the end. His most remarkable poem, the splendid though fragmentary *Quest of the Sangraal* (1863), is instinct with his sympathy with the spirit of the old legend, and therefore provides a most suggestive contrast with Tennyson's thoroughly modernised version in the *Idylls of the King*. After this his most interesting work is to be found in his vigorous Cornish ballads. One of these—the *Song of the Western Men*—had a curious history. Evolved out of a traditional refrain and published anonymously in a Plymouth paper in 1825, this at first deceived such good judges of the antique as Scott and Macaulay, both of whom accepted it as a genuine old ballad.

The year 1803 also saw the birth of Richard Henry (or

as he later called himself, Richard Hengist) Horne, whose
life was as varied as that of Hawker was externally uneventful.   After a few years at Keats's old school
Horne.   at Edmonton, Horne was sent to Sandhurst to
prepare for the Army, but, being expelled for insubordination, he entered the Mexican naval service, saw a good
deal of fighting, and afterwards travelled much. At
twenty-five he plunged into journalism in London ; but
went to Australia in 1852, and remained there till 1869.
He then returned to England and to literary work, and
died in 1884. Horne wrote much in verse and prose,
but his one outstanding production is his epic poem,
Orion (1843), known in history as the "farthing epic,"
for at that price he actually published it, as a caustic
commentary on the apathy of the public regarding poetry.
Though such a trick was of course calculated to discredit
it, *Orion* is really a fine poem. It is built up about a
philosophic idea, which is worked out "by means of
antique or classical imagery and associations" : the
central figure being conceived as "a type of the
struggle of man with himself, *i.e.* the contest between
the intellect and the senses." The theme is boldly and
clearly handled, and the blank verse, to some extent
reminiscent of Keats's *Hyperion*, has a stately movement
and much sonorous beauty.

Still following the chronological order, we come next
to a poet who on the strength of one acknowledged
Fitz-   masterpiece might perhaps have been given
Gerald.   a place among the greater poets of his age.
Edward FitzGerald was born in the same year as his
life-long friend, Tennyson (1809), and on leaving Cambridge in 1830 with an income sufficient to make him
independent, and no ambition for a practical career,
settled down to the life of a scholarly recluse, spending

his time in boating, gardening, reading, and generally in a busy idleness which exactly suited his disposition. He died in 1883. The only tangible fruits of his leisurely activity for many years are his delightful letters, which easily rank among the best in our literature. In 1851, however, he published *Euphranor : a Dialogue on Youth*, in Platonic form, the prose style of which was greatly admired by Tennyson. Meanwhile, at the suggestion of Prof. Cowell, he had begun to learn Spanish, and his enthusiasm for Calderon led him to make a very free translation of six of that dramatist's plays (1853). The same friend also turned his attention to Persian, and out of this new study came the work with which his name will always be associated—his version of a selection of the *Rubáiyát* (quatrains) of the eleventh-century Persian poet, Omar Khayyám. Fitz-Gerald held very liberal views regarding the duties and privileges of a translator. In handling his original, he did not scruple to reject, add, condense, amplify, re-arrange. His aim, indeed, was not literal fidelity, but a free interpretation of his poet's meaning, and his work is therefore a paraphrase rather than a translation, or, as his American friend Charles Eliot Norton put it, "a re-delivery of a poetic message." This goes far to explain its extraordinary hold upon the modern reader. FitzGerald found in the quatrains of the old tent-maker an Epicurean philosophy which, however the outward form of it may change, is the expression of a mood at least as characteristic of our own world as of Omar's. That philosophy he reproduces with such exquisite and persuasive power that, as Norton further said, "in its English dress" the poem "reads like the latest and freshest expression of the perplexity and of the doubt of the generation to which we ourselves belong." But while the philosophy itself is doubtless the main element in the poem's permanent appeal, the peculiar beauty of its form and style must also be taken into account. Even those who most vigorously dissent from the poet's doctrine of *Carpe Diem* must still be fascinated by the haunting music of the stanzas in which that doctrine is embodied.

Another of Tennyson's coevals and personal friends also deserves passing notice. Richard Monckton Milnes **Lord** (1809–85), who in 1863 became Lord Houghton, **Houghton.** was a man of varied accomplishments, but he is now remembered more as an intimate associate of greater men and a generous patron of struggling authors and artists than for his own contributions to literature. His poems of travel in Italy, Greece, and the East are without any special distinction, and his narrative poems are not now likely to be rescued from the oblivion into which they have fallen. But in his *Poems of Sentiment and Reflection* he shows delicate fancy and a faculty for easy and graceful verse. He was particularly successful with the drawing-room type of lyric and with songs for music. Slight as they are, such things as *Strangers Yet* and *The Brookside* are worthy of a place in any anthology of minor Victorian poetry.

Martin Farquhar Tupper (1810–89), who was a year younger than Houghton, is the most remarkable example **Tupper.** in nineteenth-century literature of a completely exploded reputation. Of his many books, one only, *Proverbial Philosophy*, can be said to survive, and this merely as a name. First published in 1839, but afterwards enlarged, this bulky collection of platitudes and commonplace moralisings couched in loose rhythmical prose, ran through edition after edition sold by the hundred thousand in England and America, was translated into many foreign languages, and netted £10,000 apiece to the poet and his publisher. It is now only a curiosity of literature and a signal illustration of the occasional divagations of popular taste.

No such sensational success attended the efforts of Aubrey Thomas de Vere (1814–1902), but, on the other **A. de Vere.** hand, he has never lost the respectable place which he made for himself among the lesser Victorian poets. The son of Sir Aubrey de Vere (1788–1846), whose sonnets were warmly praised by Wordsworth, this younger De Vere published a number of volumes of verse which included sonnets, lyrics, dramas, and narrative poems ; the last-named (e.g., *Legends of St. Patrick*, 1872) being intended, as he explained, " to illustrate religious philosophy or early Irish history." Such work is indicative of the bias of the poet's mind. In youth he had been, as he reports, " mainly devoted to theological studies," and in 1851 he joined the Roman Catholic Church.

We now come to a group of poets known collectively as the " Spasmodics," a happy nickname fastened upon **The "Spasmodics."** them by their satirist, Aytoun, which itself suggests their common characteristics—overstrained sentiment, forced and unnatural expression, a desire to be striking and unconventional at all costs, and as a result, affectations, conceits, gush, and frequent descents into bathos and turgidity. " Spasmodic " tendencies are apparent in other writers of the time, as notably in Mrs. Browning, but the three recognised members of the school who are important enough to have a place in our survey are Bailey, Dobell, and Alexander Smith.

Philip James Bailey (1816–1902) achieved sudden and remarkable fame on the appearance in 1839 of a philosophical poem in dramatic form entitled *Festus*, which was eagerly read by a very large public, praised by really good judges (as by Rossetti), and confidently classed by the critics with *Paradise Lost* and *Faust*. His other writings—*The Angel World* (1850), *The Mystic* (1855), *The Age* (1858), *The Universal Hymn* (1867)—were failures, but these he tried to save from complete destruction by incorporating large portions of them in his master-work. The result was that *Festus* continued to expand until in its " jubilee edition " it reached the enormous bulk of fifty-two long scenes aggregating something like 40,000 lines. The object of this prodigious poem is to set forth an interpretation of the universe and its divine purpose in terms of a mystical optimism ; but though its pretentious philosophy may impose for a time upon the unwary reader, it turns out on examination to be thoroughly commonplace. As a whole *Festus* is all but unreadable, but it contains occasional passages of really great imaginative power and lines here and there which have something of the grand style. Bailey's chief fault—and in this, as in his sententiousness, he resembles Edward Young—is his habit of piling up grandiose imagery, his incessant straining after sublimity, and in consequence the general tawdry magnificence and bombastic inflation of his work.

Bailey.

Sydney Dobell (1824–74), though as a boy he entered the counting-house of his father, a well-to-do wine merchant, later became a mere sleeping partner in the firm, and henceforth devoted himself to travelling in search of health and to literature. A closet-drama, *The Roman*, published in 1850, achieved a success which to-day it is difficult to understand. His more ambitious and more interesting *Balder* (1854), on

Dobell.

11

the other hand, was almost universally attacked by the critics, whose animosity it would seem was mainly due to the erroneous supposition that " Balderism " was held up for imitation instead of being presented merely as a dramatic study. In this poem Dobell undertook to analyse the egotistic kind of scepticism which he believed to be the special product of " our strong, great, ambitious, but perplexed and disconcerted time," and to trace the progress of his typical hero "from doubt to faith, from chaos to order." Unfortunately for the poet's design, only the first of the projected three divisions of the poem was ever written. Even this repels us by its extreme length, but it is not without high merit in parts, while as a thoughtful inquiry into modern moral and spiritual conditions it has something of the historical interest which belongs to Clough's almost contemporary *Amours de Voyage*. As both *The Roman* and *Balder* show, Dobell was one of the most unequal of writers. He rose on occasion to heights of real sublimity, but his aspiring flights were too often broken, and then he plunged head-foremost into the lowest depths of rant and bathos. He was naturally more even in his minor verse. His *Sonnets on the War* (in collaboration with Alexander Smith, 1855), and his collection of lyrics, *England in Time of War* (1856), contain some things (e.g., *The Army Surgeon, The Common Grave, Home in War Time*) of great power.

Alexander Smith (1829–67), who was born of humble parentage at Kilmarnock, and as a youth became pattern-designer in a Glasgow factory, burst upon the world at twenty-four with *A Life Drama*, of which ten thousand copies were sold in a few months, and which was received with loud applause by the London press. His popularity, though astonishing for the moment, was, however, very brief ; a critical reaction

A. Smith.

quickly set in, and very soon the faults of his work were being denounced as loudly as its merits had formerly been praised. From that reaction he never recovered, for his *City Poems* (1857) fell flat, and his Northumbrian epic, *Edwin of Deira* (1861), achieved only a very qualified success. In his last years he turned to prose, and published before his early death three still readable books —a volume of essays entitled *Dreamthorp* (1863), *A Summer in Skye* (1865), and a simple story of Scottish life, partly autobiographical, *Alfred Hagart's Household* (1866). As a poet Smith does not deserve to be altogether forgotten. With far less intellectual force than Dobell, he was also less violent and declamatory, and on the whole his work is more pleasing. Only the special student of Victorian literature is now likely to trouble himself about *A Life Drama* or *Edwin of Deira* ; but some of the *City Poems* (e.g., *Glasgow* and *The Night before the Wedding*) are really excellent, while *Barbara* (in the poem called *Horton* in the same collection) is a ballad of rare and impressive beauty.

This short account of the " Spasmodics " would be incomplete without some reference to the work of their **Aytoun.** satirist, William Edmondstoune Aytoun (1813–65), who in 1854 published *Firmilian, or the Student of Badajoz, a Spasmodic Tragedy*, under the pseudonym of T. Percy Jones. While this is in general a burlesque of " our young spirits, who call themselves the masters of the age," and either robe themselves in " philosophic mist " or come

> " Before us in the broad bombastic vein,
> With spasms and throes and transcendental flights,
> And heap hyperbole on metaphor,"

the satire is specially directed at *A Life Drama*, and Smith's style is happily travestied. Aytoun also wrote some excellent ballads both of the serious kind (*Lays of the Scottish Cavaliers*, 1848) and of the humorous (e.g., *A Massacre of the Macpherson*), and in partnership with Theodore Martin some very clever parodies of contemporary poets in the *Book of Ballads, edited by Bon Gaultier* (1855).

In their emotional intensity, their dread of convention, and their constant craving after originality, the " Spasmodics " have obviously many points of connection with romanticism. At the same time, the philosophic quality which in general is a marked feature of their work brings them into touch with a number of contemporary writers who otherwise have little in common with them. One of these is Arthur Hugh Clough, the subject of Matthew Arnold's fine memorial poem *Thyrsis*.

Clough. Born in 1819, Clough, after some years under Thomas Arnold at Rugby, went up to Oxford, where for a time he was carried away by the influence of Newmanism, like (in his own words) " a straw drawn up the draught of a chimney." But presently reaction set in, and, as his biographer tells us, " when the turmoil had subsided, he found . . . that it had shaken the whole foundations of his early faith." Henceforth the main effort of his intellectual life was directed to the painful task of reconstruction, as a result of which he seems in the end to have reached the conclusion that while the supposed historical bases of Christianity have to be abandoned, essential Christianity still stands firm on the bedrock of intuition and spiritual experience. Compelled by conscientious scruples to resign his University tutorship and fellowship, he passed some years in uncertainty, finding intellectual help in the friendship of Carlyle, and some distraction in travelling. After a year in the United States (1853), he returned to England to take up a position in the Education Office, and married. But his health soon began to give way, and he died in Florence in 1861.

Intellectually and spiritually Clough had much in common with his friend Arnold, and in his poetry we find the same reverent though searching critical spirit, the same sceptical note, the same absolute sincerity and moral earnestness. His minor poems are almost entirely personal in the narrowest sense of the term ; their subject-matter being provided by his own religious struggles, doubts, cravings, and persistent search for truth. Many of them impress us now with a certain want of strength and directness, but some (e.g., *Quâ Cursum Ventus,* " Say not the Struggle nought availeth," *Easter Day,* " Where lies the Land ") have real poetic as well as intellectual value. His longer poems, *The Bothie of Tober-na-Vuolich* and *Amours de Voyage,*—for which, unlike Arnold, he seeks his materials from modern life, and which are both written in rather slipshod hexameters of the *Evangeline* type,—can be praised only with quali-fication. The former, " a long-vacation pastoral," is, despite its appalling name, a pleasant half-serious, half-humorous love-story, in which the moral stress is thrown upon the practical and against the speculative life ; the latter is chiefly interesting for the character of the un-heroic hero Claude, in whom Clough presents an example of that " over-educated weakness of purpose " which he believed to be one of the most alarming results of the introspective habits and paralysing scepticism of the age. The fragmentary *Dipsychus,* a dramatic poem evidently fashioned on *Faust,* is, as the title suggests, another study of a mind out of balance with itself.

Deficient in imagination and passion, Clough's poetry is never likely to attract a large body of readers, but it will always find a sympathetic public among those who, like the poet himself, are interested in verse of the intellectual and speculative kind. Its great merits on the personal side are its sincerity and its fine moral spirit. Historically, like Arnold's subjective poetry, it is noteworthy as a clear expression of the sceptical temper of the mid-Victorian Age.

The realistic tendency exemplified in Clough's longer poems found a more popular exponent in Coventry Kearsey Deighton Patmore (1823–96), whose best known work, *The Angel in the House* (1854–62), is a long narrative poem about quite ordinary people in the ordinary circumstances of modern life. As a highly sentimental love-story, told with tenderness and grace, idealising the domestic affections and containing many pleasing pictures of English scenery and manners, this poem for a time enjoyed a very great vogue. But its over-facile octosyllabic verse often runs very thin ; the poet's style is weak at the best ; and he frequently lapses into utter triviality.

Patmore.

Another writer who also cultivated the novel-in-verse, though he did much work in many other lines as well, is Edward Robert Bulwer Lytton, first Earl of Lytton (1831–91), more generally known in literature under his early pen-name of Owen Meredith. The eldest son of the famous novelist, Lytton was educated at Harrow and Bonn, adopted statesmanship as his profession, had a distinguished diplomatic career in various European capitals, and from 1876 to 1880 was Viceroy of India. Notwithstanding the pressure of his public duties, he was always an industrious writer, mainly of verse, and the bulk of his production is very large. Though he had far more depth and earnestness than his father, he resembled him

The Earl of Lytton.

in his versatility, and in the singular ease with which he took up in succession many different styles. It has indeed been frequently noted as a curious feature of his poetry that it reveals, even on close examination, little of a distinctive or consistent character, while on the other hand (and this explains the charge of plagiarism made against him) it everywhere exhibits the powerful influence of one or another poet—now Byron, now Heine, now Tennyson, now Browning, now Swinburne, now Arnold—who for the moment had acquired ascendancy over his mind. Yet it may fairly be said that in one way Lytton was entirely himself ; he always wrote as an accomplished cosmopolitan man of the world, whose worldliness was, however, tempered and transfigured by a strong vein of idealism and a marked tendency towards introspection and melancholy. It is probable that, against his own wishes, he will be remembered chiefly by his *Lucile* (1860), an interesting story of modern life (in part founded on George Sand's *Lavinia*), told in easy, flowing anapaestic verse admirably suited to the subject (though he himself afterwards pronounced it " detestable "), and further noteworthy for its picturesque descriptions of the Pyrenees and the combination in it of romantic sentiment and worldly wisdom. As a novel-in-verse it is certainly far superior to *The Angel in the House*, though it labours under the disadvantage of inordinate prolixity. This defect— which was Lytton's common failing, and which even Mrs. Browning criticised—reappears in the later *Glenaveril*, an extremely long narrative poem (this time in *ottava rima*), which, like *Lucile*, is entirely modern in theme, characters, and setting, though otherwise it has few points of connection with that more popular work. Lytton also produced, among many other things, a large body of lyrics (in *The Wanderer* and elsewhere), a classical drama, *Clytemnestra*, a long mystical tale of Polish derivation, *Orval, or the Fool of Time*, and a fantastic political satire, *King Poppy*. On the whole, he is a disappointing writer. The general impression that he leaves with us is, that he was a highly gifted man of real poetic genius, whose powers were too much dissipated, who yielded too much to outside influences, and who thus never quite realised his possibilities.

Among the many threads which we can recognise in the complex texture of Lytton's writings is that of **Edwin** Oriental lore. Interest in the East was with **Arnold.** him, however, only slight and occasional. It is, on the contrary, the central inspiration in the poetry of Sir Edwin Arnold (1832–1904), who spent some years (1856–61) in India as Principal of the Government Sanskrit College at Poona before entering upon a distinguished career as a journalist in London. His one outstanding poem is *The Light of Asia* (1879), a sympathetic and impressive rendering in richly coloured and melodious verse of the life and teaching of Buddha. In *The Light of the World* (1891) he essayed a companion study of the life and teaching of Christ, but this never attained the same success. *The Indian Song of Songs* (1875), *Pearls of the Faith* (1883), and *With Sa'di in the Garden* (1888) may be named among his other writings. Arnold's work has considerable beauty of style, and possesses the merit of being well out of the beaten track.

To the beaten track we very manifestly return in the verse of Sir Lewis Morris (1833–1907), who gained an **Lewis** immediate success with his *Songs of Two* **Morris.** *Worlds* (1872–75), and established himself as one of the most popular poets of the day with his *Epic of Hades* (1876–77). His later works, which included

Gwen : a Drama in Monologue (1879), *Songs Unsung* (1883), and *A Vision of Saints* (1890)—a sort of companion to the *Epic of Hades*—did nothing to increase his reputation. He also wrote numerous occasional poems on national subjects. Lewis Morris is one more among the many poets of the nineteenth century who illustrate the extreme fluctuations of critical opinion. But both the extravagant praise with which his first books were received and the reaction which had already set in before his death may doubtless be explained by reference to the characteristic quality of his poetry as a whole. Lucid, graceful, easy to read and to understand, with an excellent moral tone and an entirely conventional view of life, it fell in with the taste which Tennyson and others had created, and was the more readily accepted because there was absolutely nothing original in its thought or style. At the same time it was precisely this want of individuality and distinction which was mainly responsible for its rapid loss of interest. The *Epic of Hades*, which seems of all his poems to have the best chance of keeping a place in literature, retells a number of stories from Greek mythology pleasantly enough, in a way to bring out their real or supposed moral meaning and in blank verse obviously fashioned on the Tennysonian model.

We get once more into touch with what is vital in literature, though the change unfortunately involves **James** a descent into the lowest depths of spiritual **Thomson.** experience, in passing to James Thomson, "the poet of despair," who wrote as "B. V."[1] The son of a sailor, Thomson was born at Port-Glasgow in

[1] The initials of his early chosen pseudonym, Bysshe Vanolis, "Bysshe" being taken from Shelley, while "Vanolis" was an anagram of the name of another of his favourite authors the German Novalis.

1834, and obtained a meagre education in an orphan asylum. In the course of a restless life he was successively Army schoolmaster, solicitor's clerk, mining-agent in America, and war correspondent in Spain. Then his friendship with Bradlaugh, the famous secularist, led him into a connection with *The National Reformer*, in which many of his poems first appeared. In his later years he yielded more and more to narcotics and alcohol, which hastened his end. He died in a hospital in 1882. The problem of Thomson's pessimism is largely pathological, and cannot therefore be discussed here. It is enough to say that melancholy hung about him like a pall, and that like a pall it hangs over every page of his principal work, *The City of Dreadful Night* (1874). The product, as the author himself told George Eliot, of "sleepless hypochondria," this remarkable poem—the most absolutely hopeless poem in our literature—is a masterpiece of gloomy power, rich imagination, and marvellous beauty of diction and verse. There is little in Thomson's other work which even approaches this one supreme effort, but mention may be made of *Sunday at Hampstead*, *Sunday up the River*, and the rather Swinburnesque " He heard her sing."

At this point we will depart for the moment from the chronological order that we may deal at once with **Robert** another Scotchman who, while his attitude **Buchanan.** towards life was fundamentally different from Thomson's, resembles him in being at once an unacademic poet and a poet of revolt. The son of a Radical journalist and lecturer, Robert Williams Buchanan was born in 1841. The influence of his studies at the University of Glasgow is clearly shown in the fine classic poems in his early volume, *Undertones*, though he soon ceased to care much for

" statuesque woes and nude intellectualities moving on a background of antique landscape." At Glasgow he formed a close friendship with a fellow-student, a weaver's son, named David Gray, and the two lads, in all the ardour of youthful ambition, set out together for London with the intention of taking the literary world by storm. But Gray soon sickened of consumption, and went back to his home in Kirkintilloch to die (1861), leaving behind him a small volume of some slight promise, *The Luggie and Other Poems*. His death produced a profound impression on Buchanan's mind ; it was to his memory that *Undertones* (1863) was dedicated ; while thirty years later a book of a very different stamp, *The New Rome*, was also inscribed with the name of the same friend of long ago. Henceforth Buchanan's life was one of enormous and varied activity as novelist,[1] dramatist, and contributor to the magazines. But though much of his time was thus given to such more lucrative work—a matter of necessity since he was entirely dependent on his pen—he continued to produce volume after volume of verse, of which the most important were *London Poems* (1866), *The Book of Orm* (1870), *Balder the Beautiful* (1877), *The City of Dream* (1888), *The Wandering Jew* (1893), and *The New Rome* (1899). He died in 1901.

As a poet, though his significance has been recognised by a few critics (mainly outside the regular professional class), Buchanan has by no means obtained the attention which is his due. Historically, however, his work is specially important because it contains the fullest and most powerful expression of the essentially modern spirit which is anywhere to be found in English poetry. As a religious and philosophic poet

[1] Of his many novels the best are *God and the Man* and *The Shadow of the Sword*, both highly melodramatic, but things of genuine power.

he avowedly addresses himself to the mature reader, and even the mature reader may at times be shocked by the audacity of his thought and his outspokenness. But, though he is a preacher of revolt against many things which the world holds sacred, he is likewise an apostle of faith and reconstruction, bitter in his animus against the whole system of ecclesiastical Christianity, yet filled with a Christlike love to which nothing in human life is common or unclean. It would, however, be a mistake to suppose that the interest of Buchanan's work inheres wholly in its intellectual quality. He was a poet of great imaginative insight and power, and those who care nothing for his militant radicalism will find in his writings a rich body of varied and beautiful verse. His *London Poems* (e.g., *Liz*, *Nell*, *Barbara*) contain admirable studies of humble life ; many of his dramatic pieces are remarkably effective in their blending of pathos and humour ; he had a genuine lyric gift ; his nature-poetry is full of sympathy and mystical feeling ; and some of the ballads (like the superb *Judas Iscariot*) deserve the highest praise.

In turning back a few years from Buchanan to John Byrne Leicester Warren, Lord de Tabley (1835–95), **Lord de Tabley.** we pass from the poetry of purpose to that of pure art. Between 1863 and 1873 De Tabley produced several volumes of verse and a couple of classic tragedies, *Philoctetes* and *Orestes* ; but it was not till the publication of his two series of *Poems Dramatic and Lyrical* (1893, 1895) that the critics suddenly discovered that in him they had to reckon with a poet whose merits had too long been overlooked. His work has few of the qualities which make for popularity, but its dramatic power, the magnificence of its style, and the concentration and beauty of its blank verse fully justify the praise which it has received from admirers here and there. De Tabley was a student of science as well as a poet, and his poetry of nature is remarkable for the accurate knowledge it displays in matters of detail, especially in connection with birds and flowers.

As Tennyson's successor in the laureateship, De Tabley's coeval, Alfred Austin (1835–1909), might of **Austin.** course be very fittingly placed among the poets of the post-Tennysonian age ; but in general character his work belongs so unmistakably to the earlier generation that it will be more satisfactory to deal with it here. He came of a Catholic family ; took his degree at the University of London in 1853 ; was called to the Bar in 1857 ; but on the death of his father in 1861 abandoned law for political and literary journalism. In 1854 he published his first volume of verse, *Randolph : A Tale of Polish Grief,* inspired by his sympathy with Poland and bitter hatred of Russia ; and in 1861 created a considerable stir with a pungent satire, *The Season.* From that time on he continued to produce steadily in prose and verse ; his verse including dramas (e.g., *Savonarola, England's Darling, Flodden Field*), dramatic poems (e.g., *The Tower of Babel,* " a celestial love-drama," *Prince Lucifer, Fortunatus the Pessimist*), narrative poems (e.g., *The Human Tragedy*), and numerous volumes of a more miscellaneous kind. His appointment to the laureateship in 1896, though obviously a compliment, was in reality the heaviest blow which his reputation ever sustained. The fact that he should be chosen when men like Swinburne and Morris were still alive, was itself a challenge to the critics. Moreover, comparison between him and his predecessor—between " Alfred the Little " and

" Alfred the Great "—at once became inevitable, and his work suffered as a result of the over-severe standard which was applied to it. The consequent injustice may now be corrected. There is, it is true, nothing in the least great about Austin's poetry; but it represents something more than merely respectable accomplishment. His diction is clear and pure; he is happily free from extravagances and affectations; he has abundant fancy, and at times a good deal of personal charm. Some of his longer works, like the graceful *Fortunatus* and *Madonna's Child* (part of Canto II. of *The Human Tragedy*, though also published independently), make at least very pleasant reading. But it is in his simple, flowing, musical lyrics that he is at his best. His poetry of nature also deserves a word of special commendation, for it is full of genuine freshness and feeling (*cp.* his prose books, *The Garden that I Love*, *Veronica's Garden*, etc.). Love of the English soil, of English flowers, and even of the vagaries of the English climate (e.g., *A Defence of English Spring*), was one aspect of the intense patriotism in which he resembled his precursor in the laureateship.

Nine years Austin's junior, Arthur William Edgar O'Shaughnessy (1844–81) was warmly welcomed by the O'Shaugh-reviewers when in 1870 he published his *Epic* nessy. *of Women and Other Poems*, a volume in which, notwithstanding his obvious indebtedness to Gautier, Baudelaire, and Swinburne, the individual quality was strong enough to give promise of greater things. But this first success was not repeated either with *Lays of France* (1872) or with *Music and Moonlight* (1874), which indeed suggested rather that the poet was already coming to the end of his resources. O'Shaughnessy's range was narrow and his work deficient in substance.

" Music and Moonlight " is, in fact, a good general description of it, for its principal merits are its melodiousness and a certain vague beauty of feeling and form. He belongs to the order of poets of whom he speaks in his first volume as " music-makers " and " dreamers of dreams."

It may be added that O'Shaughnessy married the daughter of John Westland Marston (1819–90), the author of some poetic dramas (e.g., *The Patrician's Daughter*, *Strathmore*) of little importance, and sister of **Marston.** the blind poet, Philip Bourke Marston (1850–87), whose three small volumes—*Song Tide* (1871), *All in All* (1875), and *Wind Voices* (1883)—contain some pretty lyrics and a few meritorious sonnets.

The traditions of light verse were carried on successfully during the Victorian Age by a number of writers, a **LightVerse** few of whom only can here be referred to as **Writers.** perhaps the most excellent examples of a fairly large class. In the *London Lyrics* (1857) of Frederick **Locker-** Locker-Lampson (1821–95) we have some of **Lampson.** the best society verse in the language, light in touch, delicately playful, and at times (e.g., *To my Grandmother*) imbued with true pathos. The *Verses and Translations* (1862) and *Fly Leaves* (1872) of Charles **Calverley.** Stuart Calverley (1831–84) are the work of a scholarly wit whose humour is quite delightful in its kind (e.g., *Ode to Tobacco*, *Lines suggested by the Fourteenth of February*), and whose parodies deserve a place beside the *Rejected Addresses* of the brothers Smith. The *Vignettes in Rhyme* (1873), *Proverbs in Porcelain* (1877), *Old-World Idyls* (1883), and the numerous other volumes of Henry **Dobson.** Austin Dobson (b. 1840) are marked by the elegance and airy grace, and something of the modishness of the Queen Anne men, but they have also a depth of poetic feeling which the Queen Anne men rarely suggest. Mr. Dobson is an avowed admirer of the eighteenth century, to the study of which he has made substantial contributions in his lives of Goldsmith, Walpole, Fanny Burney, Richardson, Hogarth, and his three series of *Eighteenth-Century Vignettes*. The

Lang. versatile and accomplished Andrew Lang (1844–1912), who won distinction in many fields — as critic, historian, biographer, translator, anthropologist—also produced a good deal of very excellent light verse in *Ballads and Lyrics of Old France* (1872), *Ballades in Blue China* (1880), *Rhymes à la Mode* (1884), and other collections. Like Mr. Dobson, he was particularly successful in the use of old French forms of verse—the *ballade*, the *roundel*, the *villanelle*, etc., which enjoyed a remarkable vogue in the seventies and eighties of the century.

The Victorian Age produced a very large number of women poets, but few of these, after Mrs. Browning

Women Poets. and Christina Rossetti, are important enough to find a place in a short sketch of nineteenth-century literature. Mention may, however, be made of three of the sisterhood, Eliza Cook, Jean Ingelow, and Adelaide Anne Procter.

Eliza Cook (1818–89) was for many years extremely popular with that large reading public which, with no

Eliza Cook. sense of the higher values of poetry, is always pleased with pretty sentiments expressed in graceful verse. Her writing was thoroughly wholesome, and her tender touch upon the domestic feelings, as in *The Old Arm-Chair*, suffices to explain her vogue.

Jean Ingelow. Jean Ingelow (1820–97) was a writer with greater claims to critical consideration, for her lyrics have often a note of true pathos, and she wrote some excellent ballads. Though most of her work is already forgotten, a few of her poems (e.g., *High Tide on the Coast of Lincolnshire*) will serve to keep her name **A. A. Procter.** alive. Adelaide Anne Procter (1825–64) was the daughter of Bryan Waller Procter (" Barry Cornwall," 1787–1874), who was a friend of many of the most famous men of his day, and himself the author of poems once admired though now no longer read. Many of her own verses, afterwards collected with additions in volume form under the title of *Legends and Lyrics*, first appeared in Dickens's *Household Words* and *All the Year Round*, the great novelist being one of her warmest admirers. Her writing is tender, delicate, and graceful, but is totally destitute of strength and distinction.

It remains for us to deal with a few writers who have some standing among Victorian poets, though they **Prose Writers who were also Poets.** won their principal laurels in prose. Macaulay's fame as a verse writer rests mainly on his *Lays of Ancient Rome* (1842). Vigorous, dashing, clear, but at the same time hard and metallic, these have the characteristic qualities which we **Macaulay.** shall presently note in his prose. No one would think of calling them great poetry, but their high rhetorical merits are not to be denied, and they reproduce with splendid effect the spirit of antique patriotism. The martial note which rings out so strongly in these *Lays* is also heard elsewhere in Macaulay's verse, as in the stirring ballads of *Ivry* and *The Battle of Naseby*.

Astonishingly versatile and restlessly ambitious of achieving success in many fields, Bulwer Lytton made **Bulwer Lytton.** various attempts to establish himself as a poet, but despite his cleverness and industry his bulky work in verse added nothing to his fame. *The*

New Timon, a Romance of London (1845), which contained a ferocious attack on Tennyson, is now remembered, if at all, only on account of Tennyson's reply in *Punch* (a portion of which is retained in his collected Works under the title of *Literary Squabbles*). An experiment in serio-comic romantic epic, *King Arthur* (1848), ended in complete disaster. *The Lost Tales of Miletus* (1866) are much better than this, but even these hardly rise above the level of well-made verse.

Thackeray, on the other hand, had a real poetic vein, and his serious verse, though small in amount in **Thack-** comparison with his ever-delightful humorous **eray.** ballads and burlesques (e.g., *The Ballads of Policeman X*, *The Willow Tree*, *The Sorrows of Werther*), is of very exquisite quality. Once at least, in his *May-Day Ode*, he showed himself capable of maintaining a very high level of thought and style, while the rough vigour of *The White Squall* is extremely striking. But the poems in which he is at his best are those in which the underlying tenderness of his nature is most fully revealed (e.g., *At the Church Gate*), and even more particularly those in which his constant sense of the pathos of things is blended with his characteristic satiric humour (e.g., *The Ballad of the Bouillabaisse*, *The Age of Wisdom*). The melancholy philosophy of life which pervades his novels is epitomised in such eminently personal utterances as *The End of the Play* and *Vanitas Vanitatum*.

The Brontë sisters also take a small, though a very small, place among the novelists who also wrote verse, **Emily** by virtue of a little volume of *Poems* which they **Brontë.** published together in 1846. Of the sixty-one pieces in this collection, however, only those of Emily Brontë have any real merit. Several of these, among them *The Old Stoic* and *Last Lines*, are certainly remarkable, but the praise which has been lavished upon them by too enthusiastic admirers must be dismissed as extravagant.

George Eliot's poetry is not only considerable in quantity, but also markedly varied in character ; but **George Eliot.** the fact that she was forty-four before she began to write verse at all supports Leslie Stephen's contention that in her the poetic impulse " was acquired rather than innate." Carefully wrought, often admirable in matter and expression, and generally characterised by a stately dignity of style, her poetry has indeed all the qualities which we should naturally expect in the work of a woman of such massive intellectuality and high moral temper. What it lacks is simply that mysterious but indispensable element which we call inspiration. Her most ambitious poem, *The Spanish Gypsy,* a long romantic narrative in blank verse, is undoubtedly a great effort rather than a great achievement ; but its fine presentation of the ethical motive which recurs so often in the writer's novels— the conflict between the life of self-sacrifice and that of self-gratification—makes it a very noble poem on the moral side ; while as a work of art it is saved from total failure by occasional passages of real beauty and by scenes, like the first interview between Fedalma (the gypsy) and Zarca, of genuine dramatic power. But while it is by *The Spanish Gypsy* that George Eliot's claims as a poet are commonly supposed to stand or fall, a higher place should, I think, be given to *The Legend of Jubal,* in which the story of the invention of music is told with much simplicity and charm, and in rimed couplets which flow with an ease and melody beyond her customary command. Two other poems of great personal interest will always remain favourites with admirers of her work at large. One of these is the series of autobiographical sonnets, *Brother and Sister*, in which we have a record of the childish experiences and memories which went to the making of Maggie Tulliver's early story in *The Mill on the Floss*; the other, her famous Positivist hymn—" O may I join the Choir Invisible "—in which she voices her faith in impersonal immortality as a well-spring of hope and inspiration for those, like herself, to whom belief in personal immortality is impossible.

While George Eliot was only a poet made by effort and culture, there is no doubt that Charles Kingsley was a poet born. His *Saint's Tragedy* (1848),

Kingsley. in which he makes the story of Elizabeth of Hungary the vehicle of his own social and religious teaching, is indeed overweighted with purpose, and despite its feverish energy, has little vital power. But *Andromeda* (1858) is a work of very high poetic quality, and its hexameters have been praised even by critics who generally condemn that classic measure as a clumsy innovation in English verse. Some of Kingsley's minor poems are also excellent, like the vigorous *Ode to the North-East Wind*, *The Three Fishers*, *A Farewell*, the delightful "When all the World is Young" in *The Water Babies*, and the wonderful ballad *The Sands of Dee*. It may perhaps be said that no poet of his time built for himself so secure a poetic reputation as Kingsley upon so small an output.

In order of time, George Meredith was a poet before he became a novelist, for his first publication was a book

Meredith. of *Poems* in 1851; and though after *The Ordeal of Richard Feverel* (1859) his energies were mainly given to prose fiction, he continued, in *Modern Love* (1862), *Poems and Lyrics of the Joy of Earth* (1883),

Ballads and Poems of Tragic Life (1887), *A Reading of Earth* (1888), and other volumes, to make occasional noteworthy appearances in the poetic rôle. Altogether, therefore, his work in verse is considerable in quantity, while, like his novels, it is marked throughout by a pronounced individuality of thought and style. His greatest single work as a poet is unquestionably *Modern Love*, which deals with the tragic story of an unhappy marriage in a rather fragmentary and obscure way, but with much subtlety and pathos. Among his minor poems special note should be taken of those which, like *The Old Chartist* and *Juggling Jerry*, are remarkable for their touches of quaint humour and their power of characterisation. One extremely important aspect of Meredith's poetry is his treatment of nature. His poetry is essentially poetry of the open air, fresh, breezy, and wholesome ; he is as near in sympathy to the common earth as his own Melampus in the poem of that name ; and the "joy of earth" pervades his pages (e.g., *The Lark Ascending, The South Wester*). But though he is alive to nature's mystical meanings, and (a continually recurring thought with him) to the oneness of nature and man, there is in his "reading of earth" no trace of that sentimentalism which is so usual in modern literature. He recognises to the full the hardness and severity of nature ; judged by our "shrinking nerves" she appears "a Mother whom no cry can melt," and who is always ready to sacrifice her best (*Thrush in February*) ; "all round we find cold nature slight the feelings of the totter-knee'd" (*Whimper of Sympathy*). But he does not recoil before these stern facts ; according to his thoroughly masculine philosophy, nature's harsh discipline is a stimulating factor in the evolution of all higher life ; and thus the lesson which he spells out from "the lines dear Earth designs" is uncompromisingly optimistic. It is much to be regretted that a poet of such fine quality should too often have placed a barrier between himself and his readers by the unnecessary intellectual strain which he continually imposes upon them. Like Browning, whom in many ways he resembles, he is frequently obscure, not through depth of thought, but through imperfection of expression. Like Browning, again, he is often careless of form, giving us, as some even of his greatest admirers have acknowledged, "poetry in the ore" rather than the finished product of art.

CHAPTER IV

GENERAL PROSE

FIRST in order alike of time and of importance among the prose writers of his age, Thomas Carlyle was born **Carlyle.** on 4th December 1795, at Ecclefechan, Dumfriesshire, where his father was a stone-mason. It is a fact of capital significance that he thus sprang straight from the rugged Scotch soil and from a severely Puritan stock, for his early surroundings and the stern old Calvinism in which he was bred left a lasting impression on his mind. From the Annan Grammar School he proceeded to the University of Edinburgh, where he matriculated in 1809. Leaving without a degree, and having in the meantime been compelled, through radical changes in his religious ideas, to give up his original thought of the ministry, he turned to schoolmastering, to which he gave some years of unprofitable toil. Already he had fallen a victim to the acute dyspepsia which was thereafter to be a source of untold misery to him, and which coloured his whole view of life. Moreover, he was now engaged in a fierce spiritual struggle, the history of which is written with tremendous power in that masterpiece of transfigured autobiography, the narrative of Teufelsdröckh's experiences in the second book of *Sartor Resartus*. That struggle ended for him as for Teufelsdröckh, in a moment of mystical illumination and "spiritual new birth."

But it is important to remember that though he was thus restored, not indeed to his former creed, but to the mood of courage and faith, this final repudiation of the Satan of pessimism and unbelief did not mean the actual close of his intellectual conflict. Neither then nor ever after did he reach that perfect serenity which, perhaps because he knew it to be beyond his attainment, he so greatly admired in Goethe.

Meanwhile he had learned German, and had found in German literature " a new heaven and a new earth "; and he now turned his knowledge to account in a translation of Goethe's *Wilhelm Meister* (1824) and a *Life of Schiller* (1825). In 1826 he married Jane Welsh, and presently retired to his wife's lonely farm at Craigenputtock, on the Dumfriesshire moors, which was his home from 1828 to 1834. During these six years he wrote some of his best essays as well as *Sartor Resartus*, which, after rejection by one publisher after another, appeared as a serial in *Fraser* (1833–34). Then he migrated to London, where his first work, the wonderful dramatic epic, *The History of the French Revolution*, written with actual poverty staring him in the face, not only ended his financial difficulties, but also established his reputation as a new and original power in literature. His position was further strengthened by the appearance in book form in 1841 of the last of several courses of lectures which he had recently been giving with success—that *On Heroes, Hero-Worship and the Heroic in History*. Already, both in *Sartor* and *The French Revolution*, he had shown himself keenly alive to the disquieting signs of the times and the urgency of " the condition of England question," and in his pamphlet on *Chartism* (1839) he had uttered a " preliminary word " on the great subject of reform. To this subject he returned in *Past and Present* (1843), which is doubly important as the expression of his ripest thought on social matters and (in Book II., with its vivid pictures of twelfth-century England) as one of the finest examples of his extraordinary power of reviving the past. The writing of this book interrupted a work upon which he had already been for some years engaged, and which, begun as a history of the Civil War, and then transformed into a biography of its chief figure, ultimately appeared as *Oliver Cromwell's Letters and Speeches, with Elucidations* (1845). While thus living in imagination in the great days of "heroic puritanism," Carlyle was becoming more and more pessimistic in regard to the tendencies and prospects of modern society, and finally his atrabilious mood found vent in the brilliant but terribly savage *Latter Day Pamphlets* (1850). Though this "furious raid into the field of political practice," as Arnold called it, aroused a storm of indignation, it appears to have brought to Carlyle himself a measure of relief, such as frequently follows an outburst of passion. This at least we may infer from the surprisingly calm tone of his next book, *The Life of John Sterling* (1851),[1] a little masterpiece of biography. After this Carlyle embarked upon his last great undertaking, *The History of Frederick II. of Prussia, called Frederick the Great* (1858–65). This work has rightly been praised as "a monument of historical industry and acumen," and it is moreover marked by some of its author's most characteristic qualities—his marvellous skill in portraiture, his power of description, his inimitable humour. But if its merits

[1] John Sterling (1806–43), though a fairly regular contributor to the magazines, really owes his fame to this biography. He left nothing behind him of independent value, but the charm of his personality made a vivid impression on his friends.

are many, it labours under many drawbacks; it is far too long for its subject; the Prussian king, as Carlyle himself came to realise, is a very "questionable" example of the "heroism" of which he is held up as a type; the narrative is continually overburdened with wearisome details about genealogies, campaigns, and battles; and while the style is often vigorous and picturesque it exhibits all too clearly the degeneration of his peculiarities into a vicious and irritating mannerism.

The completion of this immense task was practically the end of Carlyle's literary activities. Of his remaining works two only need to be named here; his address as Lord Rector of the University of Edinburgh in 1866, which contains a kind of epitome of his teachings, and an open letter entitled *Shooting Niagara, and After?* which, prompted by the Reform Bill of 1867, renews the attack of the *Latter Day Pamphlets* upon the ideals of modern democracy.

The last fifteen years of Carlyle's life were years of ever-deepening despondency. The sudden death of his wife in 1866 was a terrible shock to him; his domestic life had indeed been rather tempestuous, from faults on both sides, but there had been real love in the strange union, and the loss of the partner of his early struggles and later triumphs left him in a "measureless solitude." Old age, as it crept upon him with slowly increasing physical disabilities, but with slight abatement of intellectual fire, softened his petulance and took some of the edge from his temper, but did little to lighten his gloom. He died of natural decay, in the house in Chelsea in which he had settled on coming to London nearly half a century before, on 4th February 1881.

Though his thought was widened and liberalised by culture and especially by the influence of German idealistic philosophy, Carlyle to the last was a characteristic representative of the rugged Puritan stock from which he sprang. He was indeed a Puritan of the Puritans alike in his strength and in his limitations— in his strenuous and uncompromising moral temper, his earnestness, his spirituality, and in the narrowness of his outlook, his inflexibility and intolerance, and his utter contempt of both science and art. This defines his position and explains his antagonistic attitude towards the principal movements of his age. He found himself in a world which, as he believed, had lost all living faith in God, which had become absorbed in material welfare and progress to the neglect of all higher things, and the moral fibre of which had been loosened by the spread of a spirit of self-complacency and easy-going optimism. To this world for upwards of fifty years he preached, from many texts, but always with a remarkable consistency of aim and purpose, the stern old Puritan gospel of God and His righteousness. From a logical point of view, his own theology was vague and uncertain, but he believed with all the intensity of his nature that spirit is the only reality, that the whole material universe is but the symbol of divine power, that a just and jealous God controls the destinies of men, and that in implicit obedience to His will lies the only hope alike for individuals and nations. In this way he read history, which was for him the " larger Bible," or plain record of God's dealings with men throughout the ages. Save indeed that he conceived God as working, not through miracle, but through the everlasting concatenation of cause and effect (his doctrine of " natural supernaturalism " on the ethical side), his interpretation of history was substantially that of the Old Testament writers; the French Revolution being for him only the latest illustration on a gigantic scale of that inexorable law in accordance with which national disaster inevitably follows national sin. And this was the lesson which he took over from history and applied to the social problems of his own time. England too was fast drifting the way of eighteenth-century France, and no political remedies, but only an entire spiritual regeneration, would suffice to save it. Such was the religious foundation of Carlyle's social teaching. But to make our summary of that teaching approximately complete, we have also to take account of his life-long antagonism to another of the great movements of the nineteenth century—the advance of democracy. His whole theory of history, based as it was upon the "great man" hypothesis, was as fundamentally anti-democratic as it was anti-scientific, and to the evidence of history he triumphantly appealed for confirmation of his contention that the masses of the people, being "mostly fools," can never be safely left to work out their own salvation; that the many who are weak and unwise need at all times the support and guidance of the strong and wise few; and that, if the destruction of sham kings and aristocracies is often a terrible necessity, true kings and aristocracies, whose virtue lies not in blood or breeding but in brains and character, are everlastingly indispensable. Democracy was for him "a self-cancelling business." The only hope for turbulent young Demos was to find his master and, having found, to obey him.

That Carlyle in many ways perversely damaged his own cause is very clear. He did so by his wilfulness, intolerance, and narrowness; by the extravagance of his statements; by the harshness of his judgments;

by his acrimonious temper ; by the general grimness of his view of life ; by his perpetual grumbling and scolding. The want of a positive quality in much of his thought was also against him ; he was indeed so much more successful in demolishing the " shams " and " simulacra " upon which he poured the vials of his wrath than in defining the " veracities " which were to take their place, that there is a measure of truth in Calverley's caustic remark that he led men out of Egypt into the wilderness—and left them there. Yet his inspirational power was so enormous that, vague as his teaching often was, it entered as a potent factor into nineteenth-century thought. As the most eloquent modern preacher of sincerity, righteousness, and the gospel of work, he stands out as the greatest moral and spiritual force in the English literature of his generation.

While it is inevitable that our attention should be fixed mainly on Carlyle as a prophet, we must not overlook his high claims as a man of letters. Despite his contempt of mere art and his preoccupation in his own critical studies, with the purely ethical aspect of his subjects, he was himself a consummate literary craftsman, supreme in narrative, description, and characterisation, and a master of passion, pathos, humour, invective, sarcasm, satire, and emotional appeal. His extraordinary style,—rugged, vehement, exclamatory, often bizarre and uncouth in phraseology, and in sentence-structure defying all the conventions of formal rhetoric, —while it owed not a little to the influence of some of his German masters, was at bottom entirely personal in quality. To many it still seems, as it seemed to the first readers of *Sartor*, a " Babylonish dialect," and we must admit that in his later writings he deliberately exaggerated its mannerisms until it became a sort of caricature of itself. Yet in his case the connection between the thing said and the actual saying of it is always so vital that our final impression is that he could have delivered his message adequately in no other way.

Though five years younger than Carlyle,—for he was born on 15th October 1800,—Thomas Babington Macaulay, the son of a West India merchant of Scottish Presbyterian descent, was already well advanced in his career of unbroken prosperity while the stone-mason's son was still grimly wrestling with fate at Craigenputtock. At Cambridge he carried off various prizes, gained in two successive years (1819 and 1820) the Chancellor's medal for English verse, and laid the foundation of his reputation as one of the most remarkable talkers of the day. At this time he also began to make a name in literature with contributions in prose and verse to *Knight's Quarterly Magazine*. The real opening of his career, however, was the publication in the *Edinburgh* in 1825 of his brilliant though rather gaudy essay on Milton. In 1830 he entered the House of Commons, and as a reward for the splendid services which he rendered to the Government in the passing of the Reform Bill, was in 1834 appointed legal adviser to the Supreme Council of India. He remained in India nearly four years, and on his return to England in 1838 re-entered public life, obtaining Cabinet rank in 1839 as Minister of War. Defeated in 1847, he was re-elected in 1852, and continued to sit in the House as member for Edinburgh till 1857, when he was raised to the peerage as Baron Macaulay of Rothley. Meanwhile he had taken advantage of his temporary retirement from politics to make a definite start with a great task which he had long had in mind, and to which henceforth his energies were to be mainly devoted—the *History of England from the Accession of James II.* The first two volumes of this work were published in 1848, and instantly scored a success far greater, it is said, than had ever before attended the production of any piece of purely historical literature. The third and fourth volumes, which appeared in 1855, were received with equal enthusiasm. But between these two instalments his health, hitherto robust, had collapsed completely, and for the short remainder of his life he had to " fly on broken wing." He died suddenly on 28th December 1859, leaving his *History* a fragment.

Even a superficial examination of Macaulay's work as essayist and historian will suffice to explain his immense and lasting popularity. He had, to begin with, a marvellous capacity for making everything he touched interesting. With an animation which is unbounded and an energy which never flags, he rarely gives us, whatever his subject, a single dull page. As a mere story-teller he can bear comparison with the greatest of his contemporaries in prose fiction, and his pictorial power is as remarkable as his power of narrative. When he has an argument to conduct, he shows himself an accomplished master of all the arts of exposition, controversy, persuasion, and appeal. Then, again, the fullness of his explanations (though on this head he is open to the charge of extreme diffuseness and over-elaboration of the trite and commonplace), his abundant use of illustrations, his constant indulgence in parallels and analogies, his love of the concrete, and his happy faculty of clothing abstract ideas in material imagery, are all elements in his unique success with that large body of readers who are specially attracted by the forcible, the incisive, and the picturesque. He is indeed one of the clearest of writers. He has a matter-of-fact, business-like way of handling his subject ; he never fumbles with it ; he knows exactly what he wants to say, and he says it in a style which, whatever may be its shortcomings, is at least always a model of precision, directness, and lucidity.

Such are some of the excellent qualities which contributed to Macaulay's amazing success. But no explanation of that success would be complete which did not at the same time take into account his intellectual and moral limitations. He caught the ear and held the interest of the great general public because he himself belonged to that public and expressed its ideas instead of combating or transcending them. Save for his exceptional endowment of genius, he was indeed a representative average Englishman of his generation, and the average Englishman liked him because of his sturdy common sense, his practical utilitarian temper, his contempt for everything vague or visionary, his comfortable view of life, his cheerful optimism, his unbounded faith in the " happy materialism " of his age. Even his superficiality—for, brilliant as he is, he is undeniably shallow—added to his attraction. His very clearness was in part the result of his want of depth. He was a great populariser—not a great discoverer, not in any sense a great thinker—and the general public went with him the more willingly because he never asked them to follow him beyond the obvious and the external. And with these familiar features of his work we may further join such others as his fondness for striking effects, his tendency to exaggeration, his love of paradox and epigram, his continual use of heavily loaded emphasis : rhetorical devices well calculated to arrest attention, though often incompatible with the moderation of judgment and temperance of statement which are necessary in the interests of sober truth. Macaulay was never deliberately inaccurate ; on the contrary, he was painstaking and conscientious to the last degree in respect of his facts. But apart from the disturbing influence of his strong personal and political bias—an influence which led him unconsciously to turn his *History* into a long argument to prove, as Carlyle put it, " that Providence was on the side of the Whigs "—his mental habits were fatal to steadiness of vision and strict impartiality. Not only in its vigour and clearness, but also in its hardness, its oratorical quality, its too confident and dictatorial tone, its total lack of finer shadings and gradations, his wonderful style is an exact index of his intellectual character.

The publication of Macaulay's first collection of essays in 1843 was coincident with the rise of another **Ruskin.** great master of prose who, as a critic of modern life, was presently to take up and carry forward Carlyle's attack upon the social and political ideals of which Macaulay was the eloquent exponent. John Ruskin was born on 8th February 1819, and though a Londoner by birth was pure Scotch by blood, his father, a wealthy wine merchant, being a native of Edinburgh, and his mother a descendant of the old Covenanters. Both parents were Evangelicals of the strictest type, and their only child was brought up in an atmosphere of the most rigorous piety. Their religious views were not, however, unfavourable to literature and art, and the precocious boy was left free to cultivate his tastes for poetry and drawing. At the same time his love of nature was quickened by many long drives through England and Wales and by a first visit to Switzerland in 1833. After a desultory education, chiefly under private tutors, Ruskin in 1837 went up to Oxford,

13

where two years later he won the Newdigate Prize with a poem entitled *Salsette and Elephanta*. A serious breakdown in health then compelled him to abandon his intention of entering the Church. But fortunately he soon found another mission in a different field. He had been working steadily at his drawing and had come more and more to feel that the first principle of all good landscape—the very principle which the schools had long neglected and indeed denied—was specific fidelity to nature. This lesson, which he had learned for himself from his own practice, was meanwhile reinforced by the reading of Carlyle's *Heroes*, in which he found the broader doctrine enunciated that sincerity is the fundamental secret of real greatness in every walk of life. At the same time his admiration of Turner, which had begun in boyhood, had grown into boundless admiration. Out of the combination of these influences came the first volume of *Modern Painters* (1843). The thesis of this remarkable book was set out on the title-page : it was to prove " the superiority " of modern landscape painters, and especially of Turner, " to all the ancient masters." While, however, the vindication of Turner was always kept in view, it was based upon an elaborate analysis of the principles of landscape painting, that of truth to nature being set in the front. Challenging as it did the deeply rooted dogmas of academic tradition and the superstition of the " grand style " in painting, the book inevitably created a critical storm. But the appearance in English art of a new movement for a " return to nature," as in the Pre-Raphaelite Brotherhood a few years later, showed that his teachings, revolutionary as they seemed, were already beginning to have their effect.

The second volume of *Modern Painters* was published

in 1846, the third and fourth in 1856, the fifth and last in 1860, by which time the work had far outrun its original design and had expanded, after its author's characteristically discursive habit, into an enormous treatise on art in general and many other things. Concurrently he had also produced two other works of kindred interest : *The Seven Lamps of Architecture* (1849) and *The Stones of Venice* (1851–53). In both of these, as in *Modern Painters,* while the thoroughness of Ruskin's expert knowledge was apparent on every page, his essentially ethical attitude towards art and the didactic temper of his mind were equally in evidence ; for the former aims to prove that all really noble architecture is the product of " right feeling," while the latter is a prolonged historical demonstration of his theory that art is inseparably bound up with moral and religious conditions. In *The Stones of Venice* also we note the distinct appearance of a powerful new element in his aesthetic philosophy—his horror of the Renaissance and growing devotion to the work of the early Catholic painters ; though such devotion is curiously combined with a stiff-necked Protestantism which made him fiercely intolerant of the " romanising " Oxford Movement and clearly ill at ease in respect of the possible developments of the Pre-Raphaelite school, whose advocate he had now become (see his pamphlet *On Pre-Raphaelitism,* 1851). *The Stones* furthermore provide conclusive proof of the rapid gravitation of his mind towards the social interests in which he was soon to be absorbed. Hitherto he had been the critic and historian of art. Henceforth his chief rôle was to be that of social theorist and reformer. By this time his aesthetic teachings were very generally accepted, and even those who dissented from them treated them with respect. He had now a new and far harder battle to fight with the orthodox political economists, whose views he boldly assailed in *Unto this Last* (1862) and *Munera Pulveris* (1863). Thus far the influence of Carlyle upon him had been only indirect. Now, as the dedication of *Munera Pulveris* attests, it had become direct. In his denunciation of modern commercialism, the régime of unrestrained competition, and the economic principles—or falsehoods, as he believed them to be—which he regarded as the source of many of the worst evils of society, he was in fact developing some of Carlyle's central ideas, though his method of elaborating and applying them was entirely his own. So intense was the hostility which his daring speculations aroused that the original periodical publication of both the treatises in question (the one in *Cornhill*, the other in *Fraser*) had to be stopped. But, nothing daunted, he continued his campaign in other writings, notably in a series of letters to a Sunderland working man, entitled *Time and Tide by Weare and Tyne* (1867), and the curious miscellany, *Fors Clavigera*, which appeared at irregular intervals between 1871 and 1884— ninety-six numbers in all. Meanwhile, with his economic inquiries as a point of departure, his restless mind had begun to travel far and wide over the whole field of modern life, and his views on all sorts of subjects— artistic, social, ethical, educational, scientific—found expression in a number of popularly written volumes, largely made up of lectures, of which *Sesame and Lilies* (1865), *The Ethics of the Dust* (1865), and *The Crown of Wild Olive* (1866), may be named as the most important. Notwithstanding all these varied activities, however, he had by no means given up his work in art. As Slade Professor of Fine Art at Oxford from 1869 to 1879, and again in 1883 (when he finally resigned his position on account of the recognition by the University of the practice of vivisection in the newly endowed physiological laboratory), he gave many courses of lectures, most of which were published in book form. But the predominance of his practical interests was now always apparent, for whatever his stated subject, it was always made to bear upon problems of character and life. Another point worthy of notice about these very unacademic academic discourses is that they mark the entire disappearance of the theological ardour and Protestant animus of his young manhood. He had passed since then through a period of pronounced scepticism, and the end of his religious pilgrimage was a mysticism which, however vague, made him more appreciative than ever of the early Catholic masters.

In 1878 he had been struck down by a sudden and serious attack of brain disease, and never completely regained his health. The resignation of his professorship in 1883 was the virtual close of his public career. He then retired to his home at Coniston, near Ambleside, where he died on 20th January 1900.

Though Ruskin's work in literature was very voluminous as well as very varied, it represents only a part of his immense and many-sided activity, for from 1854, when he joined the Rev. F. D. Maurice in the establishment of the Working Men's College, to his later efforts in starting St. George's Guild as a concrete realisation of his social teachings, he was incessantly engaged in all sorts of philanthropic enterprises, to which he gave not only his time and energy, but also the bulk of his handsome private fortune. Except, however, for the light which they throw upon his personality, his practical labours do not directly concern us. The extraordinary complexity of his intellectual character, on the other hand, must never be lost sight of by any student of his writings. Mr. Frederic Harrison has described him as an amalgam of John Knox, Sir Walter Scott, and the early Catholic painters. In other words, he was at once puritan, romantic, and mystical, and the fact that from first to last he was never able entirely to harmonise these conflicting elements in his nature is the real explanation of the amazing inconsistencies and contradictions with which he perpetually surprises and bewilders us.

These inconsistencies and contradictions make it extremely difficult to epitomise his teachings. Yet certain main lines of thought run through them all. As a critic both of art and of life he was, as we have seen, essentially a moral idealist. His view of art was uncompromisingly ethical and religious. Though he started with the principle of truth to nature, he held that the right interpretation of nature is at bottom a spiritual function. All great art is " revelation " and " praise " ; it is the expression of delight in God's work, and as such, " the type of a strong and noble life." Hence his insistence upon the intimate and vital relation of art to the society which produces it and to whose pleasure it ministers : no really great art being possible except in a " strong and noble age." Here obviously we have the connecting link between the aesthetic and the social aspects of his teaching—between his reading of the lessons of Venetian architecture and his denunciation of nineteenth-century commercialism, industrialism, mammon-worship, and infidelity. And as he had approached aesthetics from the ethical side, so in turn from the same side he approached the problems of economics. The chief ground of his quarrel with the orthodox economists was that they had left morality out of the question. By this initial error their so-called science had been vitiated at its very foundation. Convinced that what is morally wrong cannot be economically right, he set out to reconstruct economic theory upon a firm ethical basis. Wealth for him is not definable in terms of money or exchangeable values. It is definable only in terms of life. "There is no wealth but life—life including all its powers of love, of joy, of admiration. That country is richest which nourishes the greatest number of noble and happy human beings."

In his many writings on practical subjects outside economics Ruskin was a singular compound of the radical and the reactionary. He struck hard at many things in the existing social system, and some of his leading ideas are indistinguishable from socialism. Yet while he outgrew the Toryism in which he had been bred, he was always at heart a "violent illiberal," and was as intolerant as Carlyle of democracy, representative government, liberty, equality, and the whole spirit of modern progress. His social ideal, as the programme of St. George's Guild testifies, was a kind of transfigured feudalism.

Ruskin's manner of writing often gives offence to all but his most devoted disciples. Impetuous and wayward, he indulges to the full his innumerable crotchets and caprices, loads his pages with the most wildly fantastic speculations, and rarely puts the slightest check upon his constitutional habit of starting off at tangents into unwieldy digressions having little or nothing to do with the subject nominally in hand. Even more he irritates us by his frequent petulance, by his aggressively dogmatic tone, and by the unmeasured assurance with which he sets everybody right (including himself) on every possible question. Yet these faults are largely redeemed by the rare beauty of his style. In his early books, which he wrote very evidently under the influence of Hooker, Jeremy Taylor, and other masters, he is indeed often too ornate, and his sustained brilliancy (as, *e.g.*, in *The Seven Lamps*) becomes fatiguing from want of relief. But in these he has given us many unsurpassed examples of poetic prose, especially in his wonderful, highly wrought descriptions of nature. His really characteristic style is, however, that of his second period, in which his prose, pruned of its former rhetorical excesses, becomes an almost perfect model of ease, simplicity, and unforced eloquence.

Strikingly different in temper and manner from that alike of Carlyle, of Macaulay, and of Ruskin, the prose work of Matthew Arnold also presents a curious **Arnold.** contrast with his own work in verse; for, while the ground-tone of his verse is, as we have seen, pensive melancholy, his prose on the other hand is buoyant, breezy, and often even gay. This contrast may be explained largely by chronological considerations. His verse was in the main the product of his earlier manhood, with its intellectual struggles and spiritual unrest; his prose of his later years, when his mind had ripened, his thought had settled, and he had grown less introspective and more interested in the world about him. He began as an essayist, naturally enough, with a subject which lay very near to him, and which indeed had already entered into his poetry—literary criticism. Thence he passed on to write also, first of society and politics, and afterwards of religion.

Arnold's point of departure as a literary critic is his conception of literature as a "criticism" (by which he really means an interpretation) "of life." In this much discussed definition it is evident that the moral element is uppermost. He does not concern himself greatly about the technical side of literature ; except in his Oxford lectures *On Translating Homer*, this side is indeed very much in the background. Nor does he deal much with the historical side ; though he recognises the " Zeitgeist " (see, *e.g.*, his over-ingenious explanation of Gray's infertility), he expressly warns us against being misled by merely historical estimates (see *The Study of Poetry* in *Essays in Criticism*, first series). His general method is to go straight to the work of a given author and, taking this as it stands, to seek its meaning and weigh its value as a " criticism of life." In this he is guided by two cardinal principles : in the first place, the foundation of all really great literature is " sound subject-matter " ; in the second, such subject-matter must be treated in a spirit of " high seriousness." He builds no critical system ; here, as elsewhere, indeed, he distrusts system-makers, theorists, and dogmatists. His great rule is that we should train our judgment and taste by living as much as possible with what is best in literature ; and he further emphasises the importance of the study of the classics and of modern European literatures other than our own—especially French and German—the one as a check upon the vagaries and extravagances to which the English mind is prone, the other as a cure for our insularity.

As a critic of politics and society, his views of which are to be found mainly in *Culture and Anarchy* (1869) and *Discourses in America* (1885), Arnold in his own way was quite as much as Carlyle and Ruskin a determined opponent of the comfortable, self-satisfied, materialistic spirit of his age. Hence, while he agreed with Ruskin in little else, he shared his contempt for Macaulay. His quarrel was particularly with the English middle classes, whose utilitarian temper, stiff puritanism, faith in political machinery, narrowness of outlook, imperviousness to ideas, and hard unintelligence, he epitomised under the general name of Philistinism. The great need of the time, he contended, was "culture," or a knowledge of "ourselves and the world" and of "the best that has been thought and said in the world," and "criticism," or the free play of the whole mind, unhampered by prejudices, upon the facts and problems of society. The ideal which he held up as a corrective of modern one-sidedness and over-specialisation was that of "perfection," or the full development of our natures through the harmonious co-operation of all the powers—religious, intellectual, artistic, social—which go to the making of a complete human life.

From social and moral criticism Arnold passed with the same calm confidence to the criticism of religion. The inspiration of this new adventure, which he began in *St. Paul and Protestantism* (1870) and pursued in *Literature and Dogma* (1873), *God and the Bible* (1875), and *Last Essays on Church and Religion* (1877), is not far to seek. He was firmly convinced that the old foundations of faith were fast breaking up under stress of modern thought, and his desire was both to save the Bible and to liberate the essential spirit of Christianity from the husk of outworn creeds. Too orthodox for the heterodox and too heterodox for the orthodox, his views satisfied neither party. At the same time, his effort to popularise theological discussion and the critical study of the Bible was not without its use.

In respect of Arnold's style there is little difference of opinion. Though sometimes rather modish, and with occasional irritating mannerisms—like his habit of repeating favourite catchwords till we weary of them—he is one of our best masters of lucid, colloquial prose, plain in texture, but harmonious in cadence and scholarly in tone ; and his wit, irony, satire, and never-failing urbanity combine to give additional charm to his treatment of everything he touches.

While the books of John Henry Newman, to whom we may next turn, belong for the most part to theology **Newman.** rather than to literature, he is still entitled to an independent place among our great Victorian men of letters. He was born in 1801, obtained an Oriel fellowship in 1822, and in 1828 became Vicar of St. Mary's, Oxford, from the pulpit of which, for some fifteen years, he preached sermons by which, as we have more than once seen, he profoundly affected the thought of many of the younger men at the University. In 1832 he went with Hurrell Froude (James Anthony's brother) on a long tour in the Mediterranean, during which he wrote most of the poems published in his *Lyra Apostolica*, including the famous hymn, " Lead, kindly Light." He returned to Oxford in 1833, filled with the conviction that it was his special mission to revive the Catholic spirit—the ancient spirit of faith and devotion—in the Anglican Church. Hence his connection with the Oxford Movement, the issue of which, so far as he was himself concerned, was his secession in 1845 to the Church of Rome. Up to this time his prose work had been entirely theological. In *Loss and Gain : The Story of a Convert* (1848)—an imaginative reflection of his own experiences and a picture of Oxford during the Tractarian agitation—he made his first appeal to the wider reading public. Such broader interest also belongs to his *Idea of a University* (1852) and *Lectures on University Subjects* (1854–58), produced during his tenure of the Rectorship of the new Catholic university at Dublin, and even more to his second effort in prose fiction, *Callista : A Tale of*

the Third Century (1856). A controversy with Charles
Kingsley, who had rashly imputed to the Roman
Catholic clergy in general and to Newman in particular
the practice of equivocation (a controversy which ended
in complete disaster for Kingsley), is now memorable
only because it was the occasion of the *Apologia pro Vitâ
Suâ* (1864), the greatest piece of religious autobiography
of the nineteenth century. Newman's later prose
writings need not detain us, but mention must be made
of his wonderfully imaginative poem, *The Dream of
Gerontius* (1865), which though purely doctrinal in
purpose, has great beauty as poetry. He was made a
cardinal in 1879, and died in 1890. As a stylist, Newman
has received the highest praise from the most exact-
ing critics. While not faultless, his prose is on the
whole a model of clearness, strength, suppleness, and
harmony.

Among the many young men who fell under Newman's
influence, one of the most important was James Anthony
Froude (1818–94), who went up to Oxford when
Froude. the Tractarian agitation was at its height,
helped the great leader with his *Lives of the Saints*, and
himself took deacon's orders with the intention of entering
the Church. But he was soon caught by the tide of
reaction which after Newman's secession to Rome swept
so many of his disciples into scepticism ; his entire
abandonment of orthodoxy being clearly shown in *The
Nemesis of Faith* (1849), a painful study of spiritual
wreckage set in the framework of a sentimental novel.
The great work of his life—written under the influence of
Carlyle, who had now become his mentor, *vice* Newman
deposed—is his *History of England from the Fall of Wolsey
to the Defeat of the Spanish Armada* (1856–70), which,
though sadly marred by gross inaccuracies, partisanship,

and special pleading, is vivid in interest and full of dramatic power. Its immense length, however, must necessarily deter all but the special student of the period in question, and to the general reader Froude is likely to be best known by his four volumes of miscellaneous essays, *Short Studies on Great Subjects* (1867-83), which deal with a large variety of interesting topics in a most attractive manner, and in a style which is remarkably clear, unaffected, and picturesque. His other works include *The English in Ireland in the Eighteenth Century* (1872–74) ; *Oceana* (1886), an account of a tour in Australasia ; an historical romance, *The Two Chiefs of Dunboy* (1889) ; *Life and Letters of Erasmus* (1894) ; and *Lectures on the Council of Trent* (1896). His publication of Carlyle's *Reminiscences* (1881) and his *Life of Carlyle* (1882–84) brought down a storm of adverse criticism upon his head, the charge very justly made against him being that he had been guilty of bad taste and breach of confidence in his treatment of the memory of his old friend and master.

The aesthetic revival which at Oxford followed close upon the Tractarian Movement, and was in its inception a secondary product of some of the forces which had been at work in it, had also a very considerable effect on literature. It is represented in particular by two writers of nearly the same age—Pater and Symonds.

As Walter Horatio Pater (1839–94) always produced slowly and with infinite pains, the bulk of his work is **Pater.** comparatively small. His first book, *Studies in the Renaissance*, appeared in 1873 ; *Marius the Epicurean* in 1885 ; *Imaginary Portraits* in 1887 ; a collection of essays entitled *Appreciations* in 1889 ; and a course of lectures on *Plato and Platonism* in 1893. After his death, three further volumes, *Greek*

Studies, Miscellaneous Studies, and an unfinished romance, *Gaston de Latour,* were published by his literary executor.

Pater was one of the many young Oxford men whom Ruskin turned to the study of art, but while Ruskin had always associated aesthetics with ethics, Pater on the contrary was an adherent of the purely aesthetic school. In his literary criticism, and again in his attitude towards life, the aesthetic element is also uppermost, though the hedonistic philosophy which was specifically enunciated in the much-discussed *Postscript* to the *Renaissance* was afterwards considerably modified by the growing sympathy with Christianity apparent in *Marius.* While his direct criticism of art and literature is always illuminating, his most distinctive work is contained in what, for want of a better name, we may call with Mr. Gosse his "philosophic fiction." The *Imaginary Portraits* (the very title of which is indicative of his methods) are brilliant examples of his peculiar workmanship, and to these may be added the beautiful *Child in the House* and *Emerald Uthwart,* in the *Miscellaneous Studies.* Though in the form of stories, these depend for their interest upon the psychological subtlety with which their central figures are delineated. Pater was specially fond of analysing rare and curious types, and particularly natures out of harmony with their surroundings, or born out of their due time, or in periods of transition disturbed by that conflict of ideas which was ever present in his own mind. In both *Marius the Epicurean* and *Gaston de Latour,* which are really imaginary portraits on a large scale, we have a similar preoccupation with the same kind of intellectual problem.

Pater's views on style, which are fully set out in

his essay on the subject in *Appreciations*, are entirely esoteric. Style he regarded not merely as a means to an end but also as an end in itself. His position is that, while the ordinary writer is concerned with style only or at least primarily as a medium of expression, the artist in addition aims by his very manner of writing to give to the initiated reader or connoisseur that peculiar aesthetic pleasure which arises from the exhibition of consummate craftsmanship. His emphasis is thrown upon deliberation, self-restraint, economy of effort, the constant and rigorous use of the file ; and these are the principles which governed his own work. Composition was with him always a matter of immense and protracted labour ; and the result of his patient toil and scrupulous attention to every detail was a prose of extraordinary though exotic beauty, sumptuous, rich in colour, full of delicacy, subtlety, and grace, but over-elaborate, heavy, savouring too much of artifice, and wanting in spontaneity, freedom, and often even in clearness.

John Addington Symonds (1840–93) was, notwithstanding the ill-health which compelled him to **Symonds.** spend the greater part of his life at Davos Platz, an industrious and prolific writer. The catholicity of his interests is shown in the wide range of his works, which include *An Introduction to the Study of Dante* (1872) ; a valuable though extremely prolix history of *The Renaissance in Italy* (1875–86) ; *Studies of the Greek Poets* (1873–76) ; *Shakespeare's Predecessors in the English Drama* (1884) ; lives of Shelley (1886), Ben Jonson (1886), and Michael Angelo (1892), and a monograph on Walt Whitman (1893). He also published some excellent translations and several volumes of original verse. Symonds' work is scholarly without being profound, and he conveys much sound information in a very popular way. His great defect is his style, which is terribly diffuse, florid, and ornate.

We may here appropriately introduce the name of a third Oxford man, just a little older than the fore-**Swinburne.** going two, and who, with many points of difference, has something in common with them both. We have already dealt at some length with Swinburne's poetry. A far briefer consideration will suffice of his work in prose. That work, which comprises two volumes of essays and separate studies of Blake, Chapman, Ben Jonson, Shakespeare, Charlotte Brontë, and Victor Hugo, has many qualities of distinction, for it is scholarly, catholic in sympathy in spite of the writer's innumerable prejudices, and often marked by that peculiar insight into poetry which perhaps only one who is himself a poet can possess. But Swinburne's extravagances, his want of balance, and the violence of his likes and dislikes, make him entirely untrustworthy as a critic. Though he often gives us passages of splendid eloquence, his style on the whole is vitiated by many of the faults which we have already noted in his verse—extreme verbosity, inflation, over-emphasis, and the abuse of alliteration, the balanced sentence, and other rhetorical devices. It should, however, be added that to some extent he outgrew these defects ; at least his later prose shows a welcome tendency towards greater restraint and simplicity.

All the writers just dealt with are easy enough to classify by reason of their connection with well defined **Borrow.** movements in thought. We have now to turn back in time to one of the famous free lances of Victorian literature. It is indeed an open question whether Borrow would be more fittingly considered among the general prose writers or among the

novelists of his age, for while such of his books as are
supposed to be records of fact contain a plentiful admixture of fiction, his novels on the other hand are
largely autobiographical. On account of the miscellaneous character of his work, however, it seems natural
to introduce him here. The son of a captain of militia,
George Henry Borrow was born at East Dereham,
Norfolk, in 1803 ; passed a large part of his childhood
in wandering about with his father, seeing many strange
things and people, as described in *Lavengro* ; attended
the Grammar School at Norwich from 1815 to 1818 ;
and spent five years as clerk to a firm of local solicitors.
His astonishing faculty for languages was soon in evidence, for while still a youth he had picked up a knowledge of Greek, Latin, French, German, Danish, Irish,
Welsh, and Romany. On his father's death in 1843
he entered upon a long period of adventure, during
which he rambled through England and became ac-
quainted with the gypsies, and travelled in Russia,
Portugal, Spain, and Morocco (1833–39) as agent of the
Bible Society. In 1840 he married a well-to-do widow
and settled at Oulton, near Lowestoft, where, after some
further travels and a residence in London, he died in
1881. His works include (besides many translations)
The Zincali, or Gypsies of Spain (1841) ; a suspiciously
romantic account of his experiences as a colporteur,
The Bible in Spain (1843) ; two loosely constructed
novels, in which fact and fiction are inextricably
blended, *Lavengro* (1851), and its sequel, *The Romany
Rye* (1857) ; and *Wild Wales* (1862). Borrow was an
eccentric and a Bohemian, and all his life long did battle
with convention and respectability. There is a fine
spirit of the open air and a contagious zest of adventure
in all his writings, which are also marked by much

14

freshness and individuality of manner and style. He was undoubtedly a man of genius, but our enjoyment in reading him is often destroyed by the everlasting intrusion of his aggressive and not very pleasant personality, and by his innumerable and violent prejudices. We may perhaps forgive him for his egotism and his blustering insularity, and may be amused rather than annoyed by his love of prize-fighting and his praise of beer. But his religious bigotry, and especially his rabid hatred of everything Catholic, frequently become intolerable.

The enormous bulk and variety of the general prose literature of the Victorian Age make it impossible for us to attempt any comprehensive survey of it within the space of a brief chapter. Out of the many remaining writers a few only can be selected for mention, and these we will take as they come in their chronological order.

Miller. Hugh Miller (1802–56) was a Scotchman, who worked at his trade as a stone-mason till he was over thirty. He found a wide public for his popular books on geology (e.g., *The Old Red Sandstone*, 1841 ; *Footprints of the Creator*, 1849 ; *The Testimony of the Rocks*, 1857), in which he stoutly upheld the traditional view of creation against the incoming scientific theories. While these books are now entirely out of date, his autobiography, *My Schools and Schoolmasters*, may still be read with interest.

Brown. John Brown (1810–82), an Edinburgh physician, wrote but little, his output being almost wholly comprised in three volumes—the two series of *Horae Subsecivae* (1858–61) and *John Leech and Other Papers* (1882). But though small in amount, his work is exquisite in quality, with humour, pathos, tenderness, and an old-world charm of style which have often been compared with Lamb's. He is best known as the author of *Rab and his Friends*, a little masterpiece in the literature of dog-life and childhood ; but the lover of animals will find the less familiar *Our Dogs* almost if not quite as good.

Alexander William Kinglake (1809–91), whose immense history, *The Invasion of the Crimea*, in eight **Kinglake.** large volumes (1863–87), severely criticised by experts for its one-sidedness and more generally for its prolix and florid style, does not directly concern us, is named here as the author of an earlier work, *Eothen* (1844), a record of impressions of travel in the East. This too is marred by some of the faults of manner which were conspicuous on a larger scale in the history, but its brilliancy is remarkable. Kinglake expressly avowed his intention of producing a book of travel which, eschewing all " useful information," should be simply entertaining, and the continued popularity of *Eothen* is sufficient testimony to his success.

John Forster (1812–76) was an industrious though commonplace writer, who did useful work in history **Forster.** and biography. His *Goldsmith* (1854) is still regarded as an authority. But his most valuable contributions to literature were his very full lives of two contemporaries whom he had known well— *Landor* (1869) and *Dickens* (1872–74).

Sir Arthur Helps (1813–75) tried his hand in many kinds of writing, but little of his work survives. His **Helps.** name is now chiefly associated with two series of essays in dialogue form, *Friends in Council* (1847–59), which for a time enjoyed considerable popularity, the waning of which, however, is not surprising, for though their style is agreeable and their tone excellent, both their criticisms and their moralisings are entirely commonplace. His more ambitious undertaking, *The Spanish Conquest in America* (1855–61), is entirely eclipsed by Prescott's works on the same subject ; but the biographies of Las Casas, Columbus, Pizarro, and Cortes, which grew out of this, are very readable.

Mark Pattison (1813–84), a very fine type of the true University scholar, is one more among the many men **Pattison.** who fell under Newman's spell at Oxford and afterwards went their own way. Under his influence as Rector, Lincoln College was for many years a centre of intellectual life and progress. His most important work in literature is the masterly study of *Isaac Casaubon* (1875) ; but the general reader will remember him chiefly by his admirable short life of Milton in the *English Men of Letters* series, and his learned and illuminating essay, *Tendencies of Religious Thought in England*, 1688–1750. His interesting though rather painful *Memoirs* are extremely valuable, not only as a singularly frank piece of self-portraiture, but also for the light which they throw on the state of things at Oxford from 1832 to 1860.

George Henry Lewes (1817–78), who is principally known in literary history through his association with **Lewes.** George Eliot, was himself a man of brilliant talents and wonderful versatility. His works include a tragedy and a couple of novels, long since forgotten ; a popular but thoroughly sound *History of Philosophy* ; a *Life of Robespierre* ; some admirable books on science for the general reader ; a study of Aristotle ; and four massive volumes, designed as a foundation for a philosophic system, entitled *Problems of Life and Mind*. From the literary point of view,

however, his most interesting writings are his vivacious
little book on *The Spanish Drama* (1846) and his *Life of
Goethe* (1855)—long acknowledged even by the Germans
as one of the best biographical and critical studies of
their greatest author.

By far the most substantial work of Walter Bagehot
(1826–77) is to be found in his treatises on political
Bagehot. and economic questions (*The English Constitution, Lombard Street, Physics and Politics*).
But he has also a certain standing as a literary critic.
His *Literary Studies*, made up after his death from his
contributions to various periodicals, show an acute
mind and considerable independence of judgment.

Sir Leslie Stephen (1832–1904), the first editor of
the great *Dictionary of National Biography*, was a very
Stephen. skilful biographer, a critic of wide knowledge,
sanity of opinion, and sound taste, and the
master of a remarkably clear, terse, and epigrammatic
style. His *Hours in a Library* and *Studies of a Biographer*
contain many essays of great value ; his monographs on
Pope, Swift, Johnson, and Hobbes in the *English Men of
Letters* series are admirable books of their kind ; while
his large work, *A History of English Thought in the
Eighteenth Century*, is marked by great learning and
breadth of view.

John Morley (b. 1838), after a distinguished career in
journalism and literature, became an important figure
Lord in politics, entered Gladstone's Cabinet in 1886,
Morley. and was raised to the peerage in 1908. His
works include monographs on Burke (1867 and 1879),
Walpole (1889), Cromwell (1900) ; a biography of Cobden
(1881) ; a monumental *Life of Gladstone* (1903) ; many
excellent essays (*Critical Miscellanies*, 1871, 1877 ;
Studies in Literature, 1891 and 1908) ; and a series of

masterly studies of Voltaire (1871), Rousseau (1873), and Diderot (1878), which together form a contribution of the greatest value to the history of French thought in the eighteenth century and the intellectual forces behind the Revolution.

Three other writers, though, strictly speaking, their works belong to the later Victorian period, may for the sake of convenience be included in this chapter.

Jefferies. John Richard Jefferies (1848–87) began his literary career with several unsuccessful novels and tragedies, but found his real line in *The Gamekeeper at Home* (1878), the first of a number of books dealing with natural history and scenes and characters from rural life. Jefferies had a keen eye, an accurate knowledge of the ways and habits of animals, birds, and insects, and a deep, poetic feeling for nature, and he wrote in a very pleasant style. For these reasons his books will always find a public among nature-lovers, though many of such will regret his curious callousness in regard to the sufferings of animals, as shown, for example, in the chapter on deer-hunting in his *Red Deer*. A wider interest, however, attaches to his remarkable *Story of my Heart*, which he calls an "autobiography," but which is really rather the record of his bold and suggestive, if somewhat fantastic, speculations about some of the ultimate problems of life.

Grant Allen. Charles Grant Blairfindie Allen, always known as Grant Allen (1848–99), a Canadian by birth, but a resident in England, was a prolific and versatile writer. He was specially interested in science, in which he would willingly have found his life-work, but, having to look to his pen for support, he turned to fiction, and produced some thirty novels, one of which, *The Woman who did* (1895), created a temporary stir on account of the " advanced " views advocated in it. His most distinctive work, however, is contained in books like *The Evolutionist at Large* and *Vignettes from Nature*, in which, like Jefferies, he united science with literature, and showed a happy faculty for conveying sound information in an agreeable and lively manner.

William Hurrell Mallock (b. 1849) early made a reputation as a clever but rather specious writer on **Mallock.** religious, philosophical, and social questions. Two of his books in particular attracted much attention at the time of their appearance : *The New Republic* (1877) on account of its brilliant but not too scrupulous satiric portraits of Ruskin, Jowett, Arnold, Pater, and other people just then very much in the public eye ; and *Is Life Worth Living?* (1885), for its analysis of the pessimism which was widely characteristic both of the mid-Victorian, and even more of the later Victorian, Age.

CHAPTER V

THE NOVEL

WHILE, as we now see, the Victorian Age was rich both in poetry and in general prose, its typical literary form was undoubtedly the novel. Much of the work done in this fertile field was of course slight and ephemeral. Much, on the other hand, was weighty and lasting. For, absorbing as it did a great deal of the best creative energy of the time, the novel was used not only as a means of catering for the amusement of idle readers, but also as the vehicle of a serious "criticism of life." Moreover, owing to the peculiar place which it thus came to occupy in Victorian literature, it was inevitable that, more than any other form of such literature, it should be coloured by all the influences at work in the complex modern world. The spread of democracy made it social and humanitarian. The growth of the scientific spirit made it realistic and analytical. The prevalence of religious and moral controversy made it polemical and doctrinaire. At the same time, while the characteristic Victorian novel was unquestionably the novel of contemporary life, the romantic revival in art and poetry presently affected fiction also, bringing with it the rejection of the narrow principles of realism, the assertion of the rights of the imagination, a complete resulting change in manner and tone, and incidentally a return to the past. Thus in its very variety Victorian fiction is in itself an index of the many-sidedness and eclecticism of the age.

In opening what will have to be a very rapid survey of this large subject we have first to mention two belated **G. P. R. James.** followers of Scott who represent what at the moment was the waning romantic tradition. Slightly the elder of these, George Payne Rainsford James (1801–60) was also the more prolific. He is credited with seventy-seven separate works, mostly historical romances, though history, biography, and poetry help to swell the list. James had a sound knowledge of history, especially of French history, but he was wholly destitute of creative power, and all his novels (e.g., *Richelieu*, *Henry Masterton*) are manufactured according to a few well-worn formulas. The other writer whom we here associate with him, William **Ainsworth.** Harrison Ainsworth (1805–82), though not so careful a workman, had far greater faculty of invention. Poor in style, extravagant in plot, crude in characterisation, and feeble in dialogue, his thirty-nine novels (of which *The Tower of London*, 1840, and *Old St. Paul's*, 1841, are perhaps the best) have little title to rank as literature, but they have one merit—they are full of exciting incident. Here and there, too, Ainsworth showed really remarkable descriptive power, as in the famous episode of Dick Turpin's ride in *Rookwood* and the account of the great plague and fire of London in *Old St. Paul's*.

We turn next to two novelists who have many points in common and whose work impresses us to-day as belonging very distinctly to the pre-Victorian generation—Marryat and Lever.

Frederick Marryat (1792–1848) went to sea as a midshipman in 1806, saw much hard service, retired in

1830 with the rank of captain, and settled down to the life of a man of letters, his first book, *Frank Mildmay*, **Marryat.** having been published the year before. His novels (e.g., *Peter Simple*, 1834 ; *Jacob Faithful*, 1834 ; *Midshipman Easy*, 1836), which are largely made up out of his own experiences, are rattling stories, entirely formless, and full of a boisterous humour which often degenerates into extravagant farce. It would be waste of time to discuss Marryat as an artist ; but, with all his defects, he carries us along by his natural vigour, and his exciting scenes—his battles, sea-chases, and hair-breadth escapes—are often handled with much effect. His characters are mainly oddities, grotesque but amusing. His literary model was obviously Smollett, but though like Smollett he deals with phases of life which are generally rough and often brutal, and is never in the least squeamish, he is happily free from his predecessor's repellent ferocity.

What Marryat did for the naval life of the Napoleonic period was done for its military life by the Irish novelist **Lever.** Charles James Lever [1] (1806–72). His best known books, *Harry Lorrequer* (1839) and *Charles O'Malley* (1841), are quite as formless as Marryat's, for they are little more than huge bundles of anecdotes. Lever's original vein was always extremely thin, and in later tales of the same kind (such as *Arthur O'Leary*, 1844) it was manifestly getting exhausted. Thereupon he changed his manner entirely and began to write novels of Irish society and Continental life (e.g., *Roland Cashel*, 1850 ; *The Daltons*, 1852). These have had their admirers, but they have never

[1] As also by two minor writers, William Hamilton Maxwell (1792–1850), author of *Stories of Waterloo* (1834), etc., who gave Lever his cue, and James Grant (1822–87), who in turn followed Lever with *The Romance of War* (1845) and many other tales of military adventure.

approached in popularity his earlier and more characteristic work.

We now come to the first writer on our list who properly belongs to the new generation. The career of **Lytton.** Edward George Earle Lytton Bulwer, later Bulwer Lytton, was one of extraordinary and varied activity. Born in 1803, he won the Chancellor's prize at Cambridge with a poem on sculpture; entered Parliament in 1831; was made a baronet in 1838; became Colonial Secretary in 1858; was raised to the peerage in 1866; and died in 1873. But though much of his energy was thus given to politics, he was from first to last an industrious and prolific man of letters, his large output including poems (see *ante*, p. 177), essays, and some successful plays (e.g., *The Lady of Lyons*, 1838; *Richelieu*, 1839; *Money*, 1840), besides the novels which concern us here. In these again his versatility is apparent. He first made his mark with *Pelham, or the Adventures of a Gentleman* (1828), a satiric picture of fashionable life conceived in a spirit of persiflage and pretentious cleverness. His next important works were *Paul Clifford* (1830) and *Eugene Aram* (1832), both melodramatic and sentimental tales of crime. A visit to Italy turned his restless mind in a new direction, and two brilliant but rather tawdry historical romances, *The Last Days of Pompeii* (1834) and *Rienzi* (1835), were the result. In *Ernest Maltravers* (1837) and its sequel, *Alice, or the Mysteries* (1838), he then made an attempt to combine sensationalism with a plentiful admixture of German transcendental philosophy; in *Night and Morning* (1841) he cultivated pure melodrama; while in *Zanoni* (1842) he plunged deep into the occult doctrines of Rosicrucianism. *The Last of the Barons* (1843) and, five years later, *Harold, the Last of the Saxon Kings* (1848), mark his return to history, though this time to the history of his own country. Sounder and less theatrical than their Italian forerunners, these two works are for this reason much more satisfactory, and Lytton was justified in claiming that in them he had "intellectualised" historical fiction. Meanwhile public taste had been setting strongly towards domestic themes, and, yielding to this, as he yielded to every fresh current, he now produced a group of family novels—*The Caxtons* (1849), its sequel, *My Novel* (1853), and *What will He do with It?* (1858)—much quieter in tone and mellower in thought than any of his previous writings. To the last, however, he continued to experiment. In *The Haunted and the Haunters* (1860) and *A Strange Story* (1862) he returned to the supernatural; *The Coming Race* (1871) is a quasi-scientific Utopian romance; while *Kenelm Chillingly* (1873) and the posthumous *Parisians* may be roughly classed with the *Caxton* group as novels of contemporary manners.

Such versatility is amazing, and not less amazing is the success which Lytton won in so many different lines, for he never really failed in any of them. But his want of concentration was against him. All that extraordinary cleverness joined with industry no less extraordinary could accomplish, he undoubtedly did accomplish, but if his writings keep to what is in the circumstances a surprisingly uniform level, he never (with the solitary exception of his powerful little ghost story, *The Haunted and the Haunters*) did any one thing which can be placed incontestably in the highest class of its kind. His work, moreover, has suffered greatly from its want of reality, sincerity, and depth. It is, we feel, essentially showy work; his sentimentalism is unwholesome; his learning and philosophy, which he is fond of parading in immense digressions, often savours of charlatanism ; while, save in his very latest writings, his style is intolerably stilted and florid.

The combination of statesmanship and literature which is a remarkable feature of Lytton's career re-appears in that of Benjamin Disraeli (1804–81), **Disraeli.** who was three times Chancellor of the Exchequer and twice Prime Minister of England, and who in 1876 became Earl of Beaconsfield ; but in his case the connection is far closer, because most of his novels were written to expound his political views. Before he entered the House of Commons in 1837 he had already published *Vivian Grey* (1827), *The Young Duke* (1831), *Contarini Fleming* (1832), and *The Wondrous Tale of Alroy* (1833), while *Venetia* (which deals with an episode in the life of Byron) and *Henrietta Temple* appeared in the year in which he took his seat. Of these, the last two stand in a class by themselves, because they are love-stories of an extremely sentimental kind, having nothing to do with politics. The others, on the contrary, are specially interesting on the biographical side for the light which they throw upon the young writer's ideas in the days before he abjured Radicalism and went over to the Tories. In matter and manner these early novels strikingly resemble the contemporary work of Lytton. More important, however, from the personal and historical, if not perhaps from the purely literary, point of view, are the three novels which followed Disraeli's change of political creed—*Coningsby* (1844), *Sybil* (1845), and *Tancred* (1847), which are all political manifestoes, the progress of the narrative being in each case interrupted by long disquisitions on subjects connected with its theme. After this the cares of office naturally interfered with Disraeli's literary activity. But he reappeared as a novelist in 1870 with *Lothair*, the great success of which must, however, be attributed in part to the fact that some of the prominent public personages of the day figured among its characters under very thin disguises. *Endymion* (1880) was universally regarded as an anti-climax. Several clever satires of his early manhood—*Ixion in Heaven*, *The Infernal Marriage*, and *Pompilia* (all 1828)—have to be added to complete the tale of his work in fiction.

Disraeli's novels are as enigmatical as his character and career, though for obvious reasons there is more unanimity of opinion regarding his qualities as a writer than in respect of his claims as a statesman. No one will question his brilliancy, his wit, his rhetorical power ; no one, on the other hand, will deny that his taste and sentiment are often false, his habitual tone cynical and flippant, and his style gaudy and meretricious. His fundamental defect—and in this, as in many other ways, he resembles Lytton—is his artificiality. His novels do not depict life ; they remind us rather of Sidonia's gallery in *Coningsby*, because, like that, they are " fantastic, glittering, variegated, full of strange shapes and dazzling objects." Yet no reader of *Sybil* can doubt his sincerity in this one book at least. It is in its own way as thoroughly earnest an attempt to grapple with the great economic and social problems of the time, though these are of course approached from a very different point of view, as *Alton Locke*, and if Disraeli necessarily lacked Kingsley's first-hand knowledge of the masses, he had done his best to acquaint himself with their condition during a tour in the North, and, as he declared, had " written from his own observation." The trilogy of political novels, of which *Sybil* is the middle term, will always remain valuable as documents in the history of the transformation of feudal Toryism into Tory democracy, and Disraeli's entire work for the revelation it affords of the aims and ambitions of one who played so conspicuous a part on the public stage of his time.

The foregoing pages, added to those already devoted to the men of the older generation who were still active in the early thirties,[1] will give us some idea of the state of prose fiction in England in the years immediately preceding the advent of the best beloved of all our novelists. It was while serious fiction was represented in the main by Lytton and Disraeli, and the laughter-loving public, beginning to weary of Hook and Pierce Egan,[2] was finding a fresh fund of amusement in the sea-

Dickens. yarns of Marryat, that Charles Dickens sprang suddenly into fame. The son of John Dickens, then a clerk in the Navy Pay Office, he was born at Portsea, Portsmouth, on 7th February 1812. When barely ten, he was put to work in a blacking-factory at a shilling a day, and as a neglected child about the London streets laid the foundations of his wonderful knowledge of the life of the great city in many of its most sordid phases of poverty and wretchedness. Later he was released from his drudgery and sent to a private school, where he remained till he was fifteen, after which, and a year in a lawyer's office, he became a reporter, soon drifting from journalism into literature. His first book was a collection of descriptive and narrative papers, entitled *Sketches by Boz* (1836), the success of which was

[1] See Part I. Chap. V.

[2] Pierce Egan (1772–1849) was a sporting journalist and miscellaneous writer whose *Life in London* (or *Tom and Jerry*), the issue of which in monthly numbers began in July 1828, and its sequel, *Finish to the Adventures of Tom, Jerry, and Logic* (1828), had a long run of popularity. These sketches of cockney Bohemian life possess a certain amount of historical interest because they have to be reckoned among the precursors of *Pickwick*.

soon eclipsed by *The Posthumous Papers of the Pickwick Club* (1836–37). Before this masterpiece of humour was half complete, Dickens, assured of his position as incomparably the most popular writer of the day, was already immersed in other work, and *Oliver Twist* and *Nicholas Nickleby* having, like *Pickwick*, first run their course in monthly parts, appeared in volume form, the one in 1838, the other in 1839, while *The Old Curiosity Shop* followed in quick succession (1840). In *Barnaby Rudge* (1841) Dickens turned for the nonce from contemporary life to the past, setting a tale of private adventure in an historical framework provided by the No-Popery Riots of 1780. Then in 1842 came a visit to the United States, an account of which was given in the extremely unflattering *American Notes* (1842), and which further yielded much excellent material for *Martin Chuzzlewit* (1844), a work of great variety and power, which stands well to the front among all his novels. Meanwhile he had struck a fresh vein with his Christmas stories (*The Christmas Carol*, 1843 ; followed by *The Chimes*, 1845 ; *The Cricket on the Hearth*, 1846, etc.), little things, perfect in their kind, unique, and inimitable. A second travel-book, the admirable *Pictures from Italy* (1846), also belongs to this period. His next work on a large scale, *Dombey and Son* (1846), the weakest of all his novels, showed a temporary failure of power, but the lost ground was soon recovered in the splendid triumph of *David Copperfield* (1850), his own favourite among his books, probably the favourite also with the vast majority of readers, and one of the outstanding masterpieces of English fiction. Its publication is commonly regarded as the culminating point in his career as a writer, and though I cannot myself agree with the critics who speak of his remaining twenty years as a period of decline, various changes in the general character of his work from this time on are very apparent. One of these may be noted in passing. His earlier books had belonged for the most part to what Scott called "the loose and incoherent" class of novel, and were obviously deficient in structural unity. He now turned his attention to plot, and henceforth, instead of depending for his interest mainly upon a succession of episodes, he sought to build up the materials of his stories into organic wholes in accordance with a carefully devised general plan. This change of method is first marked in *Bleak House* (1853), while the resulting increase of unity also characterises his two remaining novels on the old immense scale—*Little Dorrit* (1857) and *Our Mutual Friend* (1865), as well as three shorter books, *Hard Times* (1854), *A Tale of Two Cities* (1859), and *Great Expectations* (1861). The two last-named of these—the one a powerful tragedy of French revolutionary times, the other a capital plot-story, rich alike in dramatic interest and in humour—provide conclusive disproof of the statement that "after *David Copperfield*" Dickens "never wrote anything altogether first-rate"; and if *Bleak House*, *Little Dorrit*, and *Our Mutual Friend* suffer in places from a certain failure of freshness and spontaneity, we note in all of them, among the various qualities which help to compensate for the loss of buoyancy and overflowing fun, a decided deepening in the treatment of character. This is also apparent in the admirable series of miscellaneous papers—a sort of later *Sketches by Boz*—*The Uncommercial Traveller* (1860).

A man of tremendous vitality, Dickens always lived at high pressure, undertaking an amount of work outside his novels—including towards the end his famous public readings—which might well have taxed the strength of

15

half a dozen ordinary people. He paid the penalty of overstrain in an early collapse of health, and died of an apoplectic stroke on 9th June 1870, leaving behind him a fragment of a new novel of great promise, *The Mystery of Edwin Drood.*

The distinctive qualities of Dickens's work—his copious and irresistible humour, his immense dramatic power, the unsurpassed vividness of his descriptive writing, the marvellous vitality (within certain easily defined limits) of his characterisation—are so familiar that it is unnecessary for us now to expatiate upon them. Nor need we linger much over his defects, which recent critics are perhaps inclined to force into undue relief. The most serious of these undoubtedly sprang from his craving for theatrical effects. It is in respect of his extravagant and often mawkish sentimentalism and of his fondness for lurid melodrama that he has suffered most from the general change which has come over popular taste since his time. In regard to characterisation, the charges continually brought against him are that, with all his apparent diversity, his true range was extremely circumscribed, that his psychology was poor and often bad, that he always failed when he ventured beyond his own particular world of middle-class and low life into the circles of culture or the upper regions of society, and that even within his special field he depended upon exaggeration for his success. There is undoubtedly a measure of truth in these allegations, though they cannot be accepted without considerable qualification. But even if they were admitted to the full, the unique greatness of his achievement is still beyond challenge. The theatrical bent of his genius, which prompted him on the one side to melodrama, led him on the other towards farce, and for this reason his humorous characterisation frequently (though by no means always) runs into caricature. But his great comic creations—his Pickwick, Sam Weller, Dick Swiveller, Pecksniff, Mrs. Gamp, Micawber, Silas Wegg, and the rest of them—are none the less among the triumphs of our imaginative literature. No other writer in that literature, with the solitary exception of Shakespeare, has called into being so many men and women who have become part and parcel of that great humorous tradition into which we of the English-speaking race are privileged to be born.

Dickens belongs entirely to the humanitarian movement of the Victorian Age, and is indeed by far its most important representative in literature. By his large and generous sympathy with " the complaining millions of men," by his hearty scorn of religious hypocrisy, greed, hardness of heart, and the vulgar pride of caste, and by his noble championship of the cause of the poor, the weak, the oppressed, he exercised an influence for good the value of which it would be impossible to exaggerate. Nor is his general spirit alone to be considered. We must also recognise the specific social purpose with which he was almost always inspired, for in nearly all his novels he sets out to attack some particular abuse or abuses and to advocate some much-needed reform. Fortunately he was by instinct so completely the dramatic artist that he rarely made the mistake of sinking the novelist in the preacher. Yet the ethical aim of his work is always clear, and it must be kept steadily in view in our estimate of him.

Dickens's one great contemporary rival, William Makepiece Thackeray, was just seven months his senior, **Thackeray.** for he was born on 18th July 1811 at Calcutta, where his father held a post in the service of the East India Company. Brought to England as a child, he was placed in the Charterhouse, whence in 1829 he proceeded to Cambridge. Leaving abruptly the following year, he next spent two years on the Continent, partly in travel, partly in studying art in Weimar and Paris, meanwhile seeing life in many phases and accumulating a fund of experience which he was afterwards to turn to good account. A small private fortune which he inherited on coming of age having been squandered through injudicious investments, he was now thrown on his own resources, and discouraged with the outlook in art (which he had meant to make his profession), he turned to journalism and literature. The work which he did during the next ten years was very miscellaneous and unequal, but it included some things which, though little noted at the time, were as thoroughly representative of his genius as anything that followed. This is the case with three at least of his many contributions to *Fraser*: the *Memoirs of Mr. C. J. Yellowplush* (1838–40), with their powerful pictures of the seamy side of high life; *Catherine* (1839–40), a disagreeable story of crime, designed expressly to destroy the romantic glamour which had been thrown over the criminal classes by some of the writings of Harrison Ainsworth and Lytton; and *Barry Lyndon* (1844), another realistic study of rascality, this time in the ironical form of an *apologia* from the pen of the consummate rascal himself. No less characteristic are the brilliant *Novels by Eminent Hands* (1847) and the fierce and bitter *Book of Snobs* (1848), both of which were first printed in *Punch*, for the former burlesques the romantic absurdities of some of the popular contemporary writers of fiction, while the latter is compact of scathing satire of the shams and affectations of English society.

It was not till he had thus served a long apprenticeship to literature that Thackeray at length took his place beside Dickens with the publication of *Vanity Fair* (1847–48), if not the greatest, at least the most entirely characteristic of all his books, for it is the one in which he most openly repudiates both the romantic tradition in fiction and the romantic falsification of life. His next long work—the rambling, chaotic, and in part auto-biographical *History of Pendennis* (1849–50)—was less ferocious and gloomy, but it was no less a protest against heroics (see Preface), Pendennis himself being pre-sented, not as an idealised fancy-picture of English youth, after the fashion of the ordinary novelist, but as a faithful full-length portrait of one of " the gentlemen of our age," with all his weaknesses and follies. The same determination to keep close to the plain truth of life is equally apparent in *The History of Henry Esmond* (1852), though here Thackeray turns to the past for his theme. As the re-creation of a bygone age—the Age of Anne, the very style of which is reproduced with mar-vellous perfection—*Esmond* is universally recognised as one of the masterpieces of historical fiction. Yet it is historical fiction of a kind which neither Scott nor any of his imitators in the " big bow-wow " line had ever essayed. Its narrative moves, it is true, through some of the great scenes of the early eighteenth century, and some of its famous figures are introduced in it ; but incidents and characters alike are stripped of the gaudy trappings of romance, while the absence of those picturesque descriptions which had become part of the historical novelist's stock-in-trade is a further illus-tration of the writer's realistic aim. *The Virginians*, four years later (1858–59), dealing as it does with the fortunes of Esmond's grandsons in the third quarter of the eighteenth century, was a kind of sequel to this great work, but fell very far below its level. Nor can unqualified praise be given to another novel, this time of modern life, *The Newcomes*, which he had published in the meanwhile (1854–55), though we are willing to forgive a good deal that is relatively poor and tedious in these " memoirs of a most respectable family " for the sake of Colonel Newcome, one of the noblest figures in English fiction. While still engaged on *Esmond*, Thackeray had turned his attention to another though closely connected field, and had prepared a series of lectures on *The English Humourists of the Eighteenth Century*, which, like a companion course on *The Four Georges*, he gave with success in England and the United States (1852–53 and 1856–57). The business of lecturing naturally interfered with his novel-writing, and this may help to explain the decline which after *Esmond* was manifest in all his work—unless, indeed, an exception be made in favour of the delightful, gossipy essays, *The Roundabout Papers*, which are certainly excellent in their kind. These appeared at intervals in the newly established *Cornhill*, which he edited from 1860 to 1862. To the same magazine he also contributed his two remaining novels, the slight but amusing *Lovel the Widower* and *The Adventures of Philip on his Way through the World*, a sort of later *Pendennis*, much inferior to its precursor, but containing many passages of great tenderness, and characterised by all the old peculiar charm of style. Judged by age only, Thackeray was still in the prime of life. But he had grown old prematurely, and for some years his health had been failing. He had just begun to occupy himself with a new novel, *Denis Duval*, when he was found dead in his bed on the morning of 23rd December 1863.

Though the influence of Fielding, for whom his

admiration was boundless, may be seen in many of the characteristics of his work, there was one important respect in which Thackeray did not follow his master. He praised *Tom Jones* for the organic perfection of its design, but it is precisely in the matter of design that he himself was weakest. Only once did he take the trouble to think out carefully the whole of his story in advance, and *Esmond*, which is also the only one of his novels which did not first appear in serial form, is from beginning to end a piece of well-proportioned art. But as such it is a striking exception among his works. Elsewhere he allowed his story to take care of itself, with the result that he gives us, as Anthony Trollope put it, " strings of incidents and memoirs of individuals " rather than novels in the ordinary sense of the term. In fact, he thought nothing about plot or plan. His method, according to his own statement, was simply to create at the outset two or three of the chief persons of his drama and then to follow their course from chapter to chapter with little anticipation of what was to happen next ; allowing everything in the progress of his narrative to depend upon the natural evolution of his characters and their relations with one another. Whatever was lost by this leisurely hand-to-mouth method, one thing was gained : truth to life was never sacrificed to the mechanical necessities of plot.

From this point of view, therefore, his indifference to the mere technique of construction may be regarded as one illustration of the principles on which his art was founded. An uncompromising realist, he took his stand by Fielding : " If truth is not always pleasant, at any rate truth is best from whatever chair—from those whence graver writers or thinkers argue, or from that at which the story-teller sits." It was in the interests of truth that he pricked the bubbles of pretty fancy in his early burlesques, attacked the "Newgate school" of fiction in *Catherine*, parodied the popular fashionable writers of the day in *Novels by Eminent Hands*, and in *Rebecca and Rowena* covered *Ivanhoe* with ridicule ; it was in the interests of truth that he painted his black picture of the world in *Vanity Fair* ; it was in the interests of truth that he still held up the mirror to nature in the novels which followed. But while fundamentally a realist, he was not a realist of the so-called scientific kind. He does not, like Flaubert, for example, stand apart from life and analyse it with cold-blooded impartiality. On the contrary, he feels intensely the ugliness of vice and the beauty of virtue, and strives to make us share his hatred of the one and his admiration of the other. For this reason his realism has a firm ethical basis. It is better for morality as well as for art that the world should be represented, not in the delusive colours of sentimental romance, but as it actually is— a world where our brightest dreams seldom come to fruition, where folly, hypocrisy, and base passion too often have their way unchecked, and where poetic justice is very rarely done. Hence his constant pre-occupation with evil and the merciless satire which is so prominent a feature of his work—satire directed in particular against the falsehoods and conventions which are like cankers eating at the heart of our social life ; for it was through satire that his moral spirit found its most natural expression. Hence, too, the charge of cynicism which has been brought against him. Thackeray, it must be admitted, had his cynical moods : witness many of his caustic "asides." But to describe him as a cynic is to misinterpret the quality and purpose of his satire. Cynicism means radical unbelief in the elementary instincts of human nature itself. There is no such unbelief in Thackeray. It is indeed to these elementary instincts that he makes his constant appeal. Thus, sweeping as his satire is, it leaves the sanctities of life untouched.

It must, however, be noted that, in contrast with most men, who grow harder with age, Thackeray became gentler and more mellow. He began by dwelling almost exclusively upon the ugly things in life. His first great characters—his Barry Lyndon and Catherine— were studies in unmitigated scoundrelism. In *Vanity Fair*, in which he essays to give a much fuller picture of society, the larger place which the good had come to occupy in his thought is shown by his sympathetic if depressing delineation of Dobbin and Amelia. Yet here still the emphasis is thrown heavily upon the wickedness of the world. But in the books which followed, while the general view of life remains essentially the same, the focus is somewhat changed, the beauty and pathos of love, friendship, and forgiveness are brought into relief, and the writer's effort is largely directed to the creation of characters like Esmond, Harry Warrington, Colonel Newcome, Ethel Newcome, and the Little Sister, in whom nobility, purity, and simple goodness are in the ascendant. And this growth of tenderness and pity was accompanied by an immense expansion of sentiment. Thackeray abhorred sentimentalism, and in his early writings often made merry over it. But he was always a good deal of a sentimentalist at heart, and he became more and more openly so with the general change in the temper of his mind. Even the restraint which he had formerly put upon himself now disappeared ; the habit of brooding over his pathetic incidents grew upon him ; and his later pages, as perhaps most conspicuously in *Philip*, are often moist with tears. But though his satire became less sweeping and ferocious and his tone more sympathetic and humane, his reading of life remained to the end as profoundly melancholy as ever. Indeed, increasing pity deepened his sadness. His favourite phrase, *Vanitas vanitatum*, was from first to last the epitome of his philosophy. This we should gather easily enough from the whole drift and tenor of his books. But lest we should miss his meaning he reinforces it again and again in those informal essays-in-little with which he continually interrupts and plays chorus to his narratives, and which are at once so inartistic and so charming a feature of his work.

While by his persistent and telling attacks on snobbery Thackeray helped to cleanse the social atmosphere, **Reade.** he knew nothing of Dickens's zeal for reform. We get back to the humanitarian movement in the novel in the work of Charles Reade (1814–84), who further resembles Dickens in the strongly pronounced histrionic turn of his genius. All through life indeed he repeatedly tempted fortune as a playwright, though in this direction he achieved only a measure of success. He found his real line when, on the advice of an actress, he made his play, *Masks and Faces*, into the tale of *Peg Woffington* (1853). But the theatrical element is uppermost in his work in fiction. Like Dickens in his melodramatic moods, he writes habitually, as it were, with an eye to the footlights, and his novels are full of sensational scenes conceived and handled according to the recognised principles of stage effect. Yet though many of the incidents in his plots may seem to us in the last degree extravagant, his own reply to adverse criticism was that truth is stranger than fiction, and that in every case he could justify himself by the plain evidence of fact. This is a point to be emphasised in connection with his specifically humanitarian novels—*It is Never too Late to Mend* (1856), an exposure of the abuses of prison administration and the Australian gold-fever ; *Hard Cash* (1863), an attack on private lunatic asylums ; *Foul Play* (written in conjunction with Dion Boucicault, 1869), the theme of which is the nefarious practices of the " knackers " who make money out of rotten ships ; and *Put Yourself in His Place* (1870), which deals with trade-unionism and strikes. Though a man of impetuous and headstrong temper, Reade did not allow himself to be carried away by his passionate desire to redress social wrongs. He made it his business to master his subject in all its details by patient and laborious research, and what he wrote was always based upon an immense collection of carefully compiled and tabulated documents gathered from Blue books, newspapers, and other repositories of information. Despite their essentially melodramatic quality these books are often overloaded with didactic purpose, and the best of his work is therefore rather to be found in those which are less aggressively polemical. From the point of view of pure art *Peg Woffington*, an episode from the annals of the eighteenth-century stage, is the finest thing that he ever did ; but his recognised masterpiece is *The Cloister and the Hearth* (1861), " a matter-of-fact romance " of the fifteenth century, combining scholarly accuracy with wonderful imaginative power. Reade's work is much marred by eccentricities of manner, childish tricks of style, and astonishing lapses of taste. But it is the work of a man of real dramatic genius, and some of his characters have in them the true red blood of life.

While, with many points of difference, Reade has also many points of contact with Dickens, Anthony

Trollope. Trollope (1815–82), on the other hand, belongs unmistakably to the school of Thackeray. Though during his best years he was a hard-working postal official, Trollope was, from the publication of his first book, *The Macdermots of Ballycloran* (1847), onward, one of the most prolific of our novelists. With him, indeed, as he explains at length in his *Autobiography*, literature was reduced to a business, and as a result of his unflagging industry he manufactured upwards of fifty novels, most of which reached, while a few rose decidedly above, the level of respectable workmanship. Among the best of these are *Orley Farm* (1862) and the series collectively entitled *Chronicles of Barsetshire* (1855–67). He also wrote several books of travel and short lives of Caesar (1870) and Thackeray (1879). In principle and practice he was a thoroughgoing realist, and his minutely faithful pictures of Victorian middle-class and upper-class society are already beginning to have an historical value. He was especially successful in depicting clerical life and character, as in the *Barsetshire* books, but he also did well with political life, as in the *Phineas Finn* trilogy (1869–76). Though often more than a little heavy and commonplace, he could tell a story in a way to hold attention, and he had the faculty, to use his own phrase, of making his men and women " stand upright on the ground."

In some excellent remarks on novels in general in his *Autobiography*, Trollope very justly pointed out that

Charlotte Brontë. truth to life does not preclude what we call sensational interest, provided only that such interest be properly related to character. The special importance of the next writer on our list may perhaps be indicated by the statement that she showed how the novel of passion, then commonly conceived as romance, could be cast in the realistic mould. Born in 1816, Charlotte Brontë spent her childhood at Haworth, on the bleak Yorkshire moors, whither her father, a clergyman, had settled in 1821. After a short sojourn at a school at Cowan Bridge, near Leeds—the institution described with such grim realism in the early chapters of *Jane Eyre*—she and her sister Emily presently went to Brussels to qualify for work as governesses. There the former studied and taught from 1842 to 1844, her experiences providing the basis of *Villette*. In 1846 the three girls, Charlotte, Emily, and Anne, under the pseudonyms of Currer, Ellis, and Acton Bell, published the small volume of verse to which we have already referred (see *ante*, p. 178). Then they turned to novel-writing, Charlotte producing *The Professor*, Anne, *Agnes Grey*, and Emily, *Wuthering Heights*. *The Professor* being rejected on the ground that it was deficient in plot, Charlotte set to work on another book, *Jane Eyre*, which, in the story of Fairfax Rochester, the Byronic hero, and his mad wife, provided sensation enough for even the most exigent reader (1847). While public interest in this book was still hot, the shadows were gathering darker about its author's life. Her only brother, Bramwell, died of drink and opium in 1848. In the same year she lost her sister Emily, and the next year Anne—both victims of the hereditary family disease of consumption. But though now left alone in the solitary parsonage with her austere and melancholy father, she courageously continued her work, publishing *Shirley* in 1849, and *Villette* in 1853. In 1854 she became the wife of her father's curate, the Rev. Arthur Bell Nicholls, and died in 1855. *The*

Professor, which is little more than a first sketch of *Villette*, appeared after her death.

While Charlotte Brontë's place is undoubtedly among the greater Victorian novelists, her reputation rests upon very narrow foundations. Her range was extremely circumscribed. Except in the melodramatic parts of *Jane Eyre*, which were written as a concession to public taste, she hardly ever went beyond the range of her personal experience. What is best in her work is indeed practically a direct transcript from life, and when we remember that her own knowledge of life was unfortunately confined in the main to its more disagreeable phases, and that her temper, while remarkable for strength, was stiff and hard, we have no difficulty in understanding the unsympathetic tone which generally characterises her work and the prejudices which often distort her judgment of men and things. Reflecting as they do her gloomy and rebellious spirit, her books are anything but pleasant, but their power is very great, while by the intensity of the passion with which they are charged, and which at the time of their appearance considerably disturbed the equanimity of Mrs. Grundy, they struck a distinctly new note in the domestic fiction of their time.

It is frequently said that the one novel of Emily Brontë (1818–48), *Wuthering Heights* (1847), shows greater genius than anything that her more famous sister ever wrote. It is certain that it equals even *Jane Eyre* in passion and strength, while the gloom which pervades it is all the deeper because it is entirely without the relief in which Charlotte occasionally indulged. This grim and ghastly story is a difficult work to appraise. In construction it is almost incredibly bad ; in style it is immature and violent ;

Emily Brontë.

and its character-drawing is crude. Yet there is something stupendous about its sustained and undiluted horror, while its wonderful descriptions of moorland scenery deserve the highest praise.

The third of the Brontë trio, Anne (1820–49), is remembered now only in connection with her sisters, with whom she presents a singular contrast both in the sweetness of her nature and in her entire want of strength. Her two novels, *Agnes Grey* (1847) and *The Tenant of Wildfell Hall* (1848), give her no independent place in literature.

Anne Brontë.

Charlotte Brontë's first biographer, Elizabeth Cleghorn Gaskell (1810–65), is well to the fore among humanitarian novelists in virtue of two works of direct social purpose, *Mary Barton* (1848), a strong story of Manchester factory life, and *North and South* (1855), which deals with the contrast between industrial and agricultural interests. She is best remembered, however, for a little book belonging to quite a different class, the exquisitely pathetic and humorous village-idyl, *Cranford* (1853), than which there is no more charming thing of the kind in our literature. But we mention her in this particular place because in yet another of her works, *Ruth* (1853), she may be said to have first suggested that deepening of interest in the inner life and its problems which was soon to transform the novel of manners into the psychological novel. As a carefully elaborated sermon on the text that "all deeds, however hidden and long passed by, have their eternal consequences," *Ruth* clearly anticipates the work of the great moralist who next demands our attention.

Mrs. Gaskell.

Marian Evans, always known by her pen-name of George Eliot, was born near Nuneaton, Warwickshire, in 1819, and spent her first twenty years in the quiet Midland country which she so often described in **George Eliot.** her books. In 1841 she moved with her father to Coventry, and there under the influence of two local families, the Brays and the Hennells, with whom she formed a close friendship, she abandoned the evangelical Christianity in which she had been bred and became an agnostic. Her first piece of literary work was a translation of Strauss's rationalistic *Leben Jesu*. After this, and a year on the Continent, she settled in London, and presently became sub-editor of *The Westminster Review*, in which she published many articles on literary and philosophic subjects. From these critical labours her mind was turned to the writing of fiction by George Henry Lewes (see *ante*, p. 212), with whom in 1854 she had formed an irregular union, her first three stories, collectively entitled *Scenes of Clerical Life*, appearing in *Blackwood* in 1857. Two years later *Adam Bede*, on the whole her greatest work, placed her in the front rank of contemporary novelists. This was followed by the partly autobiographical *Mill on the Floss* (1860), *Silas Marner* (1861), *Romola* (1863), a tale of the Italian Renaissance and her only excursion into the distant past, *Felix Holt the Radical* (1866), *Middlemarch* (1871–72), *Daniel Deronda* (1876), and a series of essays entitled *Impressions of Theophrastus Such* (1879). Lewes died in 1878; in the spring of 1880 she married John Walter Cross, and died on the 22nd December of the same year.

The foundations of George Eliot's art were firmly laid in realism. Dickens gathered his materials in the main from the London streets and people he had known in childhood and youth; Thackeray his from the clubs and drawing-rooms of Vanity Fair. George Eliot's true field was her girlhood's quiet world of old-fashioned village and country town. To this world she habitually keeps very close ; hence, with the exception of *Romola*, her novels are substantially (in Balzac's classification) "Scenes of Provincial Life," painted by one who conceived the novel as a faithful representation of things as they are, and whose guiding principle it was never to think of "mere effect," but to be satisfied (as she once complained that even Mrs. Gaskell was not always satisfied) with the "subdued colourings and half-tints" of life itself. Superficially, therefore, her work closely resembles that of Jane Austen, but only superficially ; for she does precisely what Jane Austen never attempted to do—she penetrates beneath the placid surface of the apparently commonplace existence which she describes in search of the great passions, conflicts, and disasters which even there shape life to tragic issues. Thus, while the author of *Pride and Prejudice* had produced nothing but exquisitely finished social comedy, the author of *Adam Bede* weaves out of her home-spun material a tragedy as pitiful, poignant, and profoundly moral as anything to be found on the stage of Æschylus or Shakespeare. The novel, which was social and satiric in the hands of Thackeray, and democratic and humanitarian in those of Dickens, becomes in hers didactic, philosophic, and religious.

We must not, indeed, be misled by the purely ethical significance of her work into a mistaken idea of its value as art. Her real greatness as a novelist ultimately depends upon her genuine dramatic power—the power which is exhibited, for example, in her wonderful revelation of the rustic mind in *Silas Marner*, in the record of Maggie Tulliver's childhood in the first part of *The Mill on the Floss*, and pre-eminently in the great comedy figure of Mrs. Poyser in *Adam Bede*. And this explains why her

16

earlier books are so much fresher and more attractive than her later ; for she began by letting her imagination play upon materials provided by memory, but afterwards, with the exhaustion of these materials, came more and more to rely upon pure thought as a substitute for waning creative power. Hence, as contrasted with those which had preceded, *Romola* and the novels which followed seem lacking in vitality, laboured, and sometimes dull. None the less, what gives its distinctive quality to her work is unquestionably the pervading presence in it of an extraordinarily rich and suggestive philosophical commentary and interpretation. No other English novelist ever brought so ripe a knowledge to bear upon the problems of conduct ; no other has ever been so well equipped for the task of the analytical psychologist. For this reason her novels have enduring value as essays on life.

Her philosophy has its roots in religion. Emotionally conservative, though intellectually radical (a point which she herself emphasises in *Theophrastus Such*), she never outgrew the spirit of the creed she had once believed in, and while her theories were agnostic, her temperament was ascetic and her spiritual outlook almost mystical. Conceiving religion as man's response to the everlasting reality of irreversible law, she seized upon the thought that all religions, however much they may vary one from another, are at one in this, that they have all sought to proclaim the eternal truth that obedience to a rule of life outside and above our own petty desires and caprices is the only way to salvation. Hence her profound sympathy with all forms of religion—Mr. Tryan's, Dinah Morris's, Savonarola's—which have helped to lift men out of themselves. For the thought that runs through all her teaching is that of the supremacy of duty, interpreted habitually in terms of self-renunciation, or the subjection of the individual will to that which (whatever may be the terminology employed) is recognised as the divine. Hence her great theme is the struggle between the higher and the lower impulses in our natures, and the way in which, the choice once made, that choice entails inevitable consequences for good or evil to self and others. This theme she generally works out tragically, for her novels are for the most part studies of the weakness which leads to sin, and of the sin which brings inevitable Nemesis in its train. With her, human nature is always plastic ; she focuses attention upon the dynamics of character ; and her finest triumphs as a psychologist are achieved in those exhaustive studies of temptation in which (as in the case of Tito in *Romola*) she traces stage by stage the slow but fatal process of moral deterioration. For the rest, there is little place for personal happiness in her scheme of things : duty must be done without thought of earthly or heavenly reward. Hence the impression left by her novels is profoundly sad. But their sadness, like the sadness of all great tragedy, is purifying and ennobling. Whatever rank may ultimately be assigned to George Eliot as a novelist, her place must always be among the greatest moral teachers of her time.

Born at Holne Vicarage, Dartmoor, in the same year as George Eliot—1819—Charles Kingsley, after a dis-
Charles tinguished career at Cambridge, entered the
Kingsley. Church, and was rector of Eversley, Hampshire, from 1844 till his death in 1875. Early in life he fell under the influence of Carlyle and F. D. Maurice, and threw himself with passionate ardour into the cause of Christian Socialism. Such ardour dominates his first two novels, *Yeast* (1848), which deals with the condition of the agricultural labourer, and *Alton Locke* (1850), which,

in the form of an autobiography of a young " tailor and poet," attacks the sweating system, and at once expounds and criticises the aims and methods of Chartism. A third novel, *Two Years Ago* (1857), though written in a more temperate tone, is also occupied with social themes. It was inevitable that such work should suffer artistically from over-stress of didactic purpose, and it is generally agreed that Kingsley is most successful as a novelist when he more or less completely frees himself from moral theory ; as pre-eminently in *Westward Ho !* (1855), an Elizabethan romance of Devonshire and the Spanish Main ; and in a lesser degree in *Hypatia* (1853), a tale of fifth-century Alexandria, and *Hereward the Wake* (1866). Yet Kingsley habitually carried something of the present with him into the past ; for in *Hypatia,* as in *The Saint's Tragedy* (see *ante*, p. 180), modern problems are still uppermost in his mind ; while *Westward Ho !* is largely an idealisation of the fighting Protestantism which he so greatly admired. Among his numerous other writings one only need here be named, the charming prose fantasy, *Water Babies* (1863).

Kingsley's work is characterised by a vigorous, healthy, chivalrous spirit, and boundless optimism. The ideal of religion which he everywhere preached was as far removed from Tractarianism (" sham popery," as he called it) on the one side as from narrow and repressive Puritanism on the other. Religion was for him always a practical thing, whose function was the saving of men in this life no less than in the life to come ; and his advocacy of field sports and manly exercises earned for his creed the nickname of " muscular Christianity."

His younger brother, Henry Kingsley (1830–76), was also a novelist of some distinction. His first novel, *Geoffrey Hamlyn* (1859), contains some vigorous pictures of life and manners in Australia, where he had spent five years. To this subject he returned in *The Hillyars* **Henry** *and the Burtons* (1865). But his best work **Kingsley.** is *Ravenshoe* (1861), a tale of the time of the Crimean War, rambling in plot, but with some clear-cut characterisation, humour, and a strong dramatic interest. The spirit of Henry Kingsley's books is manly and wholesome. He had not his brother's depth or intensity, but he had this advantage over him, that he never confused the functions of the novelist with those of the preacher. Like Charles, he was excellent in description.

After a biography of his father, William Collins the artist (1848), and an experiment in historical romance, **Collins.** *Antonina or the Fall of Rome* (1850), William Wilkie Collins (1824–89) found his real line in *Basil* (1852), a tale of modern life. Soon after this he became intimate with Dickens, for whose *All the Year Round* he wrote *The Woman in White* (1860), in which, as in *The Moonstone* (1868), he proved himself our greatest master of pure sensation and the art of unravelling an intricate plot. Among his many other novels *No Name* (1862) and *The New Magdalen* (1873) alone even approach the level of these two really remarkable books. While Collins's strength unquestionably lay in melodrama, he was not so deficient in other qualities as is sometimes alleged. His Count Fosco in *The Woman in White* is a genuine creation, and here and there he shows a good deal of pleasant humour, as in Gabriel Betterton and Drusilla Clack in *The Moonstone*, Abraham Sage and Miss Gwilt in *Armadale*, and Captain Wragge in *No Name*. Dickens inspired him to write at times with a didactic purpose, vivisection, the marriage laws, and the modern craze for athletics being among the objects of his attack.

George Meredith was born in Hampshire on 12th February 1828, and, as we have already seen (*ante*, p. 180), published his first book, *Poems*, in 1851. His **Meredith.** first productions in prose were *The Shaving of Shagpat* (1856), an Oriental extravaganza full of humour and fancy, and *Farina : a Legend of Cologne* (1857), a half-serious, half-burlesque excursion into German romance. His real career, however, opened with *The Ordeal of Richard Feverel* (1859), which, as the sub-title explains, is " A History of a Father and a Son," and more specifically, of the tragedy which results from the father's ill-advised attempt to fashion his son's character in accordance with an artificial system of education devised by him for the purpose. The fact that this very striking and original book appeared in the same year as *Adam Bede* shows that though Meredith to some extent carried forward George Eliot's work in the psychological novel, and did so under the influence of that scientific movement of which she was herself a product, he was not directly affected by her. His next novel, *Evan Harrington* (1861), a comedy of a tailor's son who would be a gentleman, is in much lighter vein, and, while it labours under the disadvantage of a far-fetched plot which also drags in places, it contains some capital scenes and one of Meredith's very best characters, Evan's sister, the Countess de Saldar de Sancorvo. *Sandra Belloni* (1864) and its sequel *Vittoria* (1867), both books of marked distinction, were in part inspired by the writer's enthusiasm for the cause of Italian freedom, the scene of the latter being laid in Italy at the time of the political commotions of 1848. *Rhoda Fleming* (1865), which on the other hand is essentially English in tone and character, is like *Richard Feverel* a tragedy, and is the most simply human and natural, and therefore (as some readers at least will feel) the most impressive, of all Meredith's books. Then came *The Adventures of Harry Richmond* (1871), a poetic comedy, which, brilliant as it is, often lapses in interest (as in the entire episode of Harry's love for the Princess Otillia), but is noteworthy for the great outstanding figure of the hero's father, Richmond Roy. Its successor, *Beauchamp's Career* (1876), is in one respect an exception among Meredith's novels. Generally his motive is love narrowly treated as the concern only of the persons immediately involved or at most of the small group to which they belong, the result being a certain want of breadth which we note in most of his work. Here he deals with larger issues, giving us in fact a wonderfully fresh and vigorous picture of mid-Victorian politics. His next work, *The Egoist* (1879), is commonly regarded as the most representative, if not the greatest, of his novels, and indeed it is pre-eminently character-istic both in its fine qualities and in its defects. As a searching and remorseless study of refined selfishness in the person of the hero, Sir Willoughby Patterne, it deserves the highest praise ; but it is so long drawn out, so overloaded with analysis, so meticulous in its elabora-tion of insignificant detail, that it often becomes in the last degree wearisome. In *The Tragic Comedians* which followed (1880), Meredith gave a close rendering of that painful episode in the life of the German social democrat Ferdinand Lassalle, which led to his miserable death. *Diana of the Crossways* (1885), which is also based on history, is often placed by Meredith's admirers in the very front rank of his writings, yet though its brilliancy of wit is certainly astonishing, it really inaugurates the period of his decline. His later books—*One of our Conquerors* (1891), *Lord Ormont and his Aminta* (1894), *The Amazing Marriage* (1895)—are so intricate in their

thought and expression, so over-subtle in their handling
of character, so cryptic and elusive in their style, that
only the confirmed Meredithian can be expected to
enjoy them. He was engaged upon yet another novel,
The Celt and the Saxon, at the time of his death in 1909.

All Meredith's novels are essentially problem-novels,
written in accordance with his theory that " fiction . . .
is philosophy's elect handmaid." [1]   Throughout his
attention is centred upon the psychology of his characters ; his comedy and his tragedy alike spring from
the conflict of emotions and ideas ; and this conflict
he studies chiefly in direct connection with the one
subject of absorbing interest to him, the relations of the
sexes and the entanglements of love. To his task of
historian of the inner life he brings a combination of
qualities of the highest order : a subtle insight into
character ; considerable humour ; wit in abundance ;
a fine spirit of poetry. His attitude towards life is extraordinarily sane ; the sturdy optimism which we have
noted in his verse pervades his prose writing also ; his
robust temper makes him the sworn foe of sentimentalism
in every form ; while with his absolute confidence in
nature and freedom he is equally impatient of social
convention and the cramping traditions which bulk
so large in current theories of morality. His criticism
of life comes out most clearly in his treatment of women,
with whom, it is generally admitted, he is particularly
successful. Revolting entirely against the early
Victorian pinched and anæmic ideal of " the essentially
feminine," he puts his women before us as full-blooded
human creatures, with plenty of personality and wills of

[1] A good deal of light is thrown upon Meredith's aims and methods
by his *Essay on Comedy and the Uses of the Comic Spirit* (1877), which
should be read in connection with his work.

their own, and because as thoroughly human, no more perfect and no less interesting than the men beside whom they stand.

Yet great as are Meredith's powers, even his best work has many and grave defects. Though we cannot question his remarkable grasp of character, the impression left with us when we have finished one of his books is that we have been living for a time in a very artificial world among men and women who somehow do not seem quite to belong to our ordinary humanity. That he has never been widely popular need therefore cause no surprise. In his very first novel he wrote : "I am aware an audience impatient for blood and glory scorns the stress I am putting on incidents so minute." But the reason why he has failed to make a larger appeal is not that readers are not interested in psychology. It is rather to be found in his want of naturalness, of simplicity, of the real common human note. From this want his style suffers sadly ; by his very manner of writing "he has planted round his garden a hedge full of thorns" though "red with wonderful roses." We are conscious, as we read, of his perpetual straining after the unusual, the unhackneyed, the striking, and this consciousness necessarily interferes with our enjoyment. His aphorisms and witty sayings—and he has an unfortunate mania for epigram —are too frequently suggestive of premeditation, and while at first they may dazzle, they end by fatiguing us with their pretentious cleverness. For the same cause his very brilliant people at times impose a heavy tax upon our patience, while his comic eccentrics (like Jack Raikes and Anthony Hackbut), are often tiresome rather than amusing. His characterisation, too, is often marred by the intrusion of his own peculiarities ; his men and women have the habit of talking in his own way and are infested with his own mannerisms. In view of his strongly marked and aggressive individuality it is easy to understand why Meredith should have aroused so much critical controversy, and why opinion upon his work should always tend to run to the extreme either of admiration or of disparagement. It is impossible as yet to say to what extent that work will stand the test of time, or what place Meredith will ultimately come to occupy among the greater Victorian novelists.

Only a few of the remaining novelists of our period can even be mentioned here, and these must be considered with the utmost brevity.

Francis Edward Smedley (1818–64), though himself a cripple, put into his work a cheery spirit and **Other** an abounding zest of life. His *Frank Fair-* **Novelists :** *leigh* (1850), *Lewis Arundel* (1852), and *Harry* **Men.** *Coverdale's Courtship* (1854) are novels of the old-fashioned type, combining, after the formula very popular at the time, a good deal of fun and melodrama, though both of a rather elementary kind. The same remark applies to the one great success of Samuel Warren (1807–77)—*Ten Thousand a Year* (1841), poorly written and full of overwrought sentiment, but still amusing on account of the adventures of the little Cockney cad, Tittlebat Titmouse. Joseph Sheridan Le Fanu (1814–73) excelled in the grim and uncanny, as in *The House by the Churchyard* (1863), *Uncle Silas* (1864), and the five horrible tales in the collection entitled *In a Glass Darkly* (1872). George John Whyte-Melville (1821–78) wrote some fair historical novels (e.g., *The Queen's Maries*, 1862 ; *The Gladiators*, 1863, etc.) and a tale of the Crimean War (utilising his own experiences), *The Interpreter*

(1858), but was more happy in his hunting stories (e.g., *Market Harborough,* 1861). Thomas Hughes (1822–96), who was active in Christian Socialism with his friends Maurice and Kingsley, will be remembered for one book—*Tom Brown's Schooldays* (1857), entirely a boy's book, with little other claim upon attention, but interesting as a picture (though probably much idealised) of Rugby under Thomas Arnold. George Alfred Lawrence (1827–76) made a hit with the publication in 1857 of *Guy Livingstone or Thorough,* a crude tale of fashionable life, which challenged the critics with its open glorification of physical force. His other novels, though they did not repeat this first success, embodied the same creed of "muscular blackguardism," as it was happily termed. James Payn (1830–98) was for many years a prolific producer of novels for the magazines and circulating libraries. His books, with their thin vein of humour, are readable enough, but they seldom rise much above the commonplace. *Lost Sir Massingberd* (1864), which has a very good plot, and *By Proxy* (1878), a really strong Chinese story, are usually accounted his best. With the Rev. Charles Dodgson (1832–98), a distinguished Cambridge mathematician who wrote unprofessionally as Lewis Carroll, we leave the commonplace entirely behind us. His fairy fantasies, *Alice's Adventures in Wonderland* (1865), and its sequel, *Through the Looking-Glass* (1871), are little masterpieces, absolutely original and inimitable. Designed for children, they appeal just as strongly to "grown-ups," who alone perhaps are able to appreciate to the full their subtle imagination and their whimsical humour. William Black (1841–98) brings us back to the ordinary current of fiction. His novels (e.g., *A Daughter of Heth,* 1871 ; *A Princess of*

Thule, 1873 ; *White Heather*, 1885, etc.) are distinctly romantic in atmosphere and abound in excellent descriptions of the Highlands, fishing, and yachting. Romance and a healthy love of the open air are again predominant in the work of Richard Doddridge Blackmore (1825–1900), whose *Lorna Doone* (1869), a tale of Exmoor in Stuart times, has enjoyed immense popularity as one of the most full-blooded and stirring of historical novels. His other books (e.g., *The Maid of Sker*, 1872 ; *Cripps the Carrier*, 1876, etc.) are full of admirable descriptions of nature and of the racy sentiment and humour of rustic life, particularly in the West Country. Sir Walter Besant (1836–1901) belongs to the humanitarian movement in fiction in virtue of his utopian novel, *All Sorts and Conditions of Men* (1882), out of which grew the People's Palace in the East End, and of such other stories of social purpose as *Children of Gibeon* (1886) and *The Alabaster Box* (1900). But he also produced a good deal of historical fiction (e.g., *Dorothy Forster*, 1884 ; *For Faith and Freedom*, 1888 ; *The Orange Girl*, 1899, etc.). Perhaps his best work, however, is to be found in the earlier books which he wrote in partnership with his friend James Rice (1844–1882), a collaborator of much genial humour (e.g., *Ready-Money Mortiboy*, 1871 ; *The Golden Butterfly*, 1876 ; and the eighteenth-century story, *The Chaplain of the Fleet*, 1881). Both in his humour and in his pathos, no less than in his humanitarianism, he often reveals the influence of Dickens. Joseph Henry Shorthouse (1834–1903) wrote one novel of remarkable distinction, *John Inglesant* (1881), the spiritual biography of a follower of Charles I., noteworthy in particular for its accurate studies of the religious ideas of the time in question—Romanist, Anglican, Quietist—which are all sympathetically analysed, though the author's High Church bias is obvious. His other books, which are characterised by the same general tone, are of relatively slight importance, though one of them, *The Little Schoolmaster Mark* (1883), deserves mention as a poetical study of childhood. The Rev. George MacDonald (1824–1905), who began life as a Congregational minister, opened his literary career with some volumes of verse, but soon turned to prose fiction. His numerous novels (e.g., *David Elginbrod*, 1863 ; *Alec Forbes of Howglen*, 1865 ; *Robert Falconer*, 1868, etc.), which are mainly Scotch in scene and character, are serious in interest, the writer's attention being fixed in general upon religious and moral problems. They are technically rather defective, and are habitually overweighted by didactic purpose ; but they have some humour and dramatic power, and a strongly poetic quality. The dialect, which is that of north-eastern Scotland, is said by those who know to be excellent. George Louis Palmella Du Maurier (1834–96), a descendant of a French family which had settled in England at the time of the Revolution, had long been well known as an artist in black and white, and through his cartoons in *Punch* as an incomparable satirist of English society, when he took the public by surprise with *Peter Ibbetson* (1892), a very remarkable and original psychical story of dreaming and double life. *Trilby*, which followed two years later, scored an even greater success, though here the occult motive takes the much cruder and more commonplace form of hypnotism. In both books the writer drew freely and with much effect upon his own early life in Paris—in the one case as a child, in the other as a student of art.

As a matter of convenience we have in the foregoing

epitome confined our attention to men-writers. A few out of the vast crowd of women-novelists must now be mentioned to complete our survey.

Mrs. Henry Wood (1814–87) was for many years a chief favourite with that large reading public which **Women.** specially loves a good story highly flavoured with sentiment and entirely conventional in moral tone. She was remarkably successful (e.g., *East Lynne*, 1861 ; *The Channings*, 1862 ; *Mrs. Halliburton's Troubles*, 1862) in combining domestic history with sensationalism, and her often harrowing pathos strengthened her popular appeal. Mrs. Lynn Linton (1822–98) wrote didactic novels from the " advanced " or anti-orthodox point of view, of which the most widely read was the thoughtful ethical study, *The True History of Joshua Davidson, Christian Communist* (1872). Another writer of pronouncedly didactic tendency, though this time of the strictly orthodox kind, was Dinah Maria Mulock, Mrs. Craik (1827–87), who cultivated domestic fiction of a rather flabby type. Her *John Halifax, Gentleman* (1856), which deals with the industrial revolution between 1780 and 1834, is, however, a book of considerable range and power, and its historical interest should help to preserve it from oblivion. A far more important name than any of these is that of Margaret Wilson, Mrs. Oliphant (1828–97), who in industry at least, and perhaps in some other qualities, may be regarded as a sort of feminine counterpart of Anthony Trollope. There was little pause in the steady flow of her novels, save such as resulted from the production of numerous books of history and biography, from the *Life of Mistress Margaret Maitland* in 1849 to *Old Mr. Tredgold* in 1896. She was unquestionably a woman of real ability, and it is therefore to be regretted that she dissipated her talents by writing too much and too fast. She is at her best in the series entitled *Chronicles of Carlingford* (1862–66), which in many ways resembles, while it hardly suffers from comparison with, Trollope's *Chronicles of Barsetshire*. The opening work of this group, *Salem Chapel*, which may be considered her masterpiece, contains some admirable character-drawing done with much insight and humour. Mary Elizabeth Braddon, Mrs. Maxwell (1837–1915), was for upwards of half a century one of the most voluminous as well as the most popular of all our writers of fiction, her novels numbering nearly seventy. She thoroughly deserved her success, for she knew how to tell a sensational story with capital effect in a brisk and attractive style, and she was, moreover, a keen observer of life (e.g., *Lady Audley's Secret*, 1862 ; *Aurora Floyd*, 1863 ; and better than either of these, though not so well known, *Henry Dunbar*, 1864). In later life she turned her attention to deeper themes and the problems of character, as in her study of eighteenth-century Methodism in *The Infidel* (1900). Thackeray's eldest daughter, Anne Isabella, Lady Ritchie (b. 1838), calls for a word of cordial recognition as the author of a number of novels (e.g., *The Story of Elizabeth*, 1863 ; *Old Kensington*, 1873, etc.) of delicate feeling and careful workmanship. The qualities of such a writer are easily appraised. Not so those of Marie Louise de la Ramée (1839–98), who was English by birth though French by descent, and who wrote under the name of Ouida. The faults of her novels (e.g., *Strathmore*, 1865 ; *Chandos*, 1866 ; *Tricotrin*, 1869) are many and glaring ; they are gaudy in style ; their high-flown passion rarely rings true ; their overcharged pictures of fashionable life are flagrantly unreal ; and we cannot for a moment believe in their wonderful heroes, who are perfect monsters of manly strength and beauty. Yet she surprises us at times by flashes of unmistakable genius, and her power will scarcely be gainsaid by any who have read *Folle Farine*, for example, or the enthralling last chapters, describing Cigarette's ride and death, of *Under Two Flags*. The genuine pathos of some of her less pretentious writing (e.g., *Two Little Wooden Shoes*) must also be recognised. Ouida had a deep sympathy with the poor, and her intense love of animals is often apparent, as in *Puck* and *A Dog of Flanders*. Finally, to bring to a rather arbitrary close a list which, to be made even approximately complete, would have to be prolonged almost indefinitely, we may just mention the name of Rhoda Broughton (b. 1840), a clever and vivacious writer, the unconventional heroines of whose earlier books (e.g., *Cometh up as a Flower*, 1867; *Red as a Rose is She*, 1870; *Good-bye, Sweetheart*, 1872; *Nancy*, 1873) rather shocked the susceptibilities of old-fashioned readers, and who certainly helped to introduce the " new woman " into Victorian fiction.

PART III

THE VICTORIAN AGE

THE LATER PERIOD (1872–1900)

CHAPTER I

INTRODUCTORY

THAT a great chapter in the annals of our literature came to a close about the beginning of the seventh decade of the nineteenth century is universally admitted by historians and critics. As in the twenties we note the gradual exhaustion of the social and literary inspirations of the Revolutionary Epoch, so now again, fifty years later, the gradual exhaustion of the social and literary inspirations of the central Victorian Era is equally apparent. For this reason the last thirty years of the century must be regarded as forming a period by themselves. As none the less they belong to the Queen's reign, we may describe them, for purposes of distinction, as the Later Victorian Age.

This period is still so near to us that we cannot as yet see it in the clearness of historical perspective. Certain of its outstanding features may, however, be recognised.

In the first place—and in this, too, we are reminded of what had happened in the twenties—that general waning of creative power of which we are conscious in the literature of the time was manifestly due immediately to the disappearance or decline of many of the great writers of the preceding generation. Thackeray and Dickens were dead ; Browning, Carlyle, Ruskin, and George Eliot had done their best work ; Tennyson, though he still had much of value to add to his production, had ceased to be an originative force in poetry ; while even his younger contemporaries, like his own Bedivere in the *Idylls of the King*, found themselves a little out of their element " among new men, strange faces, other minds." Meanwhile, though the coming race showed plenty of talent and some real genius, it produced no writers qualified at once to fill the gaps left by the passing of the earlier giants.

Moreover, as we pursue our inquiries in the literature of the seventies onward, we are aware not only of waning power but also of a vast change in spirit and tone. This change is to be explained in part as the result of a natural reaction against a long dominant mode. A particular fashion in literature will last for a time only ; after which, as it ceases to be a living thing and degenerates into a mere convention, the healthy human craving for something fresh and original will inevitably assert itself ; and since with literary fashions, as with all other phenomena, Herbert Spencer's doctrine of the Rhythm of Motion holds good, the rebound against precedent is pretty certain to involve an extreme revulsion in judgment and taste.[1] Hence the impatience with which so many writers of the new generation rejected the ideals of their fathers : repudiating, for instance, the Tennysonian tradition in poetry, and the decorum and restraint of the earlier Victorian novel.

While, however, the change in question is in part explicable simply as a reaction, it was greatly accelerated and to a large extent directed by powerful influences from the Continent, which did much to break down the old Victorian insularity and to destroy long-accepted political and social ideas and habits of life and thought. The causes which combined to bring about the cosmo-

[1] See, *e.g.*, his brief essay, *Estimates of Men*, in *Notes and Comments*.

politanism which now began to broaden our intellectual outlook need not here be discussed. But the fact itself has to be emphasised. New literary movements abroad were now followed by English writers with eager interest, and English literature was more deeply affected by foreign literatures than at any time since the close of the eighteenth century. In studying the literature of the central Victorian period it is scarcely necessary, save here and there in an exceptional case like that of Carlyle, to make any reference to the literatures of the Continent. Without continual reference to these literatures, on the other hand, a great deal in the literature of the Later Victorian Age cannot properly be understood. The influence of the Continent is to be felt more or less as a pervading presence in almost every department of it—in poetry, in criticism, in fiction; but it was in fiction that it told most directly. The immense vogue of the Norwegian dramatist Ibsen, of the French naturalist school as represented particularly by Maupassant and Zola, and to some extent of the Russian masters Tolstoi, Turgenev, and Dostoievsky, who were " discovered " about this time, counted enormously in the development of an English school of realistic novelists, whose watchword was undeviating truth to life, whose theory of what constituted truth to life led them to concentrate their attention almost exclusively upon life's sordid and ugly sides, and whose audacious frankness made the professed realism of the earlier Victorians, even that of Thackeray, seem by contrast timid and old-fashioned.

The continued progress of physical science and the domination of the scientific spirit meanwhile strengthened this realistic tendency, and at the same time helped to deepen the pessimism by which it was generally accompanied. The science of the closing decades of the nineteenth century was uncompromisingly materialistic, and its repeated attacks not only upon the ancient edifice of dogmatic faith but also upon any and every conception of the universe which rested upon spiritual foundations, kept the thought of the time in a state of perpetual unrest and filled many devout minds with gloomy forebodings of coming disaster. Historically significant, like all his writings, Tennyson's second *Locksley Hall* (1886) will always remain interesting as the expression of the despondency of a sensitive student of contemporary thought who had once eulogised science as a saving power in the world, but had now come to believe that it threatened the religious hopes to which he was still determined to cling.[1] There were many of the rising generation of course who were willing to throw such hopes aside, and were able to do so without any loss of strength and courage. Yet on the whole the literature of the period now in question, so far as it was affected at all by the scientific movement and the philosophic materialism which went with it, was impregnated thereby with the spirit of despair. Melancholy was indeed one of its most constantly recurring characteristics.

Another well-marked feature of not a little of that literature was the tendency, as the period advanced, towards what is rather vaguely known as Decadence. "The most representative literature of the day," wrote an acknowledged authority on the subject, Mr. Arthur Symons, at the time when the tendency was at its height, "the writing which appeals to, which has done so much to form, the younger generation, is certainly not classic,

[1] Note also the violent attack made in this poem upon the "New Realism."

nor has it any relation to that old antithesis of the classic, the romantic. After a fashion it is no doubt a decadence; it has all the qualities which mark the end of great periods, the qualities which we find in the Greek, the Latin decadence "; and he goes on to tell us what these qualities are—" an intense self-consciousness, a restless curiosity in research, an over-subtilising refinement upon refinement, a spiritual and moral perversity." [1] Signs of the essential unhealth which such qualities connote—an unhealth from which the whole of Europe seemed for the moment to be suffering—were very conspicuous in the art of the Later Victorian Age (as in the work of Aubrey Beardsley) as well as in its verse and prose ; but interesting as the decadent movement is in connection with the psychology of the time, it need not detain us here, since, as Mr. Symons elsewhere said, it represented merely " a straying aside from the main road of literature," and was indeed an experiment which came to nothing. It developed for a time a taste for pose and dandyism, a love of artifice and affectation, and a horror of nature and simplicity ; but before the end of the century came it had ceased to exert any influence, and in its subsidence it left very little of permanent value behind it.

Yet while in dealing in general terms with the main currents of our later nineteenth century literature we are justified in laying stress upon the various characteristics above mentioned, we must remember that they were offset by other characteristics which arose in opposition to them. Here, as always, the principle enunciated in a previous chapter has to be recognised— that every movement sooner or later sets up a countermovement. Hence we shall find that the domination

[1] *The Decadent Movement in Literature*, in *Harper's Magazine*, November 1893.

of realism in the novel was challenged by a renaissance of romance; that the mood of pessimism inspired the mood of hopefulness and courage; that the tendency to decadence led to an outburst of robustness, and the love of artifice to a fresh return to nature; and that the long tyranny of materialism was followed by a spiritual reaction, and in particular by a revival of catholicism and mysticism. It must furthermore be noted that literature was necessarily affected by certain political and social ideas which now became powerful, whether for good or for evil it is not, of course, our business here to inquire. The day of the old cautious individualistic liberalism, of which Tennyson in his middle manhood had been the accredited poetical interpreter, was over, and a new socialistic propaganda—a propaganda which attracted many men of letters (including, as we have seen, William Morris) to its support—threw the whole country into a ferment of controversial excitement and agitation. At the same time the insular nationalism which had been the controlling sentiment of earlier Victorian foreign politics gave way before the new conception of colonial expansion and the rôle of Great Britain as a world-empire, and Imperialism became one of the rallying cries of the hour.[1]

Before passing on to give a very brief sketch of the literature of the Later Victorian Age I must remind the reader that many of the most prominent figures in that literature were survivors from the preceding generation. But while these have already been dealt with it may now be added that wherever necessary their work should be re-considered in the light of the changing

[1] The publication of Sir John Seeley's *The Expansion of England*, in 1883, may be mentioned as an important landmark in the history of this great change.

conditions noted in this chapter. Many other writers, on the contrary, who now began to take a position in the world of letters will not be included here for the simple and sufficient reason that though they appeared before the nineteenth century was out, they really belong to the twentieth. As it will not be necessary to give a separate chapter to the writers of general prose, we will confine our attention to the poets and the novelists. What little may have to be said about criticism and the drama can be said by the way.

CHAPTER II

POETRY

THE first in order of age of the poets who come within the scope of this chapter is our present laureate. **Bridges.** Robert Bridges was born in 1844 at Walmer, Kent, studied medicine at St. Bartholomew's Hospital, and practised for some years as a physician in London before devoting himself entirely to literature early in the eighties. Since that time he has produced a body of work considerable in bulk and very varied both in quality and in style. In this work by far the largest space is occupied by a number of plays, for Mr. Bridges has persisted in using the dramatic form notwithstanding the obviously non-dramatic character of his genius. All his plays, with the possible exception of *Nero* (1885), which is described simply as " an historical tragedy," are avowedly experiments in different modes : *Prometheus the Firegiver* (1883) and *Demeter* (1905) are Greek ; *The Feast of Bacchus* (1889) is founded on Terence and is " in a Latin manner " ; *The Christian Captives* (1890) and *The Humours of the Court* (1893) are derived from the Spanish ; *Achilles in Scyros* (1890) and *The Return of Ulysses* (1890) are " in a mixed manner " ; while *Palicio* (1890) is " a romantic drama in the Elizabethan manner." As experiments all these plays have a certain interest, but they lack the dynamic elements of real drama and are memorable chiefly for their occasional passages of pure poetry. In his non-dramatic verse his most ambitious production is *Eros and Psyche* (1885), a very delicate rendering in attractive seven-line stanzas of the beautiful story out of the *Metamorphosis* of Apuleius, which we can also read in Pater's *Marius*, and which furnished the material for one of William Morris's tales in *The Earthly Paradise*. Mr. Bridges' longest original work is, however, *The Growth of Love* (1876 ; enlarged edition, 1889), a fine sonnet-sequence, notable for its grave and stately tone and style and for its singularly austere treatment of its subject, which is indeed handled in so remote a way and with such a conspicuous want of ordinary passion that, as compared with most love poetry, the entire series impresses us as a little cold. But admirable as many of these sonnets are, Mr. Bridges is undoubtedly at his very best in his collection of *Shorter Poems in Five Books* (1890–94) and in the supplementary *New Poems* of a few years later (1899). Here again we note the same high spiritual temper, the same restraint, the same avoidance of all appeal to the sensuous fancy, the same " sacred aloofness from life's meagre affairs." Yet these lyrics are at the same time marked by qualities which forbid us to regard him, with some of his critics, as a mere " classical revivalist " or " poet of the study." Many of them (*e.g.*, several of the elegies, *The Downs, London Snow, On a Dead Child, Indolence, Larks, Nightingales*, to name only a few) are things of great beauty, with real inspiration in them and a strongly personal note. In their treatment of nature they are also remarkable. Mr. Bridges has the keenest sense of the familiar charm of the ordinary English landscape, with its meadows, hedgerows, woods, and common flowers, and he writes of these things not only with striking simplicity and fidelity, but also with hardly a trace of that sentimentalising tendency which has long been part of the romantic tradition in our nature-poetry in general.

The technical side of his work is extremely interesting. His exhaustive treatise on *Milton's Prosody* (new edition, 1893) shows how carefully he had studied the problems of metre and metrical effect, and in his own verse he has been a deliberate innovator. His *Poems in Classical Prosody* are indeed only experiments, and (like all other such experiments) are of a kind to appeal more to scholars than to the lover of poetry for its own sake. More importance therefore attaches to the attempt which he has made in a number of his lyrics to gain greater freedom and variety of metrical movement by sundry devices, and especially by the extension of the principle (not, of course, new to our prosody) of measuring the line not by its syllables but by its accents, and by the substitution of what he calls " natural speech stress " for the established rhythms of conventional verse. His new departure is not quite so revolutionary as is sometimes supposed ; indeed, he seems to have done little more than to carry a step farther the methods already adopted by some of his great predecessors. It is therefore not amiss to recall the fact that half a century earlier even Coleridge, himself an innovator, had found fault with Tennyson on the score of his metrical licence. Mr. Bridges' own experiments attest his skilful craftsmanship and fine ear, and their results are, on the whole, though not uniformly, felicitous.

The work of our next poet strikes a very different note. William Ernest Henley was born at Gloucester **Henley.** in 1849, adopted journalism as his profession, was editor successively of *London*, *The Magazine of Art*, *The Scots Observer*, and *The New Review*, and died in 1903. All through his life he was very much of an invalid, and often carried on his work under conditions which would have crushed a weaker man, but with the indomitable courage which is expressed in what is perhaps the best known of his poems, the one (*Life and Death*, No. IV.) beginning :

> " Out of the night that covers me,
>   Black as the pit from pole to pole,
> I thank whatever gods may be
>   For my unconquerable soul."

During an illness of twenty months in the Old Infirmary, Edinburgh, he formed a fast friendship with Robert Louis Stevenson, with whom he collaborated in the plays *Deacon Brodie*, *Beau Austin*, *Admiral Guinea*, and *Robert Macaire*. He also collected some of his critical writings in two small volumes, *Views and Reviews : Literature* (1890) and *Views and Reviews : Painting and Sculpture* (1901), which are independent in judgment, incisive in style, and rather arrogant in tone. His poetry, which is to be found mainly in his *Book of Verses* (1888), *The Song of the Sword* (1892), and *Poems* (1898), is egotistic, strong, and unconventional. Perhaps the most striking part of it is the series entitled *In a Hospital*, the material of which was provided directly by his own experiences, and which, though it grips the imagination by its unsparing realism, at the same time shows how even ugly detail can be transmuted by the sheer force of poetic magic. Here, as elsewhere, his use of irregular unrimed metres is very effective. The concentrated vigour of *The Song of the Sword* should also be noted, while the *London Voluntaries* deserve attention as significant of the taste of an age in which many poets, while not neglecting nature, were seeking fresh inspiration in the romance which lies beneath the apparently sordid surface of city life.

This salient quality is a connecting link between the work of Henley and that of John Davidson, who in the more enduring portion of his very varied production belongs even more emphatically to

Davidson.

the school of realistic poets. Born in Renfrewshire in 1857, Davidson made many experiments in finding a career—as assistant in a sugar factory, chemical analyst, teacher, and clerk in a Glasgow firm—before he settled in London in 1890 to devote himself to literature. He had already written several plays—*Bruce* (1886), *Smith : a Tragic Farce* (1888), and *Scaramouch in Naxos* (1889), and he continued to the last to produce in dramatic form, though in most of his later work in this direction the machinery of drama was adopted merely as a vehicle for his revolutionary ideas (e.g., *Theatrocrat*, 1905 ; *The Triumph of Mammon*, 1907 ; *Mammon and His Message*, 1908). But he first made his mark with his poems of London life *In a Music Hall* (1891) and the two series of *Fleet Street Eclogues* (1893, 1895), the distinctive note of which was well sustained in *Ballads and Songs* (1894), *New Ballads* (1896), and *The Last Ballad and Other Poems* (1898). In the last decade of his life he developed a spirit of fanatical hostility to the entire past in art, literature, morality, and religion, and a profoundly rebellious and pessimistic philosophy derived in large measure from Schopenhauer and Nietzsche, and much of his energy was thenceforth devoted to the task of expounding his gospel of scientific materialism in its various bearings (e.g., *The Testament of a Vivisector*, 1901 ; *The Testament of a Man Forbid*, 1901 ; *The Testament of an Empire Builder*, 1902 ; and especially *The Testament of John Davidson*, 1908): his purpose being, as he declares in a note to *The Triumph of Mammon* (1907), " to destroy this unfit world and make it over again in my own image." While staying in Cornwall in 1909 he disappeared mysteriously, and for some time his fate remained in doubt. Six months afterwards, however, his body was found at sea, and though the exact manner of his death has never been ascertained, there is little doubt that it was a case of suicide.

Davidson's most noteworthy contribution to literature is contained in his ballads, and particularly in those in which, in a thoroughly individual way as regards both matter and style, he deals with the life of the city streets. In these poems he constituted himself the interpreter of actuality : his avowed principle being that " the statement of the present is the very body and soul of poetry." His place therefore is among the poets who seek to liberate poetry from the bondage of scholastic tradition and to revitalise it by bringing it back into living touch with the everyday world. In accordance with his fundamental doctrines he adopted to the full Wordsworth's theory that there is and can be no essential difference between the language of metrical composition and that of prose, and wrote in an unconventional style in harmony with his themes. Yet though his ballads were generally done in simple rimed stanzas (and with all his newness there was nothing new in his technique), he came to regard blank verse as incomparably our highest poetic medium, and his own blank verse is carefully wrought and often of great beauty.

With William Watson, who was born at Burley, in Wharfedale, Yorkshire, in 1858, and was therefore **Watson.** Davidson's junior by a year, we return to the great main current of English verse. His first book, *The Prince's Quest* (1880), a narrative poem in romantic couplets, showed the influence of Keats and Morris, and though graceful and delicate, was of no particular significance. This was followed by a tiny volume of *Epigrams of Art, Life and Nature* (1884), which proved the writer's consummate skill as an artist in miniature, but failed very naturally to attract much attention. It was in 1885 that, with his *Ver Tenebrosum*, a series of sonnets on Gordon and the Soudan, Mr. Watson emerged as a distinct figure in the literary world of his time, though it was not till the appearance of *Wordsworth's Grave* in 1890 that his peculiar qualities were revealed to the full. From that time he has continued to publish at irregular intervals, his successive volumes being always small in bulk but of choice texture and the most careful workmanship.

The comparative paucity of Mr. Watson's production is one of its characteristic features. His muse, as he has himself confessed, is " a fitful presence, seldom tarrying long," and it is one of his rare merits, in an age when nearly everyone writes too much, that he has been satisfied to await her capricious visitations. Thus far he has attempted nothing on a large scale, but on the other hand, like Landor, he has always been solicitous to do " his little things well." There is nothing unfinished, experimental, incondite, about any of his writing ; everything in it is obviously wrought by conscientious and deliberate labour to the highest possible degree of perfection. True to the spirit of his own epigram,—

> " No record Art keeps
> Of her struggles and throes,
> There is toil on the steeps,
> On the summit repose,"—

he gives us only silver that has been seven times tried. In such work we miss inevitably the engaging note of spontaneity, and often feel that the effects of the file are too apparent. Yet it would be a mistake to suppose that the formal excellence of Mr. Watson's verse connotes any want of strength or passion. H s wonderful mastery of phrase and unerring sense of the right word and the fitting epithet are not the only qualities which impress us in his style ; equally unmistakable is his fine imaginative power—that power which at once differentiates him from the mere craftsman and places him among those master poets to whom his allegiance has been given. Moreover, he is no worshipper of Art for Art's sake. He writes as one whose interests are in the living world about him. If he does not " parade a conscious naturalness," neither has he any sympathy with those scholastic poets who " go prankt in faded antique dress." " Life as I see it lived," he declares, " is great enough for me," and in this declaration he puts himself with those who, refusing to live in the " phantom times " of the past, believe that the present will " long yield aliment of song " ; while for the rest, if in his own singing he continues to use " a mode of yesterday," it is because he is convinced that " 'twill prove to-morrow's mode as well."

This brings us to another point. At a time when, in his own words, art " affects singularity," Mr. Watson has steadily adhered to the great traditions of English verse, his acknowledged masters being Milton, Tennyson, and pre-eminently Wordsworth (for his reply to the critics who charged him with lack of originality, see his *Apologia*). Much of his own inspiration has come directly from literature, and some of his most characteristic work is to be found in his critical memorial poems ; as, e.g., *Shelley's Centenary*, *The Tomb of Burns*, *In Laleham Churchyard*, with its discriminating estimate

18

of Matthew Arnold, the superb elegy on Tennyson
—*Lachrymae Musarum*, and above all, *Wordsworth's
Grave*, one of the finest things of the kind in our literature
and remarkable not only as a study of Wordsworth but
also for its large and illuminating interpretation of the
poetry of the eighteenth century. His political poems,
though the most widely read of all his writings, are
necessarily the least enduring, and are interesting chiefly
as evidence of his fervent patriotism and his desire
that the England he loves so passionately should live
up to her highest ideals. In his treatment of nature he
is generally intensely subjective, as in his *Autumn*,
which is steeped in personal feeling and full from the
first line to the last of the " pathetic fallacy," in *The
Father of the Forest*, and in the noble elegiac *Hymn to
the Sea*. In his religious poetry he writes as a reverent
agnostic (e.g., *The Unknown God*), profoundly impressed
by the " everlasting taciturnity " of nature and the
eternal mystery of " the divine reserve."

While on this side of his work Mr. Watson represents
the sceptical mood of his generation, in that of his contemporary Francis Thompson " the wave of Catholicism
which swept over the art world of the closing years of
the nineteenth century reached its poetic fulness." [1]

The child of parents who were both converts to
Romanism, Thompson was born at Preston in 1859
and educated at the Ushaw Catholic College,
Thompson. near Durham. Much against his will he then
entered Owens College, Manchester, as a student of
medicine, but after six years of fruitless drudgery he
abandoned all thought of a profession which would have
been obnoxious to him, and tramped to London, where he
lived for three years more, unknown, and in the depths

[1] Holbrook Jackson, *The Eighteen Nineties*, p. 201.

of destitution. But his first book of *Poems* (1893) scored an immediate success, ran through several editions, and gained not only the praise of the critics but also the warm approval of such men as Browning and Coventry Patmore. This success was largely due to the presence in the volume of one poem with which, it is probable, Thompson's name will always be most closely associated, *The Hound of Heaven*, in which a strikingly original conception is worked out with splendidly sustained imaginative power. His remaining volumes of verse were *Sister Songs* (1895) and *New Poems* (1897); but he also wrote in prose *Health and Holiness* and an essay on Shelley. His constitution was early undermined by privation and the practice of opium-taking, and he died in 1907.

While Thompson's poetry broadly represents the extreme reaction against the rationalistic temper and the scientific scepticism of his time, it is still unique through the force of his own strange personality. "From the material world," writes one of his friends, Mr. Lewis Hind, "Francis Thompson wanted nothing. It did not interest him. It did not exist for him. His body, that wretched creature, ordained to house, as it best might, his ardent spirit, he, shall I say, despised. Comfort, a home, provision for the future were to him unrealities. His only realities were spiritual; his only adventures were in the land of visions." This absolute detachment from actuality is the outstanding characteristic of all his work. He writes as a Catholic mystic, and his treatment both of man and of nature tends, after the manner of mystics, towards the symbolical; and though it is true that he feels the beauty of stars and children and womanhood (e.g., *Sister Songs* and *Love in Dian's Lap*), his distinctive tone is that of mystical piety often passing into fervent emotion and asceticism (e.g., *The Mistress of Vision* in *New Poems*). Both in thought and (even more perhaps) in style he has been recognised as a spiritual kinsman of such seventeenth-century religious poets as Crashaw, Vaughan, and Herbert. The strength of his verse does not, however, lie in its intellectual quality (it is often, in fact, all but unintelligible), but in its purely imaginative power, and the wealth and splendour of its imagery. It is, in fact, to adopt his own words, "a revel, an inexhaustible wassail of orgiac imageries." In that extraordinary phrase from his *Anthem to Earth* we have indeed a fair expression both of his powers and of his weaknesses. His imagination, unchecked by any consideration of propriety, runs riot, and his style is overladen with conceits, far-fetched analogies, neologisms often bizarre, sometimes uncouth, words wrested out of their natural meanings, and rich, ornate, highly Latinised embroideries. His daringly original manner, often striking, at times marvellously effective, at other times vicious, naturally lent itself to ridicule and burlesque. His mannerisms are indeed so marked that his own verse frequently reads like a parody of itself.

While Francis Thompson was of course in no sense a popular poet, the popular note was vigorously struck **Kipling.** by a young Anglo-Indian writer who came suddenly to the front about the time when *The Hound of Heaven* first saw the light. Mr. Rudyard Kipling, who was for a few years the most prominent figure in the English world of letters, was born in Bombay in 1865, and educated at the United Services College at Westward Ho, Devon. Returning to India, he became in 1882 sub-editor of *The Civil and Military Gazette* at Lahore, and soon began to contribute stories to the Allahabad

Pioneer. His first independent book, *Departmental Ditties*, was published at Lahore in 1886. After this he travelled widely, lived for a time in England, for a time in the United States, and took up his home in England in 1896. In the meantime he had created an immense sensation by his early volumes in prose and verse, but especially by his Anglo-Indian stories, which will be considered in the next chapter. His work as a poet is to be found chiefly in his *Barrack-Room Ballads* (1892), *The Seven Seas* (1896), and *The Five Nations* (1903).

Mr. Kipling's sudden and extraordinary success—a success unparalleled in our literature since Dickens leapt into fame with *Pickwick*—is to be accounted for in large measure by considerations which take us far beyond any question of the intrinsic literary merits of his work. To begin with, he brought fresh material into literature, and he dealt with this material in a strikingly fresh and unconventional way. At the time of his appearance our poetry was rapidly decaying through excess of refinement. It was becoming more and more a poetry of the drawing-room, cultured, bookish, effeminate, dependent mainly upon the past for its motives and inspiration, a thing of much superficial grace, but of little body, and flaccid through its want of virility and actuality. These were, it will be remembered, the days of the waning Tennysonian tradition, when minor bards, like Lewis Morris, took up the strain which the great Victorian laureate had made popular, and with monotonous iteration reproduced his delicacy without his original strength. Into this world of over-fastidious taste and fragile sentiment—a world in which it seemed hardly decorous for any poet to raise his voice above a whisper—Mr. Kipling burst like a sort of elemental force and with something of Walt Whitman's " barbaric yawp," and his work not only took the critics by storm but was also eagerly read by that great public which generally cares nothing about poetry, because its very coarseness seemed to carry with it an invigorating sense of reality and life. Moreover, his own ideas and training fitted him in a peculiar way to become the mouthpiece of the new imperialistic sentiment just when that sentiment was in the ascendant. His scornful question—"What do they know of England who only England know?"—seemed a challenge thrown down to the narrowness of English insularity. He was hailed at once as the laureate of empire, the interpreter of Greater Britain, and the apostle of its "manifest destiny" as a world-power; and as Mr. Le Gallienne has said, "when one's theme is so popular as the British Empire, the Empire itself is likely to help one out with the chorus." Mr. Kipling came at the right moment for success, and as always happens when there is such a correspondence between the man and the hour, he was swept to fame by the movement which in turn he did so much to stimulate.

It is evident, however, that this kind of success is in the nature of things likely to be ephemeral, and we are already far enough away from the period when it was won with such surprising ease to realise that, whatever may be the fate of Mr. Kipling's work in prose-fiction, his poetry is not wearing well. The strength which captivated his first readers has, now that it is no longer a new thing, lost much of its original power of appeal; the sentiment which stirred them seems to us a little cheap; his peculiar manner has been somewhat vulgarised by repetition and imitation; there is rather too much bluster about his patriotism; while even his style, once praised for its amazing vigour, often impresses us as at once strident and thin. None the less

we must still recognise his heroic attempt to bring into
poetry all sorts of things which poetry in its aristocrat
and scholastic moods has been accustomed to ignore—
the feelings of the common soldier, the wonders of
machinery, the romance of trade. His ambition has
been to take the actual life of the present—the life even
of rough men amid rude surroundings—and to translate
that directly into song, faithfully and frankly, and
without sacrificing any of its native savour. He is
neither retrospective nor utopian; the God of his worship
is " the God of things as they are," and in things as they
are he has sought his sufficient inspiration. Like his
own Scottish engineer, he is impatient of the conventional
make-believe which has too often done duty for poetry:

> " I'm sick of all their quirks an' turns, the loves and doves they
> dream ;
> Lord, send a man like Robbie Burns to sing the Song o' Steam";

and in his *M'Andrew's Hymn*, from which these
characteristic lines are taken, he does himself sing the
song of steam, if not with entire success, at least effectively enough to suggest a new lead in poetry. His use
of Cockney dialect and of the colloquialisms and slang
of street and barrack-room is part of his poetic programme, and it is very much to the point to notice that
he is rarely quite himself except in dialect, and that
when he adopts a more formal language and style he
is apt to become a little stilted and bombastic. Even
his famous *Recessional*, dignified and impressive as it
certainly is in itself, owed much of its success to the
accuracy with which it interpreted the national mood
of chastened feeling on the morrow of the second Jubilee,
while only its topical quality will serve to explain the
instant popularity of the almost equally famous but
poetically quite negligible *White Man's Burden*.

A few other writers, taken from the mass, may just be mentioned as in one or another way representative of English poetry in the closing decades of the century.

Mrs. Alice Christiana Meynell (b. *circa* 1853), though the larger part of her literary work is in the form of prose essays of much suggestiveness and charm,
Mrs. Meynell. has also a distinct place among our women poets (*Preludes*, 1875 ; *Poems*, 1893 ; *Later Poems*, 1902). Her verse is marked by a subdued tone, great restraint (a rare merit with women-writers), and fine technical finish. Hence she has been particularly successful with her sonnets, one of which, *Renouncement*, was adjudged by Rossetti as " one of the three finest sonnets ever written by women." Among her miscellaneous poems the most memorable is *A Letter from a Girl to her own Old Age*, which was praised by Ruskin as " perfectly heavenly."

Most of the verse of Oscar Wilde (1854–1900), while characterised by extraordinary beauty of style, is too
Oscar Wilde. full of " sensuous classicism " and too suggestive of elaborate artifice to be satisfactory to an unsophisticated taste (e.g., *Charmides*), while in its tendency to linger over abnormal moods and ideas (e.g., *The Sphinx*) it often bears the stamp of decadence. In the small group of poems entitled *Eleutheria*, however, there is a far more robust and individual quality, and with these we may join the fine ode to England, *Ave Imperatrix*, and the sonnets *Libertatis Sacra Fames* and *To Milton*, as also indicative of a strain of real manhood and high idealism in a writer who unfortunately wasted much of his power over unworthy things. The striking *Ballad of Reading Gaol* (1898), inspired by his own experiences of imprisonment, occupies a place by itself in his verse, but has its prose parallel in the posthumous

De Profundis. It should be added that Wilde was more popularly known as a writer of plays (e.g., *Lady Windermere's Fan,* 1892 ; *A Woman of No Importance,* 1893), which are full of the brilliant and paradoxical wit which also appears in his volume of essays, *Intentions* (1891).

Stephen Phillips (1868–1915) made himself a name among contemporary poets by his *Poems* of 1897, which **Stephen** received the prize of *The Academy* as the best **Phillips.** literary work of that year. The most important item in this volume, *Marpessa,* is a blank-verse poem of considerable force and beauty, and this, together with the more original *Christ in Hades,* published the year before, led many critics to predict a very great future for the writer. This promise, however, was hardly redeemed by Phillips's later work. In 1899 he produced a blank-verse tragedy, *Paolo and Francesca,* which was successful on the stage, and after this much of his energy was devoted to the drama (e.g., *Herod,* 1901 ; *Ulysses,* 1902 ; *The Sin of David,* 1904, etc.).

Mr. William Butler Yeats deserves attention not only on account of the real excellence of his own work, **W. B.** but also because he is the central figure of a **Yeats.** significant, if somewhat eccentric, movement in our later nineteenth century literature—that of the Irish Renaissance or Celtic Revival. Born in Dublin in 1865, he spent much of his childhood in County Sligo, where he became familiar with the ancient superstitions of his countrymen ; the interest thus aroused finding its first expression in his *Tales and Folk-Lore of the Irish Peasantry* (1888). In 1891 he founded the National Literary Society, which in turn gave birth a few years later to the Irish Literary Theatre in Dublin, the object of which was the creation, or re-creation, of a really native drama. A good deal of his own literary work (e.g., *The Countess*

Kathleen, The Land of Heart's Desire, Cathleen ni Hooli-han) has also been in dramatic form. In these plays, as in his non-dramatic poetry (e.g., *Wanderings of Oisin*, 1889 ; *Poems*, 1895 ; *The Wind among the Reeds*, 1899), he has been largely inspired by the old Irish legends, which he has handled with true " Celtic magic " and tenderness, a keen sense of natural beauty, and an equally characteristic tendency towards mysticism and the vaguely symbolical. With his name we may link that of Mr. George W. Russell (b. 1867),

A. E. who under the initials A. E. has published three slender books of verse—*Homeward Songs by the Way* (1894), *The Earth Breath* (1897), and *The Divine Vision* (1904)—which are distinguished by some of the same Celtic qualities, though the writer is less pre-occupied than Mr. Yeats with legendary ideas, while his relations with life and nature are simpler and more direct.

Finally, reference must be made to two writers of lighter verse. Sir William Schwenk Gilbert (1836–1911),

Gilbert. though he first made his reputation as a humorist with his delightful *Bab Ballads* (1869, 1873), and wrote much independently for the stage, is best remembered by the witty and fanciful comic opera librettos which he provided for the music of Sir Arthur Sullivan (e.g., *The Pirates of Penzance*, 1880 ; *Patience*—a pungent satire of Oscar Wilde's aestheticism —1881 ; *The Mikado*, 1885, etc.). Sir Owen Seaman

Seaman. (b. 1861), who has been editor of *Punch* since 1906, gained a place close beside Calverley with his *Horace at Cambridge* (1894) and *Tillers of the Sand* (1895). Of greater general interest, however, is his *Battle of the Bays* (1896), with its clever parodies of Edwin Arnold, Lewis Morris, Davidson, Mr. Watson, Mr. Kipling, and other contemporary writers.

CHAPTER III

THE NOVEL

JUDGED by age alone, our greatest Later Victorian novelist, Thomas Hardy, properly belongs to the earlier **Hardy.** generation, but his work is so distinctly " modern " in character that it seems more fitting to deal with him here. Mr. Hardy was born in 1840 near Dorchester, in the heart of the West Country which he has made peculiarly his own. He adopted architecture as his profession, practised for a time in Dorchester, and in 1863 gained the medal of the Institute of British Architects and the Tite Prize for design. The fair success of his first novel, *Desperate Remedies* (1871), encouraged him, however, to further attempts in fiction, and his reputation was established and his career determined by his next books, *Under the Greenwood Tree* (1872), *A Pair of Blue Eyes* (1873), and *Far from the Madding Crowd* (1874)—all novels of extraordinary freshness and charm. These were followed by *The Return of the Native* (1878), *The Trumpet Major* (1880), *The Mayor of Casterbridge* (1886), *The Woodlanders* (1887), *Wessex Tales* (1888), *A Group of Noble Dames* (1891), *Tess of the D'Urbervilles* (1891), *Life's Little Ironies* (1894), and *Jude the Obscure* (1896). After the appearance of the fantastic tale of disillusion, *The Well-Beloved*, in 1897 Mr. Hardy formally gave up the writing of fiction, and published some poems and an immense dramatic trilogy,

The Dynasts (1904–1908), the theme of which is England's struggle with Napoleon.

Under the general title of Wessex, Mr. Hardy has taken Dorset and the neighbouring counties as his special scene, and has made that part of England classic ground. His descriptions of the West Country landscape and his strong sense of local colour are indeed among the most prominent features of his work. In the human drama which is played out against this natural background the local element again predominates; his men and women are for the most part products of the soil; and the mental habits of his peasantry are depicted and their talk reproduced with wonderful insight and much racy humour. But though his rustic comedy is excellent (and every reader of *Under the Greenwood Tree* and *Far from the Madding Crowd* will regret that it is a diminishing quantity in his later novels) the bias of his mind is very distinctly towards tragedy, and tragedy of a peculiarly gloomy and hopeless kind. Only suggested in previous books, this bias first became obvious in the sombre *Return of the Native*, after which the pessimistic tendency grew upon him till it reached its culmination in the harrowing and oppressive *Tess of the D'Urbervilles* and *Jude the Obscure*—works of immense power, in which the conventional restraints of English fiction were boldly repudiated and life was handled with a frankness which many readers found offensive. As these works in particular show, Mr. Hardy is an uncompromising realist of the new school. " Like former productions of this pen," he writes, " *Jude the Obscure* is simply an endeavour to give shape and coherence to a series of seemings, of personal impressions, the question of their consistency or their discordance, of their permanence or their transitoriness, being regarded as not of the first moment." This may be read as a declaration of the creed of pure impressionism, in accordance with which the novelist will aim to give only " a slice out of life " without concerning himself about its interpretation. But Mr. Hardy's novels do not themselves suggest this absolute detachment and impersonality. A very pronounced view of life predominates in them all. Of his Eustacia Vye in *The Return of the Native* he tells us that she had come to think of Destiny " with an ever-growing consciousness of cruelty." This thought of the cruelty of Destiny is always uppermost in his own mind. His attitude towards life is consistently fatalistic. He dwells upon the injustice wrought by brute circumstance and that blind force which men have called Providence, upon the crushing weight of heredity and environment, upon the inability of the individual to escape from the meshes of his doom. He has, too, a bitter sense of the irony of things (*cp.* his collection of stories, *Life's Little Ironies*), and his tragedies often turn upon the linking up of mere coincidences and the enormous consequences of seemingly trivial events. The general impression left by Mr. Hardy's later books, therefore, is one of unrelieved gloom, but it must be remembered that this impression is produced not merely by his pessimistic philosophy as such, but also, and far more, by the immense power with which it is expressed concretely through the steady march of his dramas towards their appointed catastrophes.

Two other writers, though they worked quite independently of Mr. Hardy, may at once be associated with him here as noteworthy exponents of the extreme realism which characterised so much of the fiction of the time—George Moore and George Gissing.

Mr. Moore was born in 1851 in Ireland, but lived for many years in Paris, where he fell under the **George** influence of the then dominant naturalistic **Moore.** school. As an avowed disciple of that school, especially of Zola, he wrote *A Mummer's Wife* (1884), a sordid narrative of life in the Potteries and on the stage, and ten years later a grimly powerful novel of horse-racing and debauchery, *Esther Waters*, which, like *Jude the Obscure*, had the distinction of being banned by the circulating libraries, and in consequence of this excellent free advertisement enjoyed a temporary " success of scandal." In his later books Mr. Moore has been less concerned about merely external detail and more with problems of psychology and the examination of morbid states of mind, as in the minutely analytical *Evelyn Innes* (1898) and its sequel *Sister Teresa* (1901).

Mr. Moore's realism is unmistakably of the new Continental type. That of George Gissing, on the other **Gissing.** hand, appears to have been but little affected by foreign influences, and may be regarded as fundamentally English in derivation and character. Gissing, who was born in Wakefield, Yorkshire, in 1857, and died at St. Jean de Luz in 1903, settled in London when he was a very young man, and there engaged in a long and desperate struggle with poverty. For years he lived amid the most squalid surroundings, sometimes in a garret, sometimes even in a cellar, often in a state of abject misery, not infrequently on the raw edge of starvation. Yet throughout he clung to his scholarly tastes (choosing on occasion to forego a meal in order to add some coveted volume to his little collection of Greek and Latin classics), while with equal strength of purpose he steadily refused to abandon his own ideals of art in the hope of achieving

a momentary popularity. In the last decade of his
life his fortunes so far improved that he was placed
beyond the reach of actual penury and was able even
to realise his long-cherished ambition of a tour in Italy
(see his charming volume of sketches, *By the Ionian
Sea*, 1901). But his bitter experiences, which provided
him with materials, also coloured most of his work :
his novels, with few exceptions, being tragedies of poverty,
in which the central theme is often the futile revolt of
some character of fine aspirations against the tyranny
of environment and the limitations of a narrow lot.
His first book to attract any general attention (in
part perhaps because he put into it a little more plot-
interest than usual) was *Demos* (1886), which is largely
a study of socialism. *Thyrza* (1887) deals with the
life of a factory girl ; *The Nether World* (1889) with
the squalor and misery of Clerkenwell ; *The New Grub
Street* (1891), which is on the whole his greatest book,
gives an appalling, and it is to be feared a truthful,
picture of the seamy side of London literary life ;
Born in Exile (1892) tells of the efforts of an ambitious
man to rise above his destiny ; *The Odd Women* (1893)
is occupied with the problem of the " superfluous
woman " under the rapidly changing industrial conditions of modern society. These novels are named
out of the mass of Gissing's writings as typical of his
work in general ; two others may be mentioned because
they diverge somewhat from his usual line : *The Town
Traveller* (1898), a very pleasant and welcome experiment in a lighter vein, and the posthumously published
Will Warburton, which (like the largely autobiographical
Private Papers of Henry Ryecroft, 1903) suggests the
lifting of the dark clouds which had hitherto hung over
his imaginary world. Gissing everywhere impresses us

by his painstaking workmanship, by his obvious sincerity, and by his undeniable fidelity to the life which he describes ; but the shadows in his pictures are so heavily painted in, and he offers us so little in the way of relief, that in their total effect his writings are extremely depressing. His acknowledged master was Dickens, and his short study of the great Victorian is one of our very best books on the subject ; but though his own matter often suggests the later Dickens, —the Dickens, say, of *Little Dorrit*,—he differs from him very widely in his concentration, his avoidance of the theatrical, his general want of humour, and his pessimism.

Though Gissing was in no sense a didactic novelist, for he had no particular views to expound and no special **Other** gospel of reform to preach, his books were **Realistic** written as serious social studies, and as such **Novelists.** they have a high value. In this way they incidentally represent the strongly sociological tendency of much of the realistic fiction of the Later Victorian Age—the tendency which we further note, for example, in the slum stories of Mr. Arthur Morrison (*Tales of Mean Streets*, 1894 ; *A Child of the Jago*, 1896) and Mr. W. Somerset Maugham (*Liza of Lambeth*, 1897). One outstanding work of this sociological school deserves special attention—the *No. 5 John Street* (1899) of Mr. Richard Whiteing (b. 1840), which, itself a kind of sequel to an earlier utopian story, *The Island* (1888), is an extraordinarily arresting book, written evidently from an intimate inside knowledge of its subject and in a style of rare distinction. With this school we may also loosely connect another novelist who, though never exactly popular, has been much praised by good judges —William Hale White (1831–1913), often known by his pseudonym of Mark Rutherford. His principal books, *The Autobiography of Mark Rutherford* (1881) and its sequel *Mark Rutherford's Deliverance* (1885), can indeed hardly be classed as novels in the ordinary acceptation of the word ; they are rather life-histories of spiritual conflict and earnest gropings towards the light ; but while lacking in form, they are of singularly absorbing though painful interest. White's other works, which are at once more regular in construction and less individual, include *The Revolution in Tanner's Lane* (1887), which describes the effect of the industrial changes between 1814 and 1840, and *Catharine Furze* (1894), an almost distressingly faithful picture of the English lower middle classes. Among the realists with a purpose, though in her case the purpose is often religious or ethical rather than social, we may also place Mrs. Humphry Ward (b. 1851), a niece of Matthew Arnold and a granddaughter of Arnold of Rugby. Mrs. Ward came into great prominence in 1888 with *Robert Elsmere*, a very long and very elaborate psychological novel, dealing with the religious controversies of the day in the form of the history of a clergyman who, after a protracted battle with doubt, finally leaves the Church, and embodying a religious philosophy which reminds us of her uncle's " sublimated Bible " and Christianity without supernaturalism. The *History of David Grieve*, which followed in 1892, is an equally elaborate discussion of socialism, marriage, secularism, revivalism, and other contemporary issues. Social and political problems are in turn uppermost in *Marcella* (1894) and its sequel *Sir George Tressady* (1896), while Mrs. Ward's many other books (e.g., *The Marriage of William Ashe*, 1905) are generally built up about some specific moral theme. Her work is profoundly earnest

19

and markedly strong upon the intellectual side. Artistically it often suffers from over-elaboration and the accompanying defect of prolixity; for which reason her brief *Story of Bessie Costrell* (1895), a little tale, swift in narrative and of great tragic intensity, should be named as a thing apart.

From these representatives of realism and didacticism we may now turn at once to the brilliant writer who **Stevenson.** stands in the van of the great romantic counter-movement of his time. Robert Louis Balfour Stevenson was born in Edinburgh in 1850. He came of a family of well-known engineers, and himself began to study for the same profession; but soon gave it up; read for the Bar; was duly " called " in 1875; and for a time helped to swell the ranks of the briefless barristers in the purlieus of Parliament House. His heart was, however, given to literature; already he was contributing essays and sketches to various magazines; and before long he made a more ambitious appearance as an author with two pleasant books of travel—*An Inland Voyage* (1878), describing a canoe-trip up the Oise and the Sambre, and *Travels with a Donkey in the Cévennes* (1879). Before this his health had given cause for alarm, and in the winter of 1873–74 lung disease had compelled him to spend some months at Mentone (see his essay *Ordered South*). This was the first of many journeys undertaken in part in the hope of checking the malady against which he fought so heroically, but in part also on the promptings of his own adventurous temper. In 1879 his wanderings took him as far as California (for an account of his experiences see *Across the Plains* and *The Amateur Emigrant*), and the next year in San Francisco he married an American lady, Mrs. Van de Grift Osbourne, who had nursed him through a serious illness, and whom he soon brought back to England. Primarily to amuse his young stepson, Lloyd Osbourne (who has since made a name for himself in American literature), he wrote his first regular novel, *Treasure Island* (1883), a story of pirates and the quest for hidden booty of a kind to appeal to all boys (old as well as young), but lifted far above the usual level of such stories by its fine literary qualities and especially the vivacity and charm of its style. This book established his reputation and henceforth his pen was always busy. As a novelist Stevenson tried many lines. *The Black Arrow* (1888), a tale of the Wars of the Roses, and perhaps the most disappointing of his writings ; the admirable *Kidnapped* (1886) and its equally admirable sequel *Catriona* (1893), dealing with Scotland in the years immediately following the last Stuart rising ; and *The Master of Ballantrae* (1889), also a tale of '45, strong, but unequal and very gloomy, are all historical romances. *Prince Otto* (1885), the scene of which is laid in an imaginary German court, is an experiment (and notwithstanding the immense labour which he bestowed upon it, not a very successful experiment) in the domain of psychological fiction and clearly suggests the influence of George Meredith, of whom he was an ardent admirer. *The New Arabian Nights* (1882) and its sequel *The Dynamiter* (1885)—both done in collaboration with his wife—are brilliant extravaganzas of a most original description, while *The Wrong Box* (1892), which bears on its title-page the name of Lloyd Osbourne as joint author, is a masterpiece of dashing and farcical humour. In *The Wrecker* (1892) he and Lloyd Osbourne made an attempt to combine " the police novel or mystery story " with " the novel of manners," and produced a curious, straggling, perplexing book, which, however, despite its structural defects, is full of exciting incident, picturesque description, and excellent characterisation. *The Ebb Tide* (1894), also written in conjunction with Mr. Osbourne, has something of the same grip, and in particular gives us a wonderful sense of the charm of the Southern Seas, but on account of the unmitigated rascality in various forms and degrees of all its characters and its repulsive catastrophe, it leaves a rather unpleasant taste in the mouth. Finally, in the marvellous and unique story of dual personality, *The Strange Case of Dr. Jekyll and Mr. Hyde* (1886), inspired, according to his own statement, by a dream, Stevenson at one and the same time preached a sermon of tremendous power and contributed a fresh thrill to literature. His other work comprises a number of short stories, some of the highest excellence, three collections of poems, the delightful *Child's Garden of Verses* (1885), and the more dubious *Underwoods* (1887), and *Ballads* (1891) ; and in prose, *Virginibus Puerisque* (1881), *Familiar Studies of Men and Books* (1882), and other volumes, which put him well to the front among modern English essayists. Amid all this steadily continuous production Stevenson had been waging incessant war against disease, and much of the work which now enchants us by its high spirits and zest of life he actually did in periods of extreme prostration ; dictating to an amanuensis when he was too weak to hold a pen, and even when forbidden to speak, dictating still—in the deaf and dumb alphabet. After many changes of residence, much wandering, and a long voyage in the Southern Pacific, he settled in Samoa in 1890 (see his *Vailima Letters*), where he died suddenly in 1894. He left behind him two unfinished romances, *Weir of Hermiston*, of which only a small part had been written, and *St. Ives*, afterwards completed by Mr. (now Sir) A. Quiller-Couch.

It was not for nothing that Stevenson was called by the native Samoans Tusitala, or the Teller of Tales. He belonged to the race of born story-tellers—of those who love and cultivate story for its own sake. There was indeed a pronounced vein of Scotch seriousness and even an odd dash of puritanism in his Bohemian nature, and in his essays he often moralises with remarkable sanity and clearness of vision. But in his fiction he habitually left "problems" of all kinds entirely alone, and his refreshing freedom from analytical and speculative bias, and his contagious delight in the picturesque tragedy and comedy of life as such, were among the chief secrets of his attraction for that large public which was beginning to weary of the overstress of purpose in so much of the literature of the time. While he was quite of his age in the subtlety of his character-drawing and in his abundant use of realistic detail, the distinctive spirit of his work is that of pure romance—an exhilarating love of adventure and heroic action. That he was far more at home with men than with women is a significant feature of his work which will be obvious to every reader; though Catriona and Barbara Grant (in the same book) show what he could do with women when he tried, the fact remains that he did not often try; the "love-interest" hardly appears in some of his novels (e.g., *Treasure Island*, *The Wrecker*) at all; while in one of them, *The Ebb Tide*, the feminine element is so inconspicuous as to be practically non-existent. Another of his characteristics which is important enough for emphasis is his curious fondness not merely for the grotesque and the gruesome, but even for the horrible, as, *e.g.*, in many of his stories (*Markheim*,

The Merry Men, Olalla, etc.) and often incidentally in his novels. Yet though he was essentially the story-teller, he was also, unlike most of the world's great story-tellers, a conscious and deliberate artist in style. From first to last he cultivated style with constant and studious care, and if fault may be found (as it has been found) with his prose on the ground that it is sometimes factitious, mannered, and even, as one of his critics has put it, "tormented," we must still recognise its delightfully debonair quality, its unfailing vivacity, and the admirable blending in it of energy and grace. Merely as stylist he ranks high among our modern prose writers.

Though Stevenson's work was extraordinarily cosmopolitan, his genius was firmly rooted in his native soil, and even from far-off Samoa his heart turned affectionately towards "the venerable city which I must always think of as my home" (Dedication to *Catriona*). Hence the purely Scotch element was often strong in his books, and this serves to connect him with other Scotch writers among his contemporaries who kept their country well to the fore in fiction. One of the most important of these is James Matthew Barrie (b. 1860, knighted 1913), **Barrie and** whose first notable books, *Auld Licht Idylls* **Others.** (1888) and *A Window in Thrums* (1889), are composed of stories and sketches all admirably done, with fine humour and pathos, a keen insight into character, a deep sympathy with humble life, and most excellent talk in dialect. "Thrums," which is the Forfarshire weaving town of Kirriemuir, where the author was born, is also the scene of his first serious attempt at a novel, *The Little Minister* (1891), a rather fantastic story, having the same general characteristics ; while *Sentimental Tommy* (1896) and its sequel *Tommy*

and Grizel (1900) have a Thrums boy for their hero.
Sir James Barrie's great success as a playwright has led
to his practical abandonment of the novel for the drama.
Another writer who achieved popularity as a painter
of Scottish manners, and was apparently inspired by
Sir James, was the Rev. John Watson (1850–1907), who,
under the pen-name of Ian Maclaren, wrote two volumes
of stories, *Beside the Bonnie Brier Bush* (1894) and *The
Days of Auld Lang Syne* (1895), besides several much
inferior works of fiction on a larger scale. Both Barrie
and Watson belong fundamentally to the realists, though
their method has little in common with that of the
extreme realists of the time. A third Scotsman, Samuel
Rutherford Crockett (1860–1914), while he began with
a series of sketches, *The Stickit Minister* (1893), after
the manner of *Auld Licht Idylls*, is rather to be regarded
as a follower of Stevenson (e.g., *The Raiders,* 1894; *The
Lilac Sunbonnet,* 1894; *The Men of Moss Hags,* 1895;
and numerous other romances, generally interesting
enough to while away an idle hour, but of no particular
importance). A much more remarkable development
of Scotch romanticism, however, is one which was connected, not with Stevenson, but with that revival of
the Celtic spirit in poetry of which we have already
spoken. In 1894 a good deal of curiosity was aroused
by a little book entitled *Pharais : a Romance of the
Isles,* bearing on its title-page the hitherto unknown
"Fiona name of Fiona Macleod. This was followed by
Macleod." other volumes by the same author, regarding
whose identity there was considerable speculation—
The Sin Eater (1895), *The Mountain Lovers* (1896),
From the Hills of Dream (1896), *Green Fire* (1896), etc.;
a legendary drama, *The Immortal Hour* (1900); a collection of verse, *Through the Ivory Gate* (1901), and of

prose poems, *The Silence of Amor* (1902). It was ultimately discovered, though the matter was made certain only after the writer's death, that Fiona Macleod was in fact the dramatic mask of William Sharp (1855–1905), who had long been known as a voluminous essayist, poet, and literary critic. As an illustration of double personality this singular case reminds us of that of Chatterton and his " Rowley " poems, for not only was the work which Sharp did as Fiona Macleod much better than that which he produced in his own name, but it was also different in character. It really seemed therefore that through his *eidolon* he came into touch with latent powers, the possession of which he would not otherwise have suspected. In earlier life he had spent much time in the Western Isles, where he had learned a great deal about the life and character of the people, and about their folk-lore and superstitions. The material thus gathered he now worked up in various ways : producing sometimes "legendary moralities" (as in *The Sin Eater*) ; sometimes allegories (as in *The Hills of Dream*) ; sometimes fantasies mingled with the stuff of real life (as in *The Dominion of Dreams*) ; sometimes domestic dramas (as in *Pharais* and *The Mountain Lovers*). All these Fiona Macleod books are marked by the imaginative and visionary quality, the fine feeling for nature, and the mysticism which we associate with the Celtic genius. They are often very striking, but are rather monotonous in character and style.

It will have been noted that among the writers mentioned in the last few pages there was a marked tendency towards the use of the short story along with, or sometimes in preference to, the regular novel. The popularity of the story as a separate branch of fiction was indeed one of the outstanding features in the literature of the closing years of the nineteenth century, and this fact brings us to Mr. Rudyard **Kipling.** Kipling, who holds the place of supremacy among his contemporaries in this particular field. In dealing with Mr. Kipling as a poet I have already spoken of the adventitious circumstances which, over and above all question of his genius, helped him in his sensational rise to fame. The entire freshness of his subjects and manner must now once more be emphasised. Young as he was when he captured his public by sudden assault, he had seen much of life in strange places, and had laid up a rich store of varied experiences, and like Dickens when he wrote his *Sketches by Boz*, he began by describing the things of which he had a first-hand and intimate knowledge. Hence, his vivid pictures came as a revelation of a new world as well as of a new power. Nor was the extraordinary fertility of the young author less astonishing than his originality and graphic force, for in the first few years of his career his books followed one another with almost bewildering rapidity: *Plain Tales from the Hills*, with their frank and unflattering descriptions of Anglo-Indian life, the clever but cynical *Story of the Gadsbys* (a tale in dialogue form), and the equally clever but still more cynical *Under the Deodars*, being all published in the same year, 1888; while hot upon these came *Soldiers Three*, noteworthy for the first appearance of Mr. Kipling's famous trio of British privates—the swaggering humorous Irishman Terence Mulvaney, the phlegmatic Yorkshireman John Learoyd, and Stanley Ortheris, the quick-tempered little Cockney —who figure again in later books, and whose doings and talk are sometimes immensely amusing and sometimes very tiresome. Then came *The Courting of Dinah*

Shad and Other Stories in 1890, and among minor things, in 1891, *The Light that Failed*, a first experiment on a larger scale which proved, notwithstanding the grim power of its tragedy of love, frustrated ambition, and blindness, that the writer's true sphere was not that of the novel. *Life's Handicap*, another volume of "stories of mine own people," was also published in 1891, and this was followed, though at longer intervals, by *Many Inventions* (1893), *The Day's Work* (1898), *Traffics and Discoveries* (1904), and *Actions and Reactions* (1909), all collections of tales, the more miscellaneous character of which suggested that Mr. Kipling's original vein was at length getting exhausted, and which, though brilliant in parts, seem on the whole more laboured and less effective than those which had preceded. In the meantime, however, he was breaking fresh ground in other directions. The *Naulahka* (1892), written in conjunction with his American brother-in-law Wolcot Balestier, is a tale of adventure turning on the contrast between the progressive and commercial West and the mysterious and superstitious East ; *Captains Courageous* (1897), a realistic romance of Newfoundland cod-fishing, which can scarcely be accounted a success ; *Stalky & Co.* (1899), a school story which has been variously praised as the best book of the kind ever written, and condemned as a brutal caricature of the English boy ; and *Kim* (1901), the life-history of a street arab of Lahore, whose loosely strung adventures serve to introduce a kaleidoscopic panorama of Indian life. More important than any of these, however,—even than *Kim*,—were the two *Jungle Books* (1894, 1895), animal stories so original in conception and so convincing in execution that they may fairly be said to represent an entirely new departure in imaginative literature. The *Just So Stories* (1902), a further excursion into the same field, suffer by comparison with these ; but in two other volumes on yet another line— *Puck of Pook's Hill* (1906) and *Rewards and Fairies* (1910), in which incidents from the past are put into a delightfully fanciful setting of the present—Mr. Kipling gained one more well-merited success as a writer for children.

Even such a cursory survey of his writings will suffice to indicate their extraordinary variety. That variety becomes even more apparent when the versatility of Mr. Kipling's genius is considered. The larger part of his earlier work was naturally concerned with Anglo-Indian life, but this life was treated under its most diverse aspects ; sometimes its strenuousness was projected against the background of the ancient and dreamy East ; sometimes "the clash of civilisations " was the underlying motive ; sometimes the theme was provided by the curiosities of British officialism ; sometimes by the manners and morals of civil and military circles ; sometimes again by the idiosyncrasies and adventures of the British soldier. He gives us pungent sketches of "society " in *Plain Tales, The Story of the Gadsbys*, and *Under the Deodars* ; tragedy in *The Man who was* and *Without Benefit of Clergy* (*Life's Handicap*); boisterous comedy in many of the records of his "Three Musketeers" and elsewhere. He writes striking stories of the psychical and the supernatural, as in *The Phantom Rickshaw*, *The Finest Story in the World* (*Many Inventions*), *The Brushwood Boy* (*The Day's Work*), *They* (*Traffics and Discoveries*), *The House Surgeon* (*Actions and Reactions*) ; and ghastly tales of crime and madness, as in *The Mark of the Beast* and *The Return of Imray* (*Life's Handicap*). In *Wee Willie Winkie* and many other places he shows his remarkable understanding of and sympathy with children, and here the note of simple pathos often comes into his work. His animal books are triumphs of insight and imaginative power ; while in ·007 and *The Ship that found Herself* (*The Day's Work*) he makes an heroic though not a very successful attempt to write in prose that romance of machinery and its marvels which, as we remember, he had tried to sing in *M'Andrew's Hymn.* Yet great as is his variety, his method throughout is very much the same ; it is essentially the method of modern journalism at its best carried over into literature. He is emphatically, as we have implied, the story-writer, and even in his longer narratives his art is still the art of the story though the scale of the work is for the time being enlarged. His rare power of concentration, of defining character and situation in a few pregnant words, and of suggesting " atmosphere "—his mastery of the incisive epigram and the vivid and telling phrase—the driving force of his descriptions : these are among the distinctive elements of his manner and style. Yet while he has an astonishing faculty for producing effects, his effects seem seldom to leave a permanent impression. He has in particular little power of creating enduring character ; as Mr. Le Gallienne has said, I think quite justly, "he is deft at giving you sufficient notion of this man and that woman to last out the story," but "mainly the story is the thing, and the characters are little more than pegs on which to hang an anecdote." As a "critic of life " he has been much eulogised and much censured ; eulogised as an apostle of manliness and heroism ; censured because of his reactionary spirit, his praise of war, his love of bloodshed, his worship of the "strong man " and mere brute force. In this matter each reader's opinion will naturally depend upon his particular temperament and ideals.

It remains for us now to touch very rapidly upon a few other representative novelists of the period under review.

Samuel Butler (1835–1902), a man of very original genius, in addition to some suggestive work in science **Other** (e.g., *Life and Habit*, 1877 ; *Evolution, Old and* **Novelists.** *New*, 1879), and in literary criticism (e.g., *The Authoress of the Odyssey*, 1897), wrote a couple of clever utopian romances, *Erewhon* (1872) and *Erewhon Revisited* (1901), and a rambling, unconventional kind of novel, or family chronicle, *The Way of all Flesh* (posthumously published, 1903), in which he aired a good many of his views on heredity, education, and other subjects. William Clark Russell (1844–1911) turned his early experiences in the merchant service to good account in some capital novels of the sea, in which the nautical traditions of our fiction were well sustained, and of which *The Wreck of the Grosvenor* (1875) may be mentioned as an example. Mr. Hall Caine (b. 1853) has delighted an immense public, though he has by no means satisfied the critics, with a series of grandiose and theatrical romances (e.g., *The Deemster*, 1888 ; *The Bondman*, 1890 ; *The Manxman*, 1894 ; *The Christian*, 1897 ; *The Eternal City*, 1901, etc.), conceived on an epic scale, and in which, through a vast amount of flamboyant writing, the emotional interest is worked up to the highest pitch of intensity. Mr. Stanley John Weyman (b. 1855) has written many good stories of the Dumas type (e.g., *The House of the Wolf*, 1890 ; *A Gentleman of France*, 1893 ; *Under the Red Robe*, 1894 ; *The Man in Black*, 1894, etc.), with plenty of " go " in them and an excellent historical atmosphere. Sir Henry Rider Haggard (b. 1856), in the highly sensational *King Solomon's Mines* (1885), *Allan Quatermain* (1887), and a large number of other romances of the thrilling kind, has catered effectively for the tastes of readers who love plenty of excitement and are not specially fastidious regarding the finer qualities of literary art. Thomas Anstey Guthrie, who uses the pen-name of F. Anstey (b. 1856), scored a well-deserved success with an amusing topsy-turvy story, *Vice Versâ* (1882), which he followed up with other clever books (*The Tinted Venus, The Brass Bottle, The Fallen Idol*) in the fantastic vein. To Olive Schreiner (b. 1859), a native of Basutoland, our fiction is indebted for one noteworthy contribution—*The Story of an African Farm* (1893), which gives a vivid and, it is said, an accurate picture of Boer character and life on the veldt. Sir Arthur Conan Doyle (b. 1859) would well merit recognition as the author of some strong and sound historical romances (e.g., *Micah Clarke*, 1888 ; *The White Company*, 1891 ; *The Refugees*, 1891), and of much good work in other fields ; but he is specially known as the creator of the now world-famous detective Sherlock Holmes (*A Study in Scarlet*, 1887 ; *The Adventures* (1892), *Further Adventures* (1893), and *Return* (1905) *of Sherlock Holmes* ; *The Hound of the Baskervilles*, 1902, etc.). Mr. Jerome Klapka Jerome (b. 1859) made a reputation as a humorist with *Idle Thoughts of an Idle Fellow* (1886) and *Three Men in a Boat* (1889), but has done more serious work, as in his really fine novel, *Paul Kelver* (1902). Another humorist who has laid us under a heavy debt of gratitude is Mr. William Wymark Jacobs (b. 1863), whose *Many Cargoes* (1896), *The Skipper's Wooing* (1897), *Sea Urchins* (1898), and numerous other volumes contain much rich comedy and are specially remarkable for their inimitable dialogue. Sir Gilbert Parker (b. 1862), a Canadian by birth, though for many years resident in England, has done some strong work in the romance of Canadian history (e.g., *The Trail of the Sword*, 1895 ; *The Seats of the Mighty*, 1896 ; *The Pomp of the Lavillettes*, 1897), and has also produced several excellent studies of French-Canadian life and character (e.g., *Pierre and his People*, 1892 ; *The Lane that had no Turning*, 1900). Hugh Stowell Scott, who wrote as Henry Seton Merriman (1863–1903), was an industrious and business-like writer who sought romance in many fields ; in Russia (*The Sowers*, 1896) ; *The Vultures*, 1902) ; in Spain (*In Kedar's Tents*, 1897 ; *The Velvet Glove*, 1901) ; in Corsica (*The Isle of Unrest*, 1899), etc. etc. Mr. Anthony Hope Hawkins, who has adopted the pen-name of Anthony Hope (b. 1863), won special fame with two dashing romances of adventure in an imaginary kingdom in Tyrol, *The Prisoner of Zenda* (1894) and *Rupert of Hentzau* (1898), and, as a master of witty dialogue, with his brilliant little *Dolly Dialogues* (1894) ; but he has also produced much excellent fiction on other lines, as in *The God in the Car* (1894), *Quisanté* (1900), *The Intrusions of Peggy* (1902), etc. Sir Arthur Quiller-Couch, who writes as " Q." (b. 1863), is also a novelist of considerable versatility, but we remember him best for his tales of the West Country, and especially his own native Cornwall (e.g., *Troy Town*, 1888 ; *Shining Ferry*, 1905 ; *The Mayor of Troy*, 1906, and others), which are marked by a breezy vigour of narrative, excellent local colour, and plenty of fresh, healthy humour. Many other names might be added—some with doubtless quite as good a right to inclusion as any of those we have just mentioned—but in a brief survey such as this we cannot attempt to make our catalogue even approximately complete. It would not, however, be fitting to close without a reference to two other writers whose appearance in the eighties and nineties, though little noticed then, must, as we can now see, be regarded as an event of importance in the literature of the time. Mr. George Bernard Shaw was born in Dublin in 1856, and settled in London in 1876, where he soon became **Mr. G. B. Shaw.** prominent as a dramatic critic and advocate of socialism. In creative work he first turned to prose fiction and wrote *The Irrational Knot* (1880 ; published 1905), *Cashel Byron's Profession* (1886), *An Unsocial Socialist* (1887), and *Love among the Artists* (1889), all " problem " novels, dealing with marriage, economics, art, morals and other matters, and showing the author's now familiar fondness for handling curious types of character (*e.g.*, Sholto Douglas, Conolly, Sidney Trefusis, Owen Jack, Amélie Szczympliça, etc.), out-of-the-way motives and bizarre combinations. A volume of interpretation, *The Quintessence of Ibsenism* (1891), which followed these, indicated his growing interest in the stage, and particularly in the class of play represented by the work of the Norwegian master, and he soon found a new field in the drama, though his first experiments were so bold in subject and unconventional in method (e.g., *Widowers' Houses*, 1892 ; *Mrs. Warren's Profession*, 1893), that in his own words they made him rather " infamous " than famous " as a dramatist." Two collections of his dramatic writings appeared before the end of the century under the characteristic titles of *Plays, Pleasant and Unpleasant* (1898) and *Three Plays for Puritans* (1900), and since then Mr. Shaw has quite conquered the theatre-going public with *Man and Superman* (1903), *John Bull's Other Island* (1904), *Major Barbara* (1905), *The Doctor's Dilemma* (1906), and various other dramas, all marked by a great fertility of ideas, caustic wit, and an abundance of paradox and epigram.

The second of the two writers now in question, Mr. Herbert George Wells, was born in 1866, began life as **Mr. H. G. Wells.** a teacher of science, and when he took to fiction, turned his knowledge and training to good account in the clever fantastic romances *The Time Machine* (1895), *The Invisible Man* (1897), *The War of the Worlds* (1898), etc. This vein he has continued to work with much success in *The First Men in the Moon* (1901), *The Sea-Lady* (1902), *The Food of the Gods* (1904), and other books all characterised by extraordinary imaginative power. But his more recent work (foreshadowed both by such realistic stories as *The Wheels of Chance*, 1896, and *Love and Mr. Lewisham*, 1900, and by the daring prophetic romance, *When the Sleeper Wakes*, 1899), has been mainly in the line of sociological fiction, as, e.g., *Kipps* (1905), *Tono Bungay* (1909), *Anne Veronica* (1909), *The New Machiavelli* (1910), *Marriage* (1912), etc. ; his interest in the vital questions of the day and the problems of the future being further illustrated in his sociological essays, *Mankind in the Making* (1903), *A Modern Utopia* (1905) and *New Worlds for Old* (1908). Like Mr. Shaw, Mr. Wells is a bold and original critic of our present society, its institutions, and its moral code, and we now recognise him as one of the intellectual forces of the time. But any further consideration of these two representative men would take us beyond the boundaries of this book. Though their earlier work falls within our period their influence did not begin to count until that period was out, and it is therefore to the twentieth century rather than to the nineteenth that they properly belong.

INDEX

Printed by
MORRISON & GIBB LIMITED
Edinburgh

Handbooks of English Literature.

Edited by J. W. HALES, M.A.,

Professor of English Literature at King's College, London; formerly
Fellow of Christ's College, Cambridge; late English Examiner in the
University of London; and Clark Lecturer at Trinity College, Cambridge.

Crown 8vo, 4s. net each volume.

THE AGE OF ALFRED (664-1154).
By F. J. SNELL, M.A.

THE AGE OF CHAUCER (1346-1400).
By F. J. SNELL, M.A. With an Introduction by the late Professor HALES. Third Edition, Revised.

THE AGE OF TRANSITION (1400-1580).
By F. J. SNELL, M.A. Two Volumes. Vol. I, Poetry; Vol. II. Prose and Drama. With an Introduction by the late Professor HALES. Second Edition.

THE AGE OF SHAKESPEARE (1579-1631).
By THOMAS SECCOMBE and J. W. ALLEN. Two Volumes. Vol. I. Poetry and Prose. With an Introduction by the late Professor HALES. Vol. II. The Drama. Fifth Edition, Revised.

THE AGE OF MILTON (1632-1660).
By the REV. CANON J. H. B. MASTERMAN, M.A. With an Introduction, etc., by J. BASS MULLINGER, M.A., Litt.D. Seventh Edition.

THE AGE OF DRYDEN (1660-1700).
By RICHARD GARNETT, C.B., LL.D. Seventh Edition.

THE AGE OF POPE (1700-1744).
By JOHN DENNIS. Eighth Edition.

THE AGE OF JOHNSON (1744-1798).
By THOMAS SECCOMBE. Seventh Edition.

THE AGE OF WORDSWORTH (1798-1832).
By PROFESSOR C. H. HERFORD, LITT.D. Ninth Edition.

THE AGE OF TENNYSON (1830-1870).
By PROFESSOR HUGH WALKER. Eighth Edition.

LONDON: G. BELL AND SONS LTD.